Media Business and Innovation

Series editor

M. Friedrichsen, Stuttgart Media University, Germany and Humboldt School Stuttgart/Berlin, Germany

More information about this series at http://www.springer.com/series/11520

Zvezdan Vukanović

Foreign Direct Investment Inflows Into the South East European Media Market

Towards a Hybrid Business Model

 Springer

Zvezdan Vukanović
Faculty of International Economics, Finance and Business
UDG – University of Donja Gorica
Podgorica, Montenegro

Media Business and Innovation
ISBN 978-3-319-80828-4   ISBN 978-3-319-30512-7   (eBook)
DOI 10.1007/978-3-319-30512-7

Printed on acid-free paper

This Springer imprint is published by Springer Nature
The registered company is Springer International Publishing AG Switzerland

A mediocre technology pursued within a great business model may be more valuable than a great technology exploited via a mediocre business model. **Henry Chesbrough**, *Business Model Innovation: Opportunities and Barriers. Long Range Planning 43 (2010):354–363.*

Foreword

Since the year 2000, we see a rapid disruption in global media business through the emergence of new technologies. The Web, new disruptive services, and changing consumer patterns shatter the world of traditional media. This has a clear and direct impact on the financial market of media businesses, increasing fragility, and requiring strategic reorientation, as well as the exploration of new financial business models. New communication and media technologies are here to stay, and a sentiment towards the "old way" will only hinder the emergence of new media products and drive media companies out of business. As new technology exponentially develops, FDI and sustainable business models become the key to success. Specifically, small and medium size media corporations require increasing of their competitive capabilities, creating innovative and novel products and services. The creation of new platforms, technologies, and innovations requires setting up of a sustainable and competitive financial media business models. Thus, the competition is not solely to develop products based on new emerging technologies; more importantly, competition shifts towards business models as such. Consequently, the rapid disruption in global media business since the year 2000 let new technologies emerge compelling innovative business models to compete in the globally competitive market.

In addition, the development in global media markets has direct impact on regional media companies. Media industry in smaller and developing countries as well as more localized media markets are not backed by a global consumer crowd and face fierce challenge in the globally competitive media market. Convergence, mergers, acquisitions, lack of innovation capability, poor adoption of new digital technologies, and market concentration (see, e.g., Lugmayr and Zotto 2015a, 2015b, 2015c; Zotto and Lugmayr 2015) are just some of the consequences that multinationals exert on regional media industries. Foreign direct investments into regional markets by multinationals seem to be a solution to drive regional innovations in the media sector. This book investigates this topic on the example of South-East European regional media markets. The book's main topic can be considered rather niche, as by my knowledge there are none or just a few studies investigating this specific topic in such a focused and direct matter. This book is a clear contribution to the body of knowledge in media industry and illustrates potentials and impact of the global media market on the example of South East European countries.

The author contributed with a rather comprehensive volume to the field of media management by investigating the relation between global corporations and regional media markets for a period of three years. He included multiple case studies from sixteen South East European countries, such as Albania, Bosnia and Herzegovina, Bulgaria, Croatia, Cyprus, Greece, Hungary, Kosovo, Macedonia, Malta, Moldova, Montenegro, Romania, Serbia, Slovenia, and Turkey. The book investigates media industry from an innovation viewpoint; thus, the author devotes a large body of the book to business model innovation research. In particular, it is this innovation-oriented approach making the current challenges of regional media industry more visible and illustrating potential pathways for new business models to create more sustainable media businesses.

A large share of the book deals with the investigation of foreign direct investments and their dynamics. In addition, the book investigates a wide range of factors and effects and illustrates the market and microeconomic relations between different stakeholders. The developed framework will help future scholars in media management and economics to gain deeper understanding that principally underlay the issues of FDI in media markets. Relatedly, this discussion culminates into the presentation of several case studies that have been conducted in South East European countries. These case studies underline the importance of the hybrid FDI media business model that has been developed by the author in a more practical setting.

I was extremely deluged to have been asked to contribute with a foreword for this exciting book. Having seen the struggle of media businesses in regions, as well as their exposure to the development in a global market, I appreciate any contribution that helps them to survive, innovate, and gain competitiveness. This book focuses on foreign direct investment as a solution and conceptualizes a framework for increasing the competitiveness of local media businesses. The reader of the book will enjoy the argumentation of the author and have exceptional insights into today's media industry in South Eastern European countries. Importantly, readers dealing with foreign direct investment in media industries on a more global scale will benefit from this work—as the knowledge of this book can also be applied to both the regional and global media markets.

Perth, Australia   Artur Lugmayr
2016

References

Lugmayr, A., & Zotto, C. D. (2015a). Convergence is NOT king - The tripe "convergence, coexistence, and divergence IS king". In: A. Lugmayr & C. D. Zotto (Eds.), *Media convergence handbook (Vol. 1): Journalism, broadcasting, and social media aspects of convergence and Media convergence handbook (Vol. 2): Firm and user perspective*. Berlin: Springer.

Lugmayr, A., & Zotto, C. D. (Eds.) (2015b). *Media convergence handbook (Vol. 1): Journalism, broadcasting, and social media aspects of convergence*. Berlin: Springer.

Lugmayr, A., & Zotto, C. D. (Eds.) (2015c). *Media convergence handbook (Vol. 2): Firms and user perspective*. Berlin: Springer.

Zotto, C. D., & Lugmayr, A. (2015). Media convergence as evolutionary process. In: A. Lugmayr & C. D. Zotto (Eds.), *Media convergence handbook (Vol. 1): Journalism, broadcasting, and social media aspects of convergence and Media convergence handbook (Vol. 2): Firm and user perspective*. Berlin: Springer.

Preface

As observer and practitioner in the world of global media, I share a deep admiration and passion for media business and industry as well as a strong conviction that they are critical institutions for the twenty-first century. I also share a genuine concern that the financial condition of media business is becoming increasingly fragile as the business models of the past and to a certain extent of the present appear to be increasingly out of sync with the rapid and continuous changes taking place in the media business. Alongside, most media companies are woefully ill-prepared to meet the changing market needs of these dynamic and innovative business changes. Relatedly, in this expanding era of global communication, traditional (old legacy) media in SEECs are in danger of residing on the sidelines or quietly disappearing—unless they can profoundly and fundamentally reexamine old assumptions and make dramatic changes in business model practice. In order to stay regionally and globally competitive and financially as well as economically both self-sustainable and profitable, SEECs media companies have to merge its economic and technological infrastructure with other competitive multinational corporations.

This monograph is the culmination of the author's 3 years' long investigation of the relationship between multinational corporations' FDI and SEECs media business markets. Multinationals are responsible for 80 % of patent and product innovations. More than one-third of world trade today takes place in the form of intra-firm transactions—that is, trade among the various parts of the same corporate network spread across borders—and the bulk of technology is transferred within the confines of integrated international production systems. This means that FDI and the operations of multinational corporations have become central to the world economy at large. Nowhere is this more important than for developing countries. Unsurprisingly, in future, competition will dominantly take place not between products or services but between business models.

Podgorica, Montenegro   Zvezdan Vukanović

Contents

Chapter 1
Introduction

The media and communication sectors have developed into a key economic sector in the modern information society. Media industries, services, and applications present a complex set of strategic challenges to economic and business analysis: challenges made more difficult by the disruptive technological changes that have been transforming the media sector. Hierarchical structures that exist to manage the work of groups are seeing their raisons d'tre swiftly eroded by the rising techno-logical tide. Business models are being destroyed, transformed, and born at dizzy-ing speeds, and the larger social impact is profound.

Research on the business/economics of media has made major advances in recent years and has contributed greatly to an increasingly sophisticated under-standing of how media are shaped by economic forces, including those unleashed by new, emerging, transformative, on-demand, and digital technologies. The new global and technological change in media business models and media FDI inflows is fast outstripping our critical frames of reference. Therefore, it is necessary to establish a diverse set of business models' methods and perspectives for studying this critical moment in media business and industry.

This volume reflects thorough discussions and enormous/unprecedented techno-logical change, media convergence, and globalization taking place within media markets' FDI sector in recent years. The study describes the latest and a wide-ranging examination of the contemporary media industry FDI inflow trends as well as micro/macroeconomic context and incorporates them into a coherent and appli-cative strategic business model. It also includes a fresh collection of media corpo-rations' multiple-case studies ripe for new types of research.

This monograph examines the variety of contexts and infrastructures in which media FDI business model innovation is applied and how these influence the regional, international, and global market. More specifically, this monograph explores the rationale, context, purpose, characteristics, development processes, and drivers of media FDI in South/East Europe. Moreover, it incorporates various micro/macroeconomic perspectives/views providing critical insight into trans-national media FDI inflows into South-East Europe market.

© Springer International Publishing Switzerland 2016
Z. Vukanović, *Foreign Direct Investment Inflows Into the South East European Media Market*, Media Business and Innovation, DOI 10.1007/978-3-319-30512-7_1

On one hand, the study draws on media industry FDI business model and profoundly complex, multifaceted, and wide-ranging empirical observation. On the other hand, the author specifically highlights and discusses the paradigm shift in business model innovation influencing the corporation's ability to flexibly change to new business models. In addition, this monograph explores a range of novel and challenging topics, perspectives, and arguments about the nature of FDI inflows into media business and industry, synthesizing and reorienting the practice and study of the topic. Based on both a wide and discrete reading and multiple-case study investigation, it offers the reader a multifaceted analysis of this important and under-researched subject.

Media industry is one of several industries to lack workable FDI inflow business models. This monograph is the first of its kind to focus on the dynamic, innovative, and transformational FDI business models in media industry. In this monograph, split into eight chapters/sections, the author offers multiple levels of FDI business model analysis on media industry. Each original chapter introduces the reader to a specific topic, reviews the literature on the development of knowledge in the field, explores critiques of the approach, and provides an understanding of empirically applying this knowledge and the implications.

The author explores the issues, limits, and challenges of business model innovation in media FDI in order to develop and reshape this rapidly and exponentially growing industry sector. In author's opinion, we are witnessing a fundamental and seismic reshaping of the international media market through increasing FDI inflows. Therefore, it is important to analyze the evolution of the dynamic/transformational business model from its very beginning of the dot.com era to the present day, exploring its conceptual framework and proposing the modifications and amendments in the sector of media FDI inflows.

The study dissects and presents advanced, wide-ranging, and varied methodological viewpoints/trajectories of competing, empirical, comparative, exploratory, and longitudinal research agendas/practices/findings—on one hand, offering a coherent conceptual and empirical analysis of contemporary business model frameworks, flow dynamics, and platforms and, on the other hand, providing the insightful critical debate, framework, and platform for discussing crucial issues in the globalized FDI media business. Moreover, it posits transnational media research as reflective of advanced globalization processes, and explores its roles and responsibilities, articulating key themes in a dynamic digital media field. In other words, the volume offers a wide-ranging micro/macroeconomic examination on the contemporary South-East Europe FDI media environment providing an empirical and methodological reflection and background knowledge on key aspects and important areas of research of the hybrid FDI business models, paradigms, as well as establishing the direction and a crucial foundation for the next phases of research in this growing arena of study; stimulating new scholarship; and resetting, proposing, and explicating new paradigmatic directions and perspectives in the domain of FDI business models.

In order to stay current and move their organizations forward in today's dynamic, profoundly transitional, increasingly networked, and rapidly evolving media environment, customer expectations, and the rules for how value is delivered, policymakers, scholars, and media managers/executives must have a clear understanding of the underlying challenges of FDI's strategies, value-added networks, delivery platforms potential, perspective, as well as an effectual grasp of critical corporate management, planning, and economic factors.

The monograph highlights the need for new perspectives, insights, drivers, growth processes, and economic expansion on FDI business model inflows into emerging South-East Europe media markets. In addition, it accentuates corporate media's FDI similarities and differences between developed and emerging country multinationals and preferred modes of FDI inflows' entry into foreign markets. Multiple-case studies from SEECs are presented, including media markets of Hungary, Malta, Slovenia, Croatia, Turkey, Romania, Bulgaria, etc.

In order to create a more competitive, profitable, and sustainable media business network value configuration, the author attempts to set as well as articulate a signaling architectural/organizational benchmark/roadmap and an agenda for future research on the implications of FDI business model innovation's paradigmatic/evolutionary shift in global media markets. These paradigmatic shifts and dynamic transformations have not only led business practices to change but also required companies to adapt to new and more dramatic competitive conditions. They also continue to map a fundamental and lasting impact on research in this area. Consequently, the author provides a systematic assessment of the current potentials and limits of the hybrid FDI business model's application and offers a detailed analysis of what could, or should, be the drivers to support its success and large-scale diffusion.

The main rationale of the monograph is twofold: first, it aims to provide media MNCs (multinational corporations) with the objective and practical knowledge as well as strategic business and economic potential of SEE media; second, it intends to provide a guidance to SEE media companies on how to more efficiently and effectively position and leverage its largely untapped and modestly integrated media infrastructure within the increasingly globalized media market. In order to increase the understanding of FDI business model in the media market, the author has conducted empirically 16-mini comparative and exploratory case studies of South-East European media market.

The monograph highlights the potential of SEECs media market and the need for reinvention of the competitive structure of FDI business model in an increasingly globalized and expanding media business and industry. In order to meet these complex and highly competitive media business demands, the author identifies and proposes a new business model—the FDI hybrid media business model consisting of seven synthetic, underlying, unique, and multidisciplinary factors/dimensions/variables/indices/principles/building blocks: (1) The Networked Readiness Index; (2) Global Competitiveness Index; (3) Global Innovation Index; (4) Media Market Concentration; (5) Forecasted Growth of GDP per capita (PPP), 2015–2025; (6) Forecasted Market Size via UN Medium variant Forecasted population prospects (%), 2015–2025; and (7) Average annual HDI growth (%), 2000–2013.

Furthermore, the author recognizes that hybrid FDI media business model can best enhance the economic and business benefits, while avoiding negative side-effects policies for media markets and domestic and multinational corporations. Correspondingly, the author points out that it is these seven indicators that are instrumental in influencing and shaping the potential for strategically intensive and sustainable FDI into increasingly competitive SEECs media industry. Moreover, the hybrid FDI business media model can be internationally applied to any global media corporation. Relatedly, this contextually nuanced study also offers new material on the current, prospective, and future evolutionary/progressive/developmental structure of multinational media corporations' FDI as well as current and future media markets in SEECs.

Importantly, this volume not only considers the economic impact and the ways in which new hybrid FDI business models emerge, develop, and are then commercialized, but also the wider societal impact and benefit of the emerging, new technologies' added network value in different digital, cyber, and hypermedia ecosystems as well as organizational architecture and platforms. The comparative, qualitative, and quantitative results and estimates provided in this publication offer important and concrete insights and recommendations on the current and future development and the deployment of both effective and efficient FDI media business model and media convergence/divergence trends. This monograph reorients the practice and study of FDI business models in media industry signaling new shifts by presenting a range of holistic strategic perspectives and arguments, proposing the new, anticipating, sophisticated, and advanced architecture of FDI media business models and serving a surefooted roadmap to new digital media ecosystem and value-network domains.

The monograph concludes by discussing the necessity for a profoundly detailed, rigorous, and stringent attitude toward the hybrid FDI business model to increase corporations' competitive advantage and added value network configurations in the dynamic digital field/ecosystem of transnational media and communications. The volume is geared toward advanced students, researchers, and academics interested in media and ICT business and strategic management, FDI, International trade, innovation, and organizational change, practitioners, policymakers within government and nongovernmental organizations, consultants, and seasoned industry executives who take interest in the ongoing debate about how to shape and implement FDI business model innovation in media industry. Moreover, this monograph will be of as much interest to economists writing in the heterodox tradition as to mainstream economists of this brave new virtual-cyber world.

Chapter 2
Business Model Research Agenda Positioning: Conceptual Frameworks, Functions, Benefits, Rationale, Dynamics, Performance, and Economic Feasibility

2.1 A Brief History of the Origin and Rise of the Business Model Concept

The concept of the BM first appeared over half a century ago in an article investigating the construction of business game revenue source model for training purposes (Bellman et al. 1957; Desmarteau and Saives 2008). The term is mentioned just once: "And many more problems arise to plague us in the construction of these business models than ever confronted an engineer" (Bellman et al. 1957: 474). The term did not see widespread use for decades. Until its reappearance in 1970s in computer science journals. Among the first who used the term business models in the context of data and process modeling were Konczal (1975) and Dottore (1977). In information management, business models were used to model a firm with all its processes, tasks, data, and communication links to build an IT system supporting the firm in its daily work.

The number of peer-reviewed journal papers on "business model" remained low until the 1990s, with only five papers containing the words "business model" in their title over the whole decade (Osterwalder et al. 2005). With the development of information and communication technologies (ICT) and the emergence of Internet companies, the concept/term quickly spread impressively gaining quick prominence among both entrepreneurial high-tech, start-up practitioners and business scholars (Verstraete et al. 2012). Congruently, the use of the term "business model" in academic papers closely followed the trend of the NASDAQ index from the early 1990s to the dot-com bubble burst. In a nutshell, the widespread use of the business model terminology seems to be intrinsically connected with technology-based

© Springer International Publishing Switzerland 2016   5
Z. Vukanović, *Foreign Direct Investment Inflows Into the South East European Media Market*, Media Business and Innovation, DOI 10.1007/978-3-319-30512-7_2

companies (DaSilva and Trkman 2014). Business models seemed to be the answer for explaining how innovative undertakings dealing with technology or any other form of unclear but potentially profitable concepts, foreign to the logic of traditional industries, were materialized in business terms (DaSilva and Trkman 2014). The sharp rise in cheap information technology, bandwidth, and communication possibilities made it much easier for companies to work in so-called value webs because coordination and transaction costs fell substantially (Tapscott et al. 2000; Amit and Zott 2001). As a result of a cheap and readily available information technology, industry boundaries became increasingly blurred, and the business model concept gradually replaced the industry as a unit of analysis (Osterwalder et al. 2005). Ghaziani and Ventresca (2005) further acknowledge that, during this period, the business model terminology spread to various communities (such as marketing, management, banking, and ICT) and has been used within various frameworks (such as business plan, business strategy, value creation, globalization, and organization design).

The term "business model" survived the dot-com bubble. The number of papers with "business model" in their title remained relatively stable between 2004 and 2007 at 25–42 papers annually. Interestingly, it began to grow again with 45, 68, and 83 papers, in 2008, 2009, and 2010, respectively. A closer look at this trend reveals that the 2004–2007 stream of papers was characterized by a change in focus from the business model of Internet companies to the analysis of business models in "general business." As the Internet and ICT had revolutionized the way companies do business in virtually all industries, the business model term quickly spread to the analysis of brick-and-mortar companies. Because companies have no previous experience in the Internet sector, entrepreneurs needed to use a diagrammatic or visual model to make their entrepreneurial projects understandable, in particular by investors who, in a perpetual search of good deals were less tolerant of financial ambiguity of current and future business investments (Verstraete et al. 2012).

Joan Magretta (2002) in HBR article "Why Business Models Matter" succinctly explains the evolutionary application of the Business Model: "The term "business model" first came into widespread use with the advent of the personal computer and the spreadsheet. The spreadsheet ushered in a much more analytic approach to planning because every major line item could be pulled apart, its components and subcomponents analyzed and tested. In other words, modeling the behavior of a business via the personal computer and the spreadsheet was something new. Before the personal computer changed the nature of business planning, most successful business models, were created more by accident than by design and forethought."

Following the advent of IT-centered businesses (1990–1995), the term Business Model rose to prominence (Stähler 2002), gaining the wider access to business peer-reviewed journals focusing on the emerging field of digital and convergent media as well as e-commerce and e-business (Timmers 1998; Kotha 1998). Accordingly, the rise of the term is closely related to the emergence and diffusion of commercial activities on the Internet. Consequently, Internet start-ups used the term to differentiate themselves from the incumbents and to explain their competitive position (Stähler 2002).

The term business model became popular only in the late 1990s, which is a result of the rapid erosion of prices in the ICT and telecom industry (Osterwalder and Pigneur 2010). In other words, cheap processing, storing, and sharing information across business units and other companies all the way to the customer created new ways of doing business. Accordingly, value chains/networks were broken up and reconfigured; innovative information-rich or -enriched products, services, and applications appeared; new distribution channels emerged; more customers were reached (Osterwalder and Pigneur 2010).

Having realized the rising prominence and high significance of the BM, there has been an increasing high-tech and media interest in delineating the concept and providing further understanding. Accordingly, the largest increase of published refereed or peer-reviewed academic papers occurred between 1998 and 2002. It was followed by the sharp rise of published master thesis and doctoral dissertations (2000–2005). Table 2.1 shows the detailed and longitudinal evolution of published academic papers, books, doctoral dissertations, and master theses in the field of business model.

Table 2.1 The chronological order of the longitudinal, comparative, and analytical framework/taxonomy of scholarly business model definitions to be found in the academic literature 1995–2013

Authors— references	Definitions	Primary sources	Citations
Slywotzky (1995)	The business system is the totality of how a company selects its customers, defines and differentiates its offerings (or response), defines the tasks it will perform itself and those it will outsource, configures its resources, goes to market, creates utility for costumers, and captures profits. It is the entire system for delivering utility to customers and earning a profit from that activity	*Harvard Business School Press*	NA
Brandenburger and Stuart (1996)	A business model is an organization's approach to generating revenue at a reasonable cost and incorporates assumptions about how it will both create and capture value	*Journal of Economics and Management Strategy*	730
Timmers (1998)	The BM primary constructs include an architecture for the products, service, and information flows, including various business actors as well as their roles and benefits in addition to sources of revenue	*Electronic markets*	2642
Venkatraman and Henderson (1998)	Business model is a coordinated plan to design strategy as an architecture of a virtual organization along three vectors: the customer interaction, asset configuration, and knowledge leverage vectors	*Sloan Management Review*	966
Maître and Aladjidi (1999)	Le business model est composé de trois éléments: une proposition de valeur, une gestion adéquate du temps et une typologie de l'écosystème puis du positionnement spécifique de l'entreprise. Le business model d'une entreprise est pour l'essentiel la structure de son offre, sa manière de générer des revenus, son organisation et la structure des coûts qui en résulte, sa manière de nouer des alliances adéquates et la position dans la chaîne de valeur qui en résulte	*Dunod*	75

(continued)

Table 2.1 (continued)

Authors—references	Definitions	Primary sources	Citations
Mayo and Brown (1999)	A business model is the design of key interdependent systems that create and sustain a competitive business	*Ivey Business Journal*	65
Selz (1999)	[A] business model is an architecture for the product, service, and information flows, including the various economic agents and their roles. Furthermore, a business model includes the potential benefits for the various agents and description of the potential revenue flow	*University of St. Gallen*	17
Eriksson and Penker (2000)	The business model is the focal point around which business is conducted or around which business operations are improved	*John Wiley & Sons Inc.*	1359
Hamel (2000)	A business comprises four major components: Core Strategy, Strategic Resources, Customer Interface, Value Network	*Harvard Business School Press*	117
Gordijn et al. (2000a)	A business model shows explicitly the exchange, flow, and communication of the value via channels—among stakeholders	*Springer*	308
Linder and Cantrell (2000)	A BM is a way in which organizations generate revenue	*Accenture Institute for Strategic Change*	29
Applegate (2000)	A business model is a description of a complex business that enables study of its structure, the relationship among structural elements, and how it will respond in the real world	*Harvard Business School Press*	129
Mahadevan (2000)	A business model is a unique blend of three streams that are critical to the business. These include the value stream for the business partners and the buyers, the revenue stream, and the logistical stream. The value stream identifies the value proposition for the buyers, sellers, and the market makers and portals in an Internet context. The revenue stream is a plan for assuring revenue generation for the business. The logistical stream addresses various issues related to the design of the supply chain for the business	*California Management Review*	986

(continued)

Table 2.1 (continued)

Authors—references	Definitions	Primary sources	Citations
Stewart and Zhao (2000)	The business model is a statement of how a firm will make money and sustain its profit stream over time	*Journal of Public Policy & Marketing*	254
Tapscott et al. (2000)	Business webs are inventing new value propositions, transforming the rules of competition, and mobilizing people and resources to unprecedented levels of performance. . .a b-web is a distinct system of suppliers, distributors, commerce service providers, and customers that use the Internet for their primary business communications and transactions	*Harvard Business School*	1161
Benavent and Verstraete (2000)	Le business model désigne un ensemble "large qui inclut les relations avec les fournisseurs, les partenariats, les interactions entre plusieurs marchés et peut se traduire par des choix qui définissent les conditions et la réalité de l'affaire"	*EMS—Editions Management et Société, Caen*	40
Kraemer et al. (2000)	The business model: consists of direct sales, direct customer relationships, customer segmentation for sales and service, and build to order production	*The Information Society*	216
Afuah and Tucci (2001)	A business model includes customer value (distinctive offering or low cost), scope (customers and products/services), price, revenue sources, connected activities, implementation (required resources), capabilities (required skills), and sustainability	*Irwin/McGraw-Hill*	NA
Amit and Zott (2001)	A business model is the architectural configuration of the components of transactions designed to exploit business opportunities An e-business models include content (exchanged goods and information), structure (the links between transaction stakeholders), and governance of transactions (the control of the flows of goods, information, and resources)	*Strategic Management Journal*	3785

(continued)

Table 2.1 (continued)

Authors—references	Definitions	Primary sources	Citations
Applegate (2001)	The business model framework, based on an I/O logic, consists of three components: concept, capabilities, and value. The business concept defines a business market opportunity, products and services offered, competitive dynamics, strategy to obtain a dominant position, and strategic option for evolving the business	*Harvard Business Review*	129
Porter (2001)	A business model is a loose conception of how a company does business and generates revenue	*Harvard Business Review*	58
Weill and Vitale (2001)	A business model includes roles and relations among a firm's consumers, customers, allies, and suppliers that identifies the major flows of product, information, and money, and the major benefits to participants"	*Harvard Business School Press*	30
Winter and Szulanski (2001)	Business model is typically a complex set of interdependent routines . . . discovered, adjusted, and fine-tuned by "doing"	*Organization science*	968
Stähler (2001)	A business model helps to understand the fundamentals of a business. It is a deliberate abstraction of a real business or a future business. It comprises of: • A description what value a customer or a partner receives from the business: it is the value proposition, and it answers the question: what value the business creates for its stakeholders? • A description of the products and services the firm is providing. It answers the question: what does the firm sell? • A description of the architecture of value creation. It answers the question: How is the value in what configuration being created? • The value and sustainability of the business is being determined by its revenue model. It answers the question: with what do we earn money?	*University of St. Gallen*	463

(continued)

Table 2.1 (continued)

Authors—references	Definitions	Primary sources	Citations
Petrovic et al. (2001)	A business model as an intermediate layer between strategy and business processes	*Proceedings of the International conference on Electronic Commerce*	376
Tapscott (2001)	Business model refers to the core architecture of a firm, specially how it deploys all relevant resources	*Strategy+Business, PwC Strategy & LLC International Business, Corporate Strategy and Management Magazine*	204
Alt and Zimmermann (2001)	A business model consists of six generic elements: mission, structure, processes, revenues, legal issues, and technology	*Electronic Markets*	398
Zott and Amit (2002)	Business model depicts the content, structure, and governance of transactions designed to create value through the exploitations of business opportunities	*INSEAD Working Paper Series*	35
Magretta (2002)	The main components of BMs include telling a logical story explaining who the customers are, what they value, and how to deliver values to them at an appropriate cost	*Harvard Business Review*	2196
Bouwman (2002)	BM is a description of roles and relationships of a company, its customers, partners, and suppliers, as well as the flows of goods, information, and money between these parties and the main benefits for those involved, in particular, but not exclusively the customer	*International Workshop on Business Models, HEC Lausanne*	20
Osterwalder and Pigneur (2002)	The business model is the missing link between strategy and business processes. More specifically, a business model is the "conceptual and architectural implementation (blueprint) of a business strategy (that) represents the foundation for the implementation of business processes and information systems"	*Proceedings of the 15th Bled Electronic Commerce Conference—eReality: Constructing the eEconomy*	713
Chesbrough and Rosenbloom (2002)	The business model represents a "coherent mediating framework" between technological artifacts, achieving economic values	*Industrial and corporate change*	2558

(continued)

Table 2.1 (continued)

Authors—references	Definitions	Primary sources	Citations
Dubosson-Torbay et al. (2002)	A business model is a conceptual and architectural implementation (blueprint) of a business strategy and represents the foundation for the implementation of business processes and information systems. A business model is nothing else than a description of the value a company offers to one or several segments of customers and the architecture of the firm and its network of partners for creating, marketing, and delivering this value and relationship capital, in order to generate profitable and sustainable revenues streams. This comprises tangible and intangible organizational assets, resources, and core competencies. comprises tangible and intangible organizational assets, resources, and core competencies	*Thunderbird International Business Review*	474
Betz (2002)	Business models are abstracts about how inputs to an organization are transformed to value-adding outputs as well as how the business profitability makes money	*Engineering Management Journal*	161
Elliot (2002a, b)	Business models specify the relationships between different participants in a commercial venture, the benefits and costs to each, and the flow of revenue. Business strategy specifies how a business model can be applied to a market to differentiate the firm from its competitors	*Willey & Sons*	67
Chesbrough (2003)	The business model consists of the value proposition, market segment, value chain structure, cost structure, the position of the firm on the value network, and the competitive strategy	*Harvard Business School Press*	10,721

(continued)

Table 2.1 (continued)

Authors—references	Definitions	Primary sources	Citations
Osterwalder and Pigneur (2003)	A business model is a conceptual tool containing a set of objects, concepts, and their relationships with the objective to express the business logic of a specific firm. Therefore, we must consider which concepts and relationships allow a simplified description and representation of what value is provided to customers, how this is done, and with which financial consequences it is delivered and captured	*Strategic Management Society Conference*	19
Hedman and Kalling (2003)	A generic business model includes seven causally related cross-sectional components: (1) customers, (2) competitors (3) offering, (4) activities and organization, (5) resources, (6) supply of factor and production inputs, and (7) a longitudinal process component	*European Journal of Information Systems*	633
Camponovo and Pigneur (2003)	A business model is a conceptual tool	*Proceedings of the 5th International Conference on Enterprise Information Systems*	176
Seddon et al. (2004)	A business model outlines the essential details of a firm's value proposition for its various stakeholders and the activity system the firm uses to create and deliver value to its customers	*Communications of AIS*	138
Mitchell and Bruckner Coles (2004a, b)	A business model is the who, what, when, where, why, how, and how much an organization uses to provide its goods and services and develop resources to continue its efforts	*Journal of Business Strategy*	103
Leem et al. (2004)	A set of strategies for corporate establishment and management including a revenue model, high-level business processes, and alliances	*Industrial Management & Data Systems*	86

(continued)

Table 2.1 (continued)

Authors—references	Definitions	Primary sources	Citations
Warnier et al. (2004)	Nous définissons le business model comme les choix qu'une entreprise effectue pour générer des revenus. Le business model apparaît comme l'ensemble des choix opérés sur un certain nombre de variables influençant la mise en oeuvre opérationnelle d'une stratégie	*13ème Conférence Internationale de Management Stratégique*	47
Morris et al. (2005)	A business model represents the way an interrelated set of decision variables in the areas of venture strategy, architecture, and economics create sustainable competitive advantage in defined markets. It has six fundamental components: value proposition, customer, internal competencies, external positioning, economic model, and personal/investor factors	*Journal of Business Research*	1330
Osterwalder et al. (2005)	The BM is an interface or an intermediate theoretical layer between the business strategy and the business processes including their IS	*Communications of the association for Information Systems*	1598
Callon and Muniesa (2005)	A business model is a "market device" defining how actors relate to markets	*Organization Studies*	781
Tikkanen et al. (2005)	BM articulates different BM components or "building blocks" to produce a proposition that can generate value for consumers and thus for the organization	*Management Decision*	271
Osterwalder et al. (2005)	A business model is a conceptual, analytic, comparative tool to help understand how a firm does business and performs, assesses, and manages communication and innovation	*15th Bled Electronic Commerce Conference Paper—eReality: Constructing the eEconomy*	127

(continued)

Table 2.1 (continued)

Authors—references	Definitions	Primary sources	Citations
Shafer et al. (2005)	A business model is a representation of a firm's underlying core logic and strategic choices for creating and capturing value within a value network	*Business Horizons*	1046
Schweizer (2005)	A business model tries to give an integrated and consistent picture of a company and the way it aims to generate revenues	*Journal of General Management*	60
Pateli and Giaglis (2005)	A business model must explicitly account for the need for partnership and provide the best possible answers to the questions regarding the type of value that each partner will contribute based on its core competence, the distribution of revenues and profits between them, the type of service offerings, and the business structures that will be required to implement the changes	*Journal of Organizational Change Management*	97
Voelpel et al. (2005)	The particular business concept (or way of doing business) as reflected by the business's core value proposition(s) for customers; its configured value network to provide that value, consisting of own strategic capabilities as well as other (e.g., outsourced, allianced) value networks; and its continued sustainability to reinvent itself and satisfy the multiple objectives of its various stakeholders	*European Management Journal*	95
Rajala and Westerlund (2005)	The ways of creating value for customers and the way business turns market opportunities into profit through sets of actors, activities, and collaborations	*18th Bled eCommerce Conference eIntegration in Action*	22

(continued)

Table 2.1 (continued)

Authors—references	Definitions	Primary sources	Citations
Lecocq et al. (2006)	Nous définissons le business model comme les choix qu'une entreprise effectue pour générer des revenus. Ces choix portent sur trois dimensions principales que sont les ressources et compétences mobilisées (qui permettent de proposer une offre), l'offre faite aux clients (au sens large) et l'organisation interne de l'entreprise (chaîne de valeur) et de ses transactions avec ses partenaires externes (réseau de valeur)	*L'Expansion Management Review*	83
Andersson et al. (2006)	The BM is a mechanism that makes the business actors' relations more explicit	*Proceedings of the 25th International Conference on Conceptual Modeling (ER2006) 6–9 November, Tucson*	117
Kallio et al. (2006)	The means by which a firm is able to create value by coordinating the flow of information, goods, and services among the various industry participants it comes in contact with including customers, partners within the value chain, competitors, and the government	*Business Process Management Journal*	37
Haaker et al. (2006)	A business model explains which organizational actor(s) (suppliers, partners, marketers, distributors, and intermediaries, competitors, customers, public organizations such as governmental bodies and agencies) is governing or being dominant in the business network	*International Journal of Mobile Communication*	88
Rasmussen (2007)	Business models define firm's competitive strategy through the design of the product or service it offers to its market, how it charges for it, what it costs to produce, how it differentiates itself from other firms by the value proposition, and how the firm integrates its own value chain with those of other firm's in a value network	*Pharmaceutical Industry Project Working Paper Series, Centre for Strategic Economic Studies Victoria University of Technology, Melbourne*	27

(continued)

Table 2.1 (continued)

Authors—references	Definitions	Primary sources	Citations
Seelos and Mair (2007)	A business model is a set of capabilities that is configured to enable value creation consistent with either economic or social strategic objectives	*Academy of Management Perspectives*	381
Rajala and Westerlund (2007)	The business model framework consists of (1) value propositions and offerings; (2) various assets and capabilities as resources needed to develop and implement a business model; (3) the revenue logic (including sources of revenue, price-quotation principles, and cost structures) that is characteristic of a particular business	*The International Journal of Entrepreneurship and Innovation*	64
Zott and Amit (2008)	The business model is a structural template that describes the organization of a focal firm's transactions with all of its external constituents in factor and product markets	*Strategic Management Journal*	706
Johnson et al. (2008)	A business model consists of four interlocking elements (customer value proposition—CVP; Profit formula; Key resources; and Key processes)	*Harvard Business Review*	1272
Rappa (2008)	According to the value network, or a multi-party stakeholder network point of view, a BM positions an organization in the value system and its relationships with different stakeholders. In other words, the business model is the method of doing business in which a company generates revenue	*TAFE*	548
Kamoun (2008)	The "BM becomes the interceding blueprint/framework of the way a business creates and captures value from new services, products, or innovations"	*Communications of the Association for Information Systems*	29
Pisano and Verganti (2008)	The business model indicates the mode of collaboration in the open or closed value network	*Harvard Business Review*	383

(continued)

Table 2.1 (continued)

Authors—references	Definitions	Primary sources	Citations
Janssen et al. (2008)	The BM describes a company from its mission perspective as well as the products-services it offers to customers	*Government Information Quarterly*	76
Richardson (2008)	Three main elements define a business model: the value proposition, value creation and delivery, and value capture	*Strategic Change*	128
Fiet and Patel (2008)	A business model explains how a venture is expected to create a profit	*Entrepreneurship: Theory & Practice*	26
Mason and Leek (2008)	. . . two cornerstones of business models (. . .): (1) structure: how firms perceive the structure of their firm, their business network, and their position within it; and (2) routines: how firms develop effective operational routines to exploit the potential value of their network	*Journal of Management Studies*	110
Patzelt et al. (2008)	Business models define how firms manage their transactions with other organizations such as customers, partners, investors, and suppliers and therefore constitute the organizations' architecture for the product, service, and information flows	*British Journal of Management*	75
Baden-Fuller and Morgan (2010)	Business models can act as recipes for management and creative managers	*Long Range Planning*	482
Teece (2010)	A business model reflects "management's hypothesis about what customers want, how they want it, and how an enterprise can best meet those needs, and get paid for doing so." A business model articulates how the company will convert resources and capabilities into economic value. It is nothing less than the organizational and financial "architecture" of a business and includes implicit assumptions about customers, their needs, and the behavior of revenues, costs, and competitors	*Long Range Planning*	1834

(continued)

Table 2.1 (continued)

Authors—references	Definitions	Primary sources	Citations
Casadesus-Masanell and Ricart (2010)	A business model is the logic of the firm, the way it operates, and how it creates value for its stakeholder	*Long Range Planning*	706
Al-Debei and Fitzgerald (2010)	BMs represents an organization's resources, their configurations, and the resultant core competencies	*Springer*	22
Zott and Amit (2010)	A business model is an activity-based perspective, including the selection of activities ("what"), the activity system structure ("how"), and who performs the activities ("who")	*Long Range Planning*	770
Al-Debei and Avison (2010)	The primary constructs and dimensions of the business model concept consists of four classes—value proposition, value architecture, value network, and value finance	*European Journal of Information Systems*	231
Osterwalder and Pigneur (2010)	A business model is a series of elements: the value proposition (product/service offering, customer segments, customer relationships), activities, resources, partners, distribution channels (i.e., value creation and delivery) and cost structure, and revenue model (i.e., value capture)	*John Wiley & Sons*	2573
Demil and Lecocq (2010)	The business model concept articulates different areas of a firm's activity designed to produce a value proposition to customers	*Long Range Planning*	456
Smith et al. (2010)	A business model is the design by which an organization converts a given set of strategic choices—about markets, customers, value propositions—into value, and uses a particular organizational architecture—of people, competencies, processes, culture, and measurement systems—in order to create and capture this value	*Long Range Planning*	163

(continued)

Table 2.1   (continued)

Authors—references	Definitions	Primary sources	Citations
Amit and Zott (2012)	A company's business model is a system of interconnected and interdependent activities that determines the way the company "does business" with its customers, partners, and vendors. In other words, a business model is a bundle of specific activities—an activity system—conducted to satisfy the perceived needs of the market, along with the specification of which parties (a company or its partners) conduct which activities, and how these activities are linked to each other	*MIT Sloan Management Review*	254
Edvardsson et al. (2012)	The business model defines the practices that the focal actor engages in and these practices influence other actors	*Review of Marketing Research*	16
Beattie and Smith (2013)	Describe business models as a holistic description on "how a firm does business"	*The British Accounting Review*	30
Beltramello et al. (2013)	Value creation is at the heart of any business model; businesses typically capture value by seizing new business opportunities, new markets, and new revenue streams	*OECD Publishing*	21

2.2   The Evolution of the ICT Exponential Growth and Influence of the Business Model

The term "business model" has been used with rapidly increasing frequency since the mid-1990s. Thus, a web search using Google in February 2003 found one million web pages using the term "business model" and 17 million using the term "strategy" (Seddon and Lewis 2003). However, a web search using Google in May 2016 found 1.24 billion web pages using the term "business model" and 606 million using the term "strategy."

Moreover, the popularity and surge of the term "business model" in scholarly peer-reviewed and non-peer-reviewed journal coincided and increased in accordance "with the advent of the Internet in the business world and the steep rise of the NASDAQ stock market index for technology-heavy companies" (Osterwalder et al. 2005). The number of times the term "business model" appeared in a business journal (peer-reviewed and non-peer reviewed) follows correspondingly a pattern that resembles the shape of the NASDAQ market index... [suggesting] that the topic of business models has a relationship with the ICT development (Osterwalder et al. 2005).

Correspondingly, part of the relationship between technology and business models stems from the business model concept's roots in transaction cost economics (TCE).

2.3 The Influence of Technology on the Creation of New Business Models

The role of technology in relation to the business model is not to be underestimated, as it is a key element in (a) determining which organizational structures and value configuration/proposition logics become feasible, (b) influencing the design of the business, i.e., its underlying architecture. Moreover, Burcham (2000), Timmers (1998), and Chesbrough and Rosenbloom (2002) accentuate that companies must acknowledge that information technology is changing the entire value chain of their business models.

Thus, the development of new technologies has been one of the great enablers in providing a strategic advantage in terms of economic growth and increasing returns to an organization within a given industry. New technologies, whether they are developed by the particular organization in research development for their specialized industry (or application) or by utilizing technology from alternative industries, are capable of providing a specialization or uniqueness of skills or operation that may not be easily matched by their competitors (Joyce and Winch 2004).

Advancements in technology, changing customer demands, or new market entrants are often seen as a necessary condition to trigger the creation of new Business Models or disruptive change in existing ones (Malmmose et al. 2014).

2.4 The Commonality and Difference Between Business Models and Strategies

Although both terms are widely used, the terms "business model" and "strategy" are often poorly defined. A systematic review of the literature, examining leading authors' definitions of both terms, reveals that there is a considerable and substantial overlap between these two terms. So the two initial questions one is tempted to ask are: "What are the nuanced and distinct differences between strategy and business model?" and "Which comes first: strategy or business model?"

The author suggests that strategy seems more concerned with competition between firms, whereas business models are more concerned with the "core logic" (Linder and Cantrell 2000) enabling a firm to create value for its customers and owners. In addition, a business model defines an abstract representation of some aspect of the firm's strategy (Seddon et al. 2004). However, unlike strategy, business models do not consider a firm's competitive positioning (Seddon et al. 2004).

More specifically, strategies are treated as ground firmly in the real world, whereas business models would be treated as abstractions of firms' real-world strategies. Such configuration of business model framework has attracted the attention of so many researchers because they are useful for evaluating alternative, potential, prospective and future ways of building profitable businesses. Also, the author suggests that much more information is required to represent a firm's strategy than is required to represent a business model. In addition, there is literally an unlimited number of different models one can build based on the one firm's strategy. On the other hand, the answer to the second question is that business model comes first, representing the building blocks and patterns for prospective and future strategies. Concurrently, the BM is the operational counterpart to strategy and covers the implementation of the strategy. Basically, the BM translates the choices made upstream of the strategic approach into operational terms and is an intermediate level of analysis between a company's strategy and its functional translations (Daidj and Isckia 2009). The BM reveals strategic choices made upstream, and articulated around four dimensions associated with clients (what is the value proposition for the client?), expertise (what are the required skills?), network (what are the modalities of collaboration between the various parties?), and revenue (how does the company make money?) which will determine the value created and the share of this value captured by the company (Daidj and Isckia 2009).

Thus, in contrast to common assumptions, the business model is neither semantically related to concepts of business process modeling and business plan (although it may be a part of one) nor the notion of strategy (although it may represent a strategic activity and strategic choice). However, the business models embody and reflect the strategy (Heikkilä et al. 2007). Along similar lines, Morris (2003) link business models to strategic management by stating that strategic choices characterize a company, while business models make the choices explicit. They see that business models have elements of both strategy and operational effectiveness, i.e., processes (Casadesus-Masanell and Ricart 2007). The main difference between the business model and the strategy is that the business model is a more concrete description of the operations of the company than the business strategy. Thus, a business model is positioned between business strategy and business processes. Consequently, the business model is a suitable test bed for the feasibility of the strategy (Casadesus-Masanell and Ricart 2007). Additionally, business models are more about adding new value network within the existing business ecosystem, while strategic management is more concerned with leading and managing the existing business portfolio of corporations.

A business model isn't the same thing as strategy, even though many people use the terms interchangeably today. Sooner or later—and it is usually sooner—every enterprise runs into competitors. Dealing with that reality is strategy's job. A competitive strategy explains how you will do better than your rivals. The business models describe, as a system, how the pieces of a business fit together, but business models neither consider nor factor in one critical dimension of performance: competition. Thus, while strategy focuses on how to prevail over competitors, the business model depicts the logic of value creation and the effective coordination of business resources (Osterwalder et al. 2005). Business models specify the relationships between different participants in a commercial venture, the benefits and costs to each, and the flows of revenue (Elliot 2002a, b). Business strategies specify how a business model can be applied to the market to differentiate the firm from its competitors, e.g., by addressing a particular segment of the market, by competing on cost and/or levels of service (Elliot 2002a, b).

A corporate or entrepreneurial strategy can be implemented through multiple business models, because the company may choose a different model to cooperate with each customer. However, the corporate business models are based on its strategy. Correspondingly, business models have been related to strategy (Teece 2010), entrepreneurship (George and Bock 2011; Huarng 2013), and international entrepreneurship (Saino et al. 2011).

The business model concept defines a business market opportunity, products and services offered, competitive dynamics, strategic positioning, and strategic option for evolving the business. From a more general management theory point of view, the business model is a framework or representation of the business logic of a company and describes the value the firm offers to one or several segments of customers, the architecture of its internal processes, as well as the network of partners needed to create, market, and deliver value to the firm's customers to generate long-term profitable, sustainable, and suitable revenue streams (Nadler and Tushman, 1997; Osterwalder et al. 2005). Business models can act in various forms: describing and classifying businesses, integrating aggregated entrepreneurial activity, and representing corporate architecture. Accordingly, business models continue to evolve from their initial states and throughout repeated application (Dunford et al. 2010) for survival and success (Javalgi et al. 2012). A business model describes the value logic of an organization, creating and capturing customer value (e.g., Osterwalder and Pigneur 2010). In essence, every company has a business model, whether that model is explicitly articulated or not (Chesbrough 2006; Teece 2010).

A business model expresses the company's strategy in a concrete form, most often at a strategic business unit (SBU) level. In the business model, the vision and strategy of a company are translated into value propositions, customer relations, and value networks. (Casadesus-Masanell and Ricart 2007). Rajala (2001) depicts a business model as consisting of four sub-models: a product development model, revenue logic model, sales and marketing model, and a servicing and implement-ation model. They also add competition, customers, resources and external financ-ing as separate but important external influences on the operating environment.

The business model is a complex, overarching conceptual tool for depicting, innovating, and evaluating business logics in start-ups and in existing organi-zations, especially in IT-enabled or digital industries (Veit et al. 2014; Demil and Lecocq 2010; Osterwalder and Pigneur 2010). Kim and Marbourgne (2000) define a business model as the firm's price and revenue model. Elliot (2002a, b) holds that a business model specifies the relationships between different participants in a commercial venture, the benefits and costs to each, and the flows of revenue.

The BM is a conceptual, architectural, financial arrangement, semantics, frame-work, alignment tool, synthesizing, articulating, positioning, mediating, leveraging, facilitating, and developing strategic goals, objectives, and constitutive elements of value proposition, value architecture, and value network. In other words, the BM is a mediating construct between technological artifacts and the strategic outcomes. The primary dimensions and spectra of the business model include value propo-sition, value architecture, value network, and value finance. On one hand, the busi-ness model is a cognitive mechanism, linking to human resource management and the management of perceptions. On the other hand, the business model is a construct for mediating technology development and economic value creation. Moreover, business model is an intermediary and the missing link between strategy and business processes, organization networks, and digitization.

From Nielsen and Bukh (2013), the following definition of a business model is provided: A business model describes the coherence in the strategic choice, which makes possible the handling of the processes and relations which create value on the operational, tactical, and strategic levels in the organization. The business model is therefore the platform, connecting resources, processes, and the supply of a service resulting in the company's long-term profitability. Additionally, the business model concept has proven a very helpful and distinct unit of analysis when conceptualized as an activity system determining the content, governance, and structure of a firm's boundary-spanning interactions (Zott and Amit 2007). In the context of the widespread digitization of businesses and society at large, the logic inherent in a business model has become critical for business success and, hence, a focus for academic inquiry (Veit et al. 2014).

On the other hand, as evidenced by the large number of studies attempting to provide business model typologies, business model researchers generally adopt a holistic and systemic (as opposed to particularistic and functional) perspective, not just on what businesses do (e.g., what products and services they produce to serve needs in addressable market spaces), but also on how they do it (e.g., how they bridge factor and product markets in serving the needs of customers). The business model perspective thus involves simultaneous consideration of content and process, which explains part of the challenge in defining and operationalizing the construct. Another insight that emerges from the author's review of the literature is that business model scholars have shifted emphasis from value capture to value creation, highlighting the latter without ignoring the former.

In sum, business models are a new unit of analysis representing a systemic, transactional, and organizational activity as well as a variable operationalizing strategy. This suggests a view of the business model as a networked, firm-centric, yet boundary-spanning, activity system. Some researchers view the business model closer to the firm (e.g., Casadesus-Masanell and Ricart 2010), others place it closer to the network (e.g., Tapscott et al. 2000), and for others still it is nested somewhere between the firm and the network (e.g., Zott and Amit 2002). All but a few business model scholars would agree, however, that it is a new, distinct concept, worthwhile of academic study and relevant in practice.

2.5 Research Methodology Aims and Approaches

This chapter is based on a longitudinal study and meta-analysis methodology.

A longitudinal survey is a correlational and observational research study that involves repeated observations of the same variables over long periods of time—often many decades. The key advantage of the longitudinal studies is that it extends beyond a single moment in time. As a result, they can establish sequences of events. Therefore, a longitudinal study is more likely to suggest cause-and-effect relationships than a cross-sectional study by virtue of its scope.

Because most longitudinal studies are observational, in the sense that they observe the state of the world without manipulating it, it has been argued that they may have less power to detect causal relationships than experiments. But because of the repeated observation at the individual level, they have more power than cross-sectional observational studies, by virtue of being able to exclude time-invariant unobserved individual differences, and by virtue of observing the temporal order of events. Longitudinal studies allow social scientists to distinguish short from long-term phenomena.

2.5.1 The Main Features and Strengths of the Longitudinal Design Research and Study

Main features of the longitudinal design research and study include:

– Single sample over extended period of time
– Enables the same phenomena, data, or individuals to be compared over time (diachronic analysis)
– Establishes a prerequisite for the micro-level analysis.

Concurrently, the main strengths of the longitudinal study are:

1. Useful for establishing causal relationships and for making reliable inferences.
2. Shows how changing properties of individuals fit into systemic change.
3. Operates within the known limits of instrumentation employed.
4. Separates real trends from chance occurrence.
5. Brings the benefits of extended time frames.
6. Useful for charting growth and development.
7. Gathers data contemporaneously rather than retrospectively, thereby avoiding the problems of selective or false memory.
8. Economical in that a picture of the sample is built up over time.
9. In-depth and comprehensive coverage of a wide range of variables, both initial and emergent—individual specific effects and population heterogeneity.
10. Enables change to be analyzed at the individual/micro-level.
11. Enables the dynamics of change to be caught, the flows into and out of particular states, and the transitions between states.
12. Individual level data are more accurate than macro-level, cross-sectional data.
13. Sampling error reduced as the study remains with the same sample over time.
14. Enables clear recommendations for intervention to be made.

2.5.2 The Main Features and Advantages of the Meta-analysis Method

"Meta-analyses" are systematic attempts to integrate the results of individual studies into a single quantitative analysis, pooling individual cases drawn from each study into a single dataset (with various weightings and restrictions). In the meta-analysis method, the author combines and contrasts the data evidences and results from two or more separate but similar studies in the hope of examining the key research questions and identifying a common statistical measures/patterns sources of disagreement among study results or other interesting relationships that may come to light in the context of multiple studies. Meta-analysis can be thought of as "conducting research about previous research." Conceptually, a meta-analysis uses and combines the results from multiple studies in an effort to increase power (over individual studies), improve estimates of the size of the effect, and/or to resolve uncertainty when reports disagree.

Basically, it produces a weighted average of the included study results and this approach has several advantages:

- Results can be generalized to a larger population.
- The precision and accuracy of estimates can be improved as more data is used. This, in turn, may increase the statistical power to detect an effect.

- Inconsistency of results across studies can be quantified and analyzed. For instance, does inconsistency arise from sampling error, or are study results (partially) influenced by between-study heterogeneity.
- Hypothesis testing can be applied on summary estimates.
- Moderators can be included to explain variation between studies.
- The presence of publication bias can be investigated.
- The ability to answer questions not posed by individual studies.
- The opportunity to settle controversies arising from conflicting claims.

Meta-analysis leads to a shift of emphasis from single studies to multiple studies. It emphasizes the practical importance of the effect size instead of the statistical significance of individual studies. The author included only methodologically sound studies (i.e., "best evidence synthesis") in a meta-analysis.

2.6 Desperately Seeking Definition: Identity Crisis of the Business Model

The lack of definitional and configured consistency as well as clarity represents a potential source of confusion, promoting dispersion rather than convergence of perspectives, and obstructing cumulative research progress on business models.

In spite of its ambiguity, as well as erroneous and haphazard use among academic scholars and corporate executives, the business model concept has become a pertinent notion in managerial vocabulary. Accordingly, it has become increasingly popular within ICT, telecommunications, media management and strategy literature, including both traditional strategy theory and in the emergent body of literature on e-business. Companies commercialize new ideas and technologies through their business models. Moreover, business models hold an increasingly dynamic and pivotal role in today's knowledge-based economies (Chapman et al. 2003).

Despite agreement on its importance to an organization's success, the BM concept is still fuzzy and vague, and there is little consensus regarding (on) its essential compositional attributes, aspects, and facets (Morris et al. 2005). Unsurprisingly, the applied analysis over the existing BM definitions within the literature illustrates the lack of consensus regarding the BM theoretical foundations (Chesbrough and Rosenbloom 2002; Magretta 2002; Morris et al. 2005; Kallio et al. 2006). The author agrees with Linder and Cantrell (2000) that researchers mean different things when they write about BMs. This applied analysis also reveals that the other BM fundamental details concerning modeling principles, reach, and functions are somehow available within the literature, but indirectly, incompletely, fragmentally lacking a consensus.

Thus, there is a need to clarify, integrate and analyze the existing views within the literature to provide a unified, tight, and sound framework of the BM concept in the media and IS domain. Such comprehensive conceptual framework is therefore required to unify the different points of view into one comprehensive framework providing a common understanding, language, and labeling in order to leverage its technological and business application (Al-Debei and Avison 2010). Thus, this chapter is motivated by the need for a comprehensive, generic, sound, and tight conceptual framework to the BM concept in the digital media business domain. The author consolidates and classifies these views, presenting a longitudinal-comparative framework and taxonomy of business model definitions in the next section which organizes these different perspectives.

The term "business model" often remains undefined lacking conceptual and contextual consensus. The literature about business model is not consistent in the usage, and, moreover, authors often do not even give a definition of the BM term. Even among its defenders there is confusion over the virtues and vices of this ambiguous business concept. Researchers have difficulty articulating what is the conceptual and methodological framework of the business model. Thus, the business model survives in a curious methodological limbo, representing a definitional morass. If "methodological limbo" exists it is not for lack of methodological discussion. Indeed, the methodological discussion on business models has been extensive over the past 20 years across the business and management literature sciences—see, for example, Amit and Zott 2000; Timmers 1998; Chesbrough and Rosenbloom 2002; Osterwalder and Pigneur 2010; Magretta 2002; Chesbrough 2013; Teece 2010; Afuah and Tucci 2000; Osterwalder et al. 2005; Osterwalder 2004; Eriksson and Penker 2000; Morris et al. 2005; Johnson et al. 2008; Zott et al. 2011; Shafer et al. 2005; Mahadevan 2000. Thus, a paradox: Although the relevance of a sound business model seems to be undisputed, a more thorough analysis of existing resources paints a different picture. At the same time, judging by recent scholarly output, the business model discipline retains considerable appeal and continues to produce a vast number of business model research papers and books, many of which have entered the pantheon of classic works (Amit and Zott 2000; Timmers 1998; Chesbrough and Rosenbloom 2002; Osterwalder and Pigneur 2010; Magretta 2002; Chesbrough 2013; Teece 2010; Afuah and Tucci 2000; Osterwalder et al. 2005; Osterwalder 2004; Eriksson and Penker 2000; Morris et al. 2005; Johnson et al. 2008; Zott et al. 2011; Shafer et al. 2005; Mahadevan 2000).

The problem is perhaps that methodological discussion of BMs study has tended to focus on its (a) conceptual, deductive, and nomothetic status, (b) theory testing case studies, (c) generalizing/universal "power." Less conspicuous, though, has been any synthesis of the discussion offering classificatory schemata for an idiographic, inductive, specific, configurative, cross-sectional, heuristic, building block, and longitudinal case studies.

Nonetheless, the author argues that the business model concept is useful in explaining the relation between FDI and media corporations. Accordingly, this monograph offers a causal, longitudinal, multiple-case study and meta-analysis outline for a hybrid FDI business model in media industry.

2.6.1 The Key Reasons for the Underdevelopment, Fragmentation, Incompleteness, Ambiguity, and Lack of a Unified Framework of the Business Model Concept

The author argues that five main reasons causing the underdevelopment, fragmentation, incompleteness, ambiguity, and lack of a unified framework of the business model concept include:

1. The youthfulness and newness of the BM investigating sector, concept and its associated research; the BM concept has only recently appeared frequently in scholarly reviewed journals (see Osterwalder et al. 2005). The number of research papers in peer-reviewed (especially high-ranking) journals is still insufficient to create an ample body of research and enable theoretical integration and conceptualization of the field.

2. The thematic multidisciplinarity (e.g., eBusiness; eCommerce; IS; strategy; business management; marketing; economics; and telecommunications). A particular case in point concerns new digital media, ICT, and telecommunications ventures along with their highly innovative products, services, and applications (e.g., IOT; WOT; 3D Printing; IPTV; Cloud Computing; Quantum Computing; Cloud Media; Cognitive Computing/Informatics/Web; Domotics—Pentaplay Bundling; Smart Grid Networks, Drones; Big Data Analytics; HCI; Gamification; Inbound Marketing; iPaaS; 5G Locative Media Technology; Micropayment; A massively multiplayer online game (also called MMOG); Neuroeconomics; Neuromarketing; Multiscreen TV; Smart Watches; Wearable Technologies; Telemedicine/Telehealth; Temporary Social Media; Social Media Networks, Web 3.0; Web 4.0; Web 5.0; UGC—User-Generated Content). The author arrived to the conclusion that the study field is still quite dispersed as practitioner-oriented publications and scholarly per-reviewed journals target a broad array of sectors, technological innovation, and management.

3. The business model varies according to the global market dynamics, length of product/service life cycles, and a change of the specific relationship between value-adding partners (e.g., suppliers, providers, and customers).

4. Another factor which makes theoretical conceptualization of the field more difficult is disjointed empirical contexts of studies. Indeed, the biggest part of the extant literature on business models examines the field of e-commerce, other industries, and business sectors being somewhat neglected.

5. The fifth factor which categorizes business models as a research field still in emergence is the absence of a clear, universally accepted definition. According to Zott et al. (2011), more than one-third of the articles the authors surveyed did not provide any explicit definition of the concept and quite often, while referring

to business model, different authors actually mean different concepts. In other words, "the business model has been referred to as a statement (Stewart and Zhao 2000), a description (Applegate 2000; Weill and Vitale 2001), a representation (Morris et al. 2005; Shafer et al. 2005), an architecture (Dubosson-Torbay et al. 2002; Timmers 1998), a conceptual tool or model (Osterwalder 2004; Osterwalder et al. 2005; Teece 2010), George and Bock 2011), a structural template (Amit and Zott 2001), a method (Afuah and Tucci 2001), a framework (Afuah 2004), a pattern (Brousseau and Penard 2006), and a set (Seelos and Mair 2007)" (Zott et al. 2011:4).

This lack of definitional consistency and clarity represents a potential source of confusion, promoting dispersion rather than convergence of perspectives, and obstructing cumulative research progress on business models. All these issues point out that the field requires (a) growing body of research which would investigate the concept of business model across a variety of empirical contexts (and not only within e-business) filling in multiple research gaps; (b) conceptual consolidation and theory-building growing from the cumulative body of research; and (c) methodological rigor, including operationalization of the concept.

2.7   A Longitudinal Analysis of the Business Models' Conceptual Frameworks, Functional Dimensions, and Modeling Principles

The main aim of this subchapter is to provide a cohesive understanding of the applicative and practical FDI business model in media industry supplying a solid and complete foundation for researchers and practitioners. To this aim, the author analyzes and synthesizes the different viewpoints relating to the BM's conceptual framework. Thus, the author systematically identifies relevant studies, appraises, assesses, and evaluates their quality and summarizes the evidence.

By analyzing the fundamental, conceptual, compositional, evaluative, and architectural dimensions as well as its the applicative principles and rationales. This unified framework synthesizes the BM compositional dimensions (structure, characteristics, reach, configuration, and functions) in a novel manner. Moreover, it provides a complete foundation for researchers and practitioners who are looking forward to utilizing the BM concept in their practices and applications. Concurrently, it represents a versatile instrument assisting to the BM scientific research community as well as practitioners since (a) it organizes and manages the BM foundational knowledge, and hence, it is helpful in assuaging the "fuzziness" problem which has been associated with the BM concept; (b) it propagates many synonyms and labels adds to the haziness of the BM concept at this stage, while both efficiently and effectively establishes a common language and terminology to reduce and clarify this problem; and (c) from a practical perspective, this unified framework enhances organizations' ability to design, create, communicate, compare, analyze, evaluate, and modify their existing and future BMs.

Retrospectively, the author finds it more useful to understand the BM concept by categorizing its current interpretations in the literature into a classification schema or a taxonomy that contains conceptually meaningful groups of objects that share common characteristics, that is, classes. Basically, taxonomy is a systemizing mechanism utilized to map any domain, system, or concept, as well as a conceptualizing tool relating its different constructs and elements.

Generally speaking, classification methods are of value in satisfying the needs of understanding data and discovery concepts (Zhifang 1988). Categorizing data based on their shared characteristics is highly useful since it represents the means by which the collected data transforms into more useful information, often called "pre-knowledge." Subsequently, this pre-knowledge can be analyzed to mine new, valuable knowledge. Furthermore, taxonomical or categorization methods provide simplicity since they aim to reduce the complexity of dealing with many instances (Parsons and Wand 2008). Parsons and Wand (2008) also agree that classifying an object supports deductions and inferences about its unobserved properties. In line with this, Clancey (1984) and Fisher and Yoo (1993) argue that classification techniques are useful means for guiding inference and for problem-solving purposes. Interestingly, all of these characteristics match the definitions of content analysis provided by Stone et al. (1966), Holsti (1969), and Agar (1980).

The employed content analysis approach uses the existing BM literature as its main source of data. In order to understand such a fuzzy concept, the author finds it more convenient to delineate the existing BM definitions within eBusiness, digital media, and IS-related literature in a comprehensive and generic manner. Therefore, definitions are extracted from the literature in IS, eCommerce, eBusiness, telecoms industry, ICT, and media business and management. The search process relies mostly on the use of digital research libraries and online academic and research databases (e.g., ScienceDirect, EBSCO, JSTOR, Proquest, Web of Science, Scopus, and ACM Digital Library, Lexis/Nexis Academic, Wiley Interscience, Journals, SpringerLink Journals, EconLit, Emerald, Google Scholar, Google Books, Sage Premier Journals, Taylor & Francis Online, Xplore IEEE/IET Electronic Library, ComAbstracts, Oxford Scholarship Online, NBER working papers), by means of keywords. The inclusion of most effective keywords included the word "model" (in particular, FDI, Business model, business model innovation, digital business model, digital media business model, eCommerce business model, eBusiness model, and business modeling).

To conduct this study the author followed Zott et al. (2011) multistep criteria and heuristic evaluation measures for literature review on business models. Accordingly, the author used the following criteria:

- Creation of a comprehensive and high-quality pool (database) of thematically as well as longitudinally analyzed/covered leading academic and practitioner-oriented management and IS journals, papers, review papers, books, book chapters, and international conferences during the inclusive time frame period from 1995 to 2013—in terms of determined impact factor and anticipated knowledge covering all the perspectives and standpoints from which the BM has been perceived and assessed. However, the theme of the business model must be really the subject of the analysis, meaning that to be included in this review, an article must also refer to the business model as a construct centered on business firms (as opposed to, for example, economic cycles).

Having the content identified—the author selected 84 articles and BM definitions that fitted these criteria as well as deemed relevant for this review. Moreover, the author based this evaluative function/framework/technique of longitudinal and meta-analysis research methods on three key compositional aspects/principles:

1. The authors' H-index factor (e.g., Michael E. Porter, h-index 127; David J. Teece, h-index 92; Henry Chesbrough, h-index 50)
2. Number of paper citations (e.g., Amit, R., & Zott, C. (2000)—3778 citations; Timmers, P. (1998)—2635 citations; Osterwalder, A., & Pigneur, Y. (2010)—2544 citations; Chesbrough, H., & Rosenbloom, R. S. (2002)—2542 citations; Magretta, J. (2002)—2185 citations; Chesbrough, H. (2013)—2044 citations; Teece, D. J. (2010)—1817 citations; Afuah, A., & Tucci, C. L. (2000)—1737 citations; Osterwalder, A., Pigneur, Y., & Tucci, C. L. (2005)—1590 citations; Osterwalder, A. (2004)—1405 citations; Eriksson, H. E., & Penker, M. (2000)—1356 citations; Morris, M., Schindehutte, M., & Allen, J. (2005)—1318 citations; Johnson, M. W., Christensen, C. M., & Kagermann, H. (2008)—1260 citations; Zott, C., Amit, R., & Massa, L. (2011)—1097 citations; Shafer, S. M., Smith, H. J., & Linder, J. C. (2005)—1041 citations)
3. High impact factor of WoS journals (e.g., Sloan Management Review, Journal of Economics and Management Strategy, California Management Review, Journal of Public Policy & Marketing, Strategic Management Journal, Harvard Business Review, Organization science, Journal of Business Strategy, Management Decision, European Management Journal, Academy of Management Perspectives, Journal of Management Studies, British Journal of Management, Long range planning, European Journal of Information Systems, The British Accounting Review).

In addition, the author follows an inductive reasoning method utilizing the collected data and information as guidelines to synthesize the BM knowledge into a generic and comprehensive but concise BM definition.

Thus, in Table 2.1 the author provides and summarizes a higher level of clarity by chronologically presenting and examining a classification of 84 selected scholarly definitions of the BM concept, covering the years 1995–2013 and showing which authors/papers have adopted these definitions.

2.8   The Multidisciplinary, Critical, Systematic, and Conceptual Research Framing of BMs' Configured Dimensions and Semantics

The Business Model (BM) is fundamental to any organization (Magretta 2002). This is because BMs provide powerful ways to understand, analyze, communicate, and manage strategic-oriented choices (Pateli and Giaglis 2004; Osterwalder et al. 2005; Shafer et al. 2005) among business and technology stakeholders (Gordijn and Akkermans 2001). The concept is also of importance as it informs the design of information systems (IS) supporting the BM of an organization (Eriksson and Penker 2000). Consequently, no one organization can afford "fuzzy thinking" about this concept (Magretta 2002).

Having realized the high significance of the BM, there has been an increasing interest (from the time when business modeling had risen to prominence by the end of 1990s with the growth of hi-tech businesses up to now) in delineating the concept and providing further understanding. For example, some attempt to define the concept (Timmers 1998; Osterwalder et al. 2005; Shafer et al. 2005; Al-Debei et al. 2008a), others understand its relationships with IS (Hedman and Kalling 2003), and other business concepts, such as corporate strategy (Mansfield and Fourie 2004), and business process modeling (Gordijn et al. 2000b), and yet others identify its constituent elements (Mahadevan 2000; Gordijn and Akkermans 2001; Chesbrough and Rosenbloom 2002; Pateli and Giaglis 2003). Researchers have also looked at the BM concept in the context of different domains. The majority of research into BMs in the IS field has been concerned with eBusiness and eCommerce, and there have been some attempts to develop convenient classification schemas. For example, definitions, components, and classifications into eBusiness models have been suggested (Alt and Zimmermann 2001; Afuah and Tucci 2003). Some researchers have applied the BM concept in the domains of business management and strategy (Linder and Cantrell 2000; Magretta 2002), the telecom sector including mobile technology along with its services (Bouwman et al. 2008; Al-Debei and Fitzgerald 2010), software industry (Rajala and Westerlund 2007), and eGoverment (Janssen et al. 2008).

Business models are sometimes presented as part of the definitions and other times described in separate lists, frameworks or ontologies. Business model frameworks and ontologies do not only specify the elements but also specify the relationships between the elements (e.g., Gordijn et al. 2005). They often also introduce some structure, in particular a two-layered model with higher-level and lower level elements (e.g., Osterwalder 2004).

Based on an extensive literature research and many years of real-world experience, different authors have developed a number of BM frameworks, for example, the Business Model Canvas (Osterwalder 2004; Osterwalder and Pigneur 2010), the Four-Box Business Model (Johnson 2010), Business Model Schematics (Weill and

Vitale 2001), Technology/Market Mediation (Chesbrough and Rosenbloom 2002), and "e3-value" (Gordijn 2002; Gordijn and Akkermans 2001). While the frameworks seem useful for describing and designing business models, most frameworks are not developed or tested via a systematic and evidence-based approach nor has their successful application been verified in a rigorous manner.

As example, the author will present the Business Model Canvas (Osterwalder and Pigneur 2010) in more detail. The Business Model Canvas presents a shared language for describing, visualizing, assessing, and changing business models. It consists of nine building blocks: (1) The value proposition of what is offered to the market; (2) The segment(s) of clients that are addressed by the value proposition; (3) The communication and distribution channels to reach clients and offer them the value proposition; (4) The relationships established with clients; (5) The key resources needed to make the business model possible; (6) The key activities necessary to implement the business model; (7) The key partners and their motivations to participate in the business model; (8) The revenue streams generated by the business model (constituting the revenue model); and (9) The cost structure resulting from the business model.

In earlier work, Osterwalder (2004) has the nine building blocks grouped into four pillars: customer interface (the "who" covered by building blocks 1, 3, and 4), product (the "what" covered by building block 2), infrastructure management (the "how" covered by building blocks 6, 7, and 8), and financial aspects (the "how much" covered by building blocks 5 and 9). In this earlier work, he also shows how the nine building blocks synthesize most of the other models at that time (covering, among others, Afuah and Tucci 2001; Hamel 2000; Magretta 2002). While there are differences between the frameworks (for example, how explicitly they include technology), the similarities are significant enough to see them as relating to the same underlying definition in terms of describing the creation and capture of customer value.

From a comparison of 18 frameworks and lists, Morris et al. (2005) state that the number of elements mentioned varies from four to eight and that a total of 24 different items are mentioned as possible elements, with 15 receiving multiple mentions. They conclude "that the most frequently cited are the firm's value offering ($11\times$), economic model ($10\times$), customer interface/relationship ($8\times$), partner network/roles ($7\times$), internal infrastructure/connected activities ($6\times$), and target markets ($5\times$). Some items overlap, such as customer relationships and the firm's partner network or the firm's revenue sources, products, and value offering."

Moreover, Al-Debei and Avison (2010) suggest a unified business model conceptual model with the dimensions value proposition, value architecture, value network, and value finance. Based on the description and discussion of business model frameworks, the findings of Morris et al. (2005), and the unified model of Al-Debei and Avison (2010), the author suggests that the higher order elements should at least cover the following dimensions: (1) Customer: the way the customer is perceived and the kind of customer that is targeted, (2) Value Proposition: the customer problem that the business initiative is trying to solve and the solution that is offered to deal with that problem, (3) Organizational Architecture: the way in which the value proposition can be provided by the different actors and their capabilities and assets, in particular the focal organization, and (4) Revenue Model: the economic considerations (possibly including nonfinancial ones) related to bringing the customer, value proposition, and architecture together, often focused on how the organizations, in particular the focal organization, can make money (Fielt 2012).

Basically, by analyzing the different components proposed by a multitude of international business scholars, the author distinguishes three groups of authors.

The first (Chesbrough and Rosenbloom 2002; Porter 2001) are interested in the appropriation of value by the firm, focusing on the financial dimension. In this first instance, the business model is assimilated to what is sometimes called the "revenue model." This notion is often found in the managerial world, as highlighted by Amit and Zott (2001). Thus, many websites describe different revenue models, such as the advertising model, or "razor and blade," which thus reduces the concept of the business model to the simple mechanism of revenue appropriation by a firm. This conception appears to be too restrictive, for two reasons. The first is that over and above the origin of the revenue, it is the profit, hence the firm's economic profitability, which would seem to be relevant, as Fiet and Patel (2008) make clear. In line with this approach, Amit and Zott (2001) clearly distinguish between revenue model and business model. While the first describes the appropriation of value, the second is interested in the creation of value, in other words, how the value is generated. This conception seems less restrictive and seems to make the revenue model a component of the business model.

A second group of authors (Mason and Leek 2008; Patzelt et al. 2008; Tikkanen et al. 2005) are particularly interested in the value generated through a company's operational methods, with or without explicit reference to its value chain. Thus, Amit and Zott (2001) define the business model as the organization of the different transactions of the central firm with all its constituent external elements. However, these authors explicitly exclude clients and products from the business model, stating they are taken into account in what they call the market strategy (see Table 1 page 5 of their article).

A third group of authors do include clients and products in the business model. Whereas for Slywotzky and Linthicum (1997) the client is the pivot, for Stähler (2002) and Lecocq et al. (2006) offers made to clients are only one component among so many others.

In addition, combining Osterwalder (2004) and Doganova and Eyquem-Renault (2009), Andersson et al. (2006) distinguish the following elements of a generic business model concept:

1. Value proposition: what value is embedded in the product/service offered by the firm
2. Supply chain: how are upstream relationships with suppliers structured and managed
3. Customer interface: how are downstream relationships with customers structured and managed

4. Financial model: costs and benefits from (1), (2), and (3) and their distribution across business model stakeholders

In this context, a business model is used as a plan which specifies how a new venture can become profitable. Doganova and Eyquem-Renault (2009) argue that a business model is an intermediary between different innovation actors such as companies, financiers, research institutions, etc., i.e., actors who shape innovation networks. In their discussion, such networks are created through what they call "narratives" and "calculations" which entrepreneurs circulate to describe their ventures and to construct markets. Here, the business model is seen as a reference point for communication among the different actors with whom entrepreneurs engage. Markets for innovations thus emerge through interaction between these actors who also interfere with different kinds of devices (e.g., support materials such as analysts' reports, presentations, software, or money). More specifically, the business model, as it connects actors through narratives and calculations (see also Magretta 2002), can be interpreted as a market device (Callon et al. 2007).

Moreover, in his overview of business model literature, Wirtz (2011) identifies three streams.

– The first stream focuses on technology. Explicating business models became popular during the Internet boom, when firms and analysts came to realize that existing ways of earning a profit were not suitable for capitalizing on new technologies: web-based products and services (e.g., Ghaziani and Ventresca 2005; Timmers 1998). Thus, there is a substantial body of literature which focuses on the consequences of particular technologies on how firms organize to earn profits. This is relevant for the field of sustainable innovation since technologies that contribute to sustainability may have a similar effect.
– The second, organizational, stream emanates from this work and deals with the business model as a strategic management tool to improve a company's value chain (e.g., Linder and Cantrell 2000; Tikkanen et al. 2005). Here, a business model serves as a development tool for business systems and architectures for representing, planning, and structuring business with an emphasis on organizational efficiency.
– A third stream is strategy oriented. It adds the element of market competition to the efficiency focus of the second stream (e.g., Afuah 2004; Casadesus-Masanell and Ricart 2010; Chesbrough 2007a; Hamel 2000; Magretta 2002). Common sense amongst strategy-oriented business model scholars is that creating and delivering customer value lies at the heart of any business model (e.g., Afuah 2004; Chesbrough 2010; Johnson 2010; Osterwalder and Pigneur 2009a, b; Teece 2010; Zott and Amit 2010).

In addition, while creating and delivering customer value, the business model itself can become a source of competitive advantage by means of business model innovation (e.g., Chesbrough 2010; Johnson 2010; Markides and Charitou 2004; Mitchell and Coles 2003). Companies striving for a competitive edge through unique value propositions can use the configuration of their business models' building blocks to execute their strategies on the market. An additional role of the business models can be changed and innovated to provide competitive advantage by changing the terms of competition (e.g., Chesbrough 2010; Demil and Lecocq 2010; Johnson 2010; Zott and Amit 2010).

2.8.1 Toward a Unified, Systematic, Integrative, Holistic, and Comprehensive BM Framework

While there has been an explosion in the number of papers and practitioner-oriented studies published, as well as an abundance of conference sessions and panels delivered on the subject of business models, it appears that researchers (and practitioners) have yet to develop a consensual—common and widely accepted paradigm that would allow them to examine business model concepts, definition, nature, structure, and its evolution through different lenses and draw effectively on each others' work (Morris et al. 2005; Tikkanen et al. 2005).

However, although the concept of Business Model is instinctively appealing and promises to "fill a niche" (Hawkins 2004), playing the pivotal role in today's complex and turbulent environment, the BM-related literature is fragmented (Chesbrough and Rosenbloom 2002) and somehow imprecise and incomplete, revealing a clear lack of consensus regarding its frameworks (Al-Debei and Avison 2010).

While academics and corporate executives agree on the importance of business models for the success of an organization, the concept is still fuzzy and vague and lacks consensus on its definition and compositional elements (Al-Debei and Avison 2010; Morris et al. 2005; Shafer et al. 2005). Since the researchers in the business area have depicted the BM from different perspectives, the BM concept is still seen to be unclear, disperse, and inconsistent in scope and focus, meaning model components and their interrelations are relatively obscure. There is a divergence of understanding among people, in particular between those who are business oriented and those who are technology oriented (Osterwalder et al. 2005). Thus, the heterogeneous understanding of the business model concept results in a relatively unstructured discussion in the media business, international business, and economic literature.

The various definitions of the business model concept highlight the fragmented nature of existing conceptualizations. A wide variety of different and multi-disciplinary approaches, views, and issues regarding the BMs' applicative concept maintain, and probably add to, the blurred, unclear, disjointed view held of the BM and keep the BM-related domain knowledge fragmented. This suggests that the domain is fuzzy and vague and still in its conceptualization phase, despite its perceived significance. Identifying the fundamental concepts, modeling principles, practical functions, and reach of the BM relevant to digital media, ICT, and telecommunications business concepts is by no means complete.

To date, the BM concept is still considered an ill-defined "buzzword" (Seddon et al. 2004; Seppänen and Mäkinen 2007) and conceptually underdeveloped (Magretta 2002; Chesbrough and Rosenbloom 2002). Furthermore, Porter (2001) suggests that the BM concept is "ambiguous" at best. In addition, the BM concept has sometimes been misperceived as a substitute of corporate strategy, business process, or business case concept (Al-Debei and Avison 2010). Regretfully, the term "business model" is a definitional morass. Frequently, the business model term is conflated with a set of disparate methodological traits that are not definitionally entailed.

2.8.2 The Synthesized Conceptual Framework

This view highlights the value proposition dimension (Magretta 2002; Hedman and Kalling 2003) of the BM concept. This dimension implies that a BM should include a description of the products/services a digital organization offers, or will offer, along with their related information. Furthermore, the BM needs also to describe the value elements incorporated within the offering, as well as the nature of targeted market segment(s) along with their preferences. Innovations relating to this particular dimension are of high concern to modern Information and Communication Technology (ICT) business organizations to attract and sustain a large proportion of customers.

The foundation of the value architecture construct is in the resource-based view (RBV). The RBV (Wernerfelt 1984; Barney et al. 2001) assumes that each company is a bundle or resources. More specifically, RBV puts emphasis on the strategic importance of resources coupled with their integration with the generation of desirable value by customers and thus sustainable competitive advantage to the company possessing the resources.

2.8.3 The Need for a Business Model Conceptual Framework

The goals of a conceptual framework are threefold. Firstly, to describe existing practice, secondly, to prescribe future practice, and thirdly, to define key terms and fundamental issues. The conceptual framework should provide the basis for future debate especially in relation to prescriptions for future practice and definitions of key terms and fundamental issues (Miller 1987). A conceptual framework aims to "...broadly define a number of key terms and concepts that can be used in identifying and debating the issues." (Miller and Islam 1988). Given the ambiguous, fuzzy, and vague state of business model research and the lack of consensus regarding definitions and constructs of business models, it seems appropriate to apply the conceptual framework in a bid to progress the research. Accordingly, the research is still in its conceptualization phase, despite its perceived importance.

2.9   Guidelines to Develop a Consensus for the Business Model

As we have seen, despite the increasing emphasis on the importance of the business model to an organization's success, there has been a lack of consensus regarding its definition and its meaning (Kallio et al. 2006). Researchers in this area have depicted business models from different perspectives. Through an analysis of definitions of the business model in the IS literature presented in the previous section, the author proposes the following reasons and guidelines for establishing a BM as a second level of clarity. These guidelines can be used as a basis on which to develop a more comprehensive definition later.

1. A way in which organizations create value (Amit and Zott 2001; Kallio et al. 2006) with two different approaches for the value proposition:

   (a) The ways in which an organization, along with its suppliers and partners (business actors), creates value for its customers (Magretta 2002; Petrovic et al. 2001; Dubosson-Torbay et al. 2002; Stähler 2002; Osterwalder et al. 2005; Haaker et al. 2006).
   (b) The ways in which an organization, along with its stakeholders (business actors), creates value for each party involved (Bouwman 2002; Stähler 2002; Haaker et al. 2006; Andersson et al. 2006).

2. A way in which an organization generates revenue (Timmers 1998; Magretta 2002; Rappa 2000; Linder and Cantrell 2000; Dubosson-Torbay et al. 2002).
3. An abstraction of the existing business and a future planned business (Stähler 2002). This suggests that the organization's business models should encompass future business outlooks.
4. An architecture for the organization, including its assets, products, services, and information flow (Venkatraman and Henderson 1998; Timmers 1998).
5. As business logic relating to the ways in which businesses are being conducted (Petrovic et al. 2001; Osterwalder et al. 2005).
6. A way in which an organization enables transactions through the coordination and collaboration among parties and multiple companies (Amit and Zott 2000; Bouwman 2002; Haaker et al. 2006).
7. An organization's strategy or set of strategies (Leem et al. 2004; Kallio et al. 2006).
8. An interface or a theoretical layer between the business strategy and the business processes (Camponovo and Pigneur 2003; Tikkanen et al. 2005; Rajala and Westerlund 2005; Morris et al. 2005).
9. A conceptual tool, a business abstraction, and a blueprint (Stähler 2002; Haaker et al. 2004; Osterwalder et al. 2005).
10. A way of understanding a single organization or a network of organizations (Bouwman 2002; Haaker et al. 2006).

2.10   Framing Future Trends of Business Model Research Agenda

The differences and the weak framework between business models, as well as a lack of strong and systematic empirical focus, prompted the author to further research the business model viability (i.e., business model conceptualization and business model implementation) with regard to the framing future trends of business model research agenda. Thus, without doubt, the field of business models is an important but yet insufficiently researched area (Boons and Lüdeke-Freund 2013). Therefore, the author's main contribution is to show how inefficient, contradictory, and antithetical operational and conceptual business model frameworks are interrelated in the current literature. The second contribution is to reflect the findings and ideas in order to offer a starting point for a more focused research agenda. Therefore, the author presents a three-dimensional future research stages intended to help building and framing a research agenda on business models. Moreover, the author suggests specific operational and contextual avenues and perspectives for future research stages/principles/approaches. Accordingly, meta-analysis, cross-sectional study, longitudinal research method, and comparative analysis are used to shed some light on the future research stage of the business model concepts and ontologies.

The proposed framework of the dimensional future research stages allows the user to design, describe, categorize, critique, and analyze a business model for any type of company. It provides a useful backdrop for strategically adapting fundamental elements of a business. By specifying the elements that constitute a model, the framework enhances the ability to assess model attributes. A model that ignores one or more of the specified components will suffer in terms of its comprehensiveness, while inconsistency can manifest itself both in terms of the fit among decision areas within a given component and the fit between components. With the proposed framework, each of forty two components is evaluated at three levels. The first stage deals with the conceptual characteristics of the business model and includes six factors such as evaluation criteria; individual business model; Social value/social business model; Business system & profit model; Strategy versus structure; and Need for a clear definition and set of components. The second stage includes design of the business model and consists of twenty different dimensions (Fit between business model strategy and business planning; Architectural value network configuration; Value offering, proposition, stream and exchange; Building block; Actor network; Dynamic capabilities, etc...—more information are available in Table 2.2). The third stage deals with the implementation and monitoring of the business model. This stage consists of sixteen factors (i.e., Market positioning; Model components in relation to operational decisions; Managing complex business models (ambidextrous organization and learning organizations; Business model implementation vs. conceptualization, etc.).

An organization's business model is never complete as the process of making strategic choices and testing business models should be ongoing and iterative (Shafer et al. 2005). Accordingly, after conceptualization and implementation, a business model should be kept up to date through time. Moreover, the influence of time on a business model is an emerging topic and requires more research.

On the other hand, one possible way to move research on business models forward could be based on the realization that scholars in different fields use the same label to explain very different things. It might be helpful, perhaps, to adopt more precise labels that indicate the researcher's main analytical focus, such as "e-business model archetype" (for studies on e-business model types), "business model as activity system" (for strategy studies focusing on boundary-spanning activities), or "business model as cost/revenue architecture" (for technology management and innovation scholars interested in explaining the economic mechanisms that allow a firm to commercialize technological innovations). This could help increase analytical focus and precision and minimize potential confusion.

The author's literature review offers a second possible avenue for advancing research on business models by suggesting the emergence of some important common ground among various business model researchers, despite the disparity of their approaches in terms of detailed concepts used and phenomena explained. It is the author's hope that the following three thematically and contextually complementary stages that were identified in this chapter pave the way for future business model research agenda as well as conceptual convergence and breakthroughs.

Also, the multicultural sensitiveness and awareness in dealing, adopting, and implementing different business models concepts is increasingly needed in the globalized world. This is particularly important as the American Business Model has undeniably dominated the whole Western world and many think that no other may be better. As professor Jean-Pierre Ubuad (2014) pointed out succinctly: "In reality other business models are emerging in other parts of the world and they might challenge the American business model very soon. It indeed appears that East Asians and Americans of European descent emphasize different aspects of problems and think through problems differently. Each civilization's members display different strengths and weaknesses in their approaches to information processing. Asians emphasize perceived contexts and relationships in their information processing to a greater extent than Westerners do. Asians also accept the validity of weaker arguments, contradicting their own views, more than Westerners do. Additionally, whereas Asians favor experiential and empirical data and reasoning to explain their worlds, Westerners favor building models of explanatory rules and using formal logic to explain theirs. It is therefore highly important for a firm that wants to operate worldwide to be able to manage throughout these very different business models and develop the skills and the flexibility required to use them in an appropriate and efficient way."

Other areas requiring further investigation include the ability of entrepreneurs and others to assess model quality. Systematic approaches for assessing model viability are needed. Methods are also needed for appraising the model's fit and implementation with(in) changing market, technological, and economics dynamics as well as conditions. One challenge concerns the translation of model components into operational decisions, where the importance of fit will likely differ by activity area. Another challenge involves experimenting with new strategic moves in ways

Table 2.2   Three-dimensional future research stages

Conceptual	Design	Implementation & monitoring
Evaluation criteria	Fit between business model strategy and business planning	Market positioning
Individual business model (Svejenova et al. 2010)	Architectural value network configuration (Amit and Zott 2001; Stähler 2001)	Model components in relation to operational decisions (Morris et al. 2005)
Social value/social business model (Dahan et al. 2010; Yunus et al. 2010)	Value offering (Gordijn 2002)	Managing complex business models (ambidextrous organization, and learning organizations) (Smith et al. 2010)
Business system & profit model (Itami and Nishino 2010)	Value Proposition (Stähler 2001; Linder and Cantrell 2000; Weill and Vitale 2001; Chesbrough and Rosenbloom 2000; Maitland and Van de Kar 2002)	Business model implementation vs. conceptualization (Sosna et al. 2010)
Strategy versus structure (Zott and Amit 2008)	Value stream (Mahadevan 2000)	IS in relation to business models—e-business and b-webs schematics (Weill and Vitale 2001; Hedman and Kalling 2003; Tapscott et al. 2000)
Need for a clear definition and set of components (Casadesus-Masanell and Ricart 2010; Magretta 2002; Pateli and Giaglis 2004; Teece 2010; Porter 2001)	Value exchange (Gordijn 2002)	Model emergence and evolution (Zott and Amit 2008)
	Building block	Ongoing, iterative and transparadigmatic business process (Shafer et al. 2005)
	Actor network (Gordijn 2002)	Organizational architecture
	Dynamic capabilities	Infrastructure management
	Distribution Channels (Weill and Vitale 2001)	Transaction leverage (Amit and Zott 2001)
	Unit of analysis	Cross-cultural, multicultural, and intercultural management, awareness, and sensitiveness (Applegate and Collura 2001)
	Activity theory (Zott and Amit 2002, 2007)	Developing value ecosystem
	Design (Zott and Amit 2002)	The trial-and-error learning (experimentation) and innovation (Sosna et al. 2010; Morris et al. 2005; Gambardella and McGahan 2010)

(continued)

Table 2.2 (continued)

Conceptual	Design	Implementation & monitoring
	Revenue stream model (Mahadevan 2000; Maitland and Van de Kar 2002; Stähler 2001; Petrovic et al. 2001; Linder and Cantrell 2000)	Assessing model quality/viability/fit (Morris et al. 2005)
	Customer Value (Afuah and Tucci 2003)	Innovation: startups vs. established firms (Sosna et al. 2010)
	Customer Segments (Weill and Vitale 2001)	Value network positioning (Chesbrough and Rosenbloom 2000)
	Customer demand (Magretta 2002)	
	Customer retention (Wirtz and Lihotzky 2003)	
	Pricing model (Afuah and Tucci 2003; Linder and Cantrell 2000)	
	Market segmentation (Gordijn 2002; Chesbrough and Rosenbloom 2000; Maitland and Van de Kar 2002)	

that do not compromise the model. Finally, further insights are needed into the dynamics of model emergence and evolution.

The following overview presents an additional agenda for three-dimensional future research stages, based on the identified gaps, and suggestions from the literature selection:

- Future research stages from the literature selection demonstrate the need for future research on basically every aspect of the business model: the concept, the design, and the implementation and monitoring.
- The influence of time on a business model is an emerging topic and requires more research.
- More research should be conducted to determine how a business model should be implemented.
- Finally, after implementation, a business model should be kept up to date through time.

Analysis of existing research on business models has enabled identification of gaps in current knowledge and has indicated avenues worthy of further investigation. These gaps can be used to draw an agenda for future research on business models as they refer both to the individual subdomains and, perhaps more importantly, to the intersections between them. While those observations that relate to individual subdomains have been documented in the previous section, some more integrative aspects are synthesized in this section.

Although quite a few researchers have worked toward constructing a conceptual framework for business model analysis from different viewpoints (including for example organizational, technological, strategic, and economic dimensions), a smaller amount of research has been devoted to synthesizing and specifying the interfaces between these largely diverse conceptual aspects. Nevertheless, such a synthesis could contribute toward specifying the boundaries and identity of each conceptual level and outlining its weight of contribution to a holistic understanding of business models (Pateli and Giaglis 2004). Above all, bridging the gaps between conceptual dimensions would undoubtedly contribute to the development of an integrated concept of a business model (Pateli and Giaglis 2004). In parallel, future research could also be directed toward visualizing the conceptual layers, the components, and the interfaces between them with the aid of computer-aided methods and tools. In this case, the area of design methods and tools would also benefit.

The review has demonstrated the need for further research toward assessing business models from different perspectives. Taking into consideration the natural differences in business actors' motivation and interests in a business model, future research should specify the stakeholders involved in each conceptual layer, identify their needs, requirements, and objectives, and define assessment criteria accordingly. The final outcome could resemble a multidimensional construct that relates conceptual levels (e.g., organizational, financial, and technical), target groups (e.g., managers, financial analysts, and system developers), evaluation objectives (e.g., market performance, profitability, and innovation), and criteria (e.g., number of customers, return on investment, and competitive differentiation) (Pateli and Giaglis 2004). The need for designing viable business models and assessing the likelihood of their real-life market success under different industry and firm-specific circumstances can be greatly assisted by integrating existing disparate research efforts in the highly interdependent subdomains of evaluation models and adoption factors. The success of a business model research design is naturally dependent on addressing holistically numerous interdependent factors such as market conditions, strategic synergies (or conflicts), competencies and assets, financial arrangements (pricing policy, revenue sharing schemes), robust technological infrastructure, effective governance schemes, and so on.

The critical analysis of the existing views toward the BM concept in this chapter has highlighted important gaps. The concern that the concept is still fuzzy and ill-defined, the consideration of BMs as substitutes for strategies, the partial views and definitions of the concept as its related knowledge is fragmented, and the fact that its practical functions are not yet clearly defined have highlighted the need for a conceptual framework that integrates the existing views and analyzes them to add novel mined knowledge to this important area of research. In the light of these arguments, the theoretical and practical implications of the constructed conceptual framework can be summarized as follows:

The BM needs to be compatible with external variables such as national culture, market opportunities, laws and regulations, customer-base size and nature, competition level, and technological advances. Therefore, researchers should provide additional insights into how digital organizations could develop compatible BMs with internal-external factors, ensuring and facilitating flexibility in terms of reengineering their existing BMs to cope with a turbulent business environment.

Finally, an important stream of research concerns the development of methodological approaches toward business model evolution or transition. Taking into account the dynamic nature of business models, as well as the rapid pace of business and technological evolutions, such methodologies would meet a timely market need and may contribute to fewer failures in business model innovation than those witnessed in hype-affected high-tech markets in recent years. This methodological BM approach summarizes the research challenges in both atomic (individual subdomains) and integrative (combinations of two or more subdomains) levels.

Now, a final word of advice comes from Henry Chesbrough, one of the most prominent business model researchers. According to him, companies should not be shy of experimenting with their business models (Chesbrough 2010). An instrumental point of departure in this process is to differentiate "failures" from "mistakes"; whereas "failures" are natural outcomes of experimentation which provide valuable learning insights, "mistakes" are poorly designed experiments which provide no learning.

2.11   The Importance of Successful Business Model

The digital era has meant that the availability of appropriate levels of information and knowledge has become critical to the success of the business. Organizations need to adapt in order to survive and succeed as their business domains, processes, and technologies change in a world of increasing environmental complexity. Enhancing their competitive positions by improving their ability to respond quickly to rapid environmental changes with high-quality business decisions can be supported by adopting suitable BMs for this new world of digital business. Thus, in rapidly changing digitized Information and Communication Technologies (ICTs)-centered businesses and environment, the BM is one of the most important as well as pivotal organizational assets, enhancing digital business managers' control over their businesses and enabling them to compete better because of the appropriate and necessary level of information that the BM provides.

With the digitization wave breaking, fundamental changes in almost all industries have been unleashed. Therein enterprises face severe challenges when shaping concrete digital business models for commercialization (BMWi 2012). The growth of the Internet has undoubtedly created greater opportunities for digitized business transactions, but this has been accompanied by an intensified competition and an accelerated pace of technological change (Veit et al. 2014). On the global scale, these developments have disrupted market forces in a novel way (Veit et al. 2014).

Such changes are putting pressure on existing firms which, in order to maintain competitiveness, have to adapt their business logic and processes to this fast-moving environment. Accordingly, the business model concept seems particularly apt to providing an overarching framework with which novel approaches in the digital era can be strategically structured, analyzed, and designed (Osterwalder and Pigneur 2013).

The Business Model (BM) is fundamental to any organization as it provides powerful ways to understand, analyze, communicate, and manage business and technology stakeholders' strategic-oriented choices (Magretta 2002; Pateli and Giaglis 2004; Osterwalder et al. 2005; Shafer et al. 2005; Gordijn and Akkermans 2001). Furthermore, the BM concept informs and supports the corporate's information systems (IS) design (Eriksson and Penker 2000).

Companies often make substantial efforts to innovate their processes and products to achieve revenue growth and to maintain or improve profit margins (Amit and Zott 2012). Innovations to improve processes and products, however, are often expensive and time-consuming, requiring a considerable up-front investment in everything from research and development to specialized resources, new plants and equipment, and even entire new business units (Amit and Zott 2012). Yet future returns on these investments are always uncertain (Amit and Zott 2012). Hesitant to make such big bets, more companies now are turning toward business model innovation as an alternative or complement to product or process innovation (Amit and Zott 2012).

Al-Debei and Avison (2010) suggest that an *explicit* depiction of the BM could be positively employed to mobilize an organizational knowledge capital useful in enhancing strategic decision-making functions and at the same time leveraging the practice of the BM in action. The business model—if explicitly based on digital technology—forms a critical organizational asset or resource promising to provide a digital organization with the longest enduring competitive advantage (Al-Debei and Avison 2010). Business model is important for entrepreneurs (Zott and Amit 2010) and as a field of study it is new and attractive to entrepreneurship research (Trimi and Berbegal-Mirabent 2012). A better understanding of business models should help entrepreneurs make more informed and thus better decisions and increase the probability of success (Trimi and Berbegal-Mirabent 2012).

Chesbrough and Rosenbloom (2002) argue that "a successful business model creates a heuristic logic that connects technical potential with the realization of economic value as the business model unlocks latent value from a technology." In line with this approach, Yuan and Zhang (2003) argue that it is not the technological application itself, but rather the BM behind the technological artifacts that makes the success and allows hi-tech companies to achieve their strategic goals and objectives.

The success of the business model is determined through the quality of management's capabilities, ability to acquire, combine, and utilize valuable resources in ways that deliver a value proposition to customers (Beltramello et al. 2013). Thus, successful companies thoroughly understand their business models via:

(a)   Knowing how the building blocks relate to each other

(b) Constantly rethinking and redesigning these blocks and their relationship to innovation before their business model is copied (Osterwalder and Pigneur 2010)

This chapter also shows that explicit BM models help digital organizations assess the intangible asset of knowledge capital more efficiently and effectively in order to support organizational strategic decision-making. Further, this mobilized knowledge signifies an organizational asset that enables a digital business to achieve sustainable competitive advantage in its market.

The BM is also an important backbone for technological artifacts as it leverages their success and facilitates the attainment of strategic aims including economic value. A successful and well-designed dynamic BM leverages, mediates, and harmonizes both digital business strategies and business processes.

Based on the technological application itself, the BM portrays a feasible, efficient, effective, and sound translating method essential to obtain and capture values from the proposed digital innovations. Thus, the concept of BM could be perceived appropriately as a backbone providing a consistent and systematic approach for designing, evaluating, and managing different technologies and their connected products and services.

Moreover, a BM for a digital business should be reviewed continually to ensure its fit with the complex, volatile, uncertain, and rapidly changing external environment. Pressing forward the body of BM scientific knowledge helps practitioners such as managers, BM designers and evaluators, and industry consultants realize the most appropriate BM to achieve their strategic goals and objectives.

In summary, the BM enhances an organization's innovation capability and could serve as executives' guidance with respect to strategic decision-making practices. Moreover, the BM is a novel strategic-oriented knowledge capital that is crucial for business organizations in an emerging, turbulent, and digital business environment.

2.12 The Benefits of the Business Model Framework

The business model framework has tangible benefits to practitioners:

1. Through the business model framework, practitioners can investigate the evolving of their business models. The business model framework provides a conceptual tool for firm-level management that also addresses operational issues. The link between operative decisions and issues regarding the business model components builds a bridge between strategic and operative management and, arguably, between middle and top management.
2. The business model framework is systemic. It demonstrates that firm processes emerge from each other and their coordination is key to maintaining competitive advantage. The major implication to management is that strongly developing one component of the business model always has network effects to other components. For example, the developing of management accounting nearly always

has implications on operations management. Likewise, strategic realignment that does not fit the other components is doomed to fail.

3. The business model is a cognitive mechanism. This implies that managing the business model in practice always has a link to human resource management and the management of perceptions. Despite the BM's abstract conceptualization, it essentially deals with pragmatic "sense-making" issues. This offers practitioners an alternative tool to conventional, prescriptive "organizational design" thinking.

4. Finally, the business model framework has proven to be a useful tool in business education. It encapsulates the key areas of management and contextualizes them in the realm of managerial action (Tikkanen et al. 2005).

2.13   Major Challenges and Constraints in Understanding, Studying, and Adopting Business Models

Zott and Amit (2007) argue that the business models of established firms are more constrained by path dependencies and inertia than more entrepreneurial firms.

Chesbrough and Rosenbloom (2002) warn that the dominant logic of the existing business model can hinder organizations in defining new business models because "the choice of business constrains other choices, filtering out certain possibilities, even as other prospects are logically reinforced."

According to Johnson et al. (2008), companies adopting novel business models confront two challenges. Firstly, there is a lack of understanding into the dynamics and process of business model development in general. Second, most companies do not understand when and how to leverage their existing as well as new business model.

Moreover, the business model's main concerns can be traced to the following four common problems:

1. Flawed assumptions underlying the core logic.
2. Limitations in the strategic choices considered.
3. Misunderstandings about value creation and value capture.
4. Flawed assumptions about the value network (Shafer et al. 2005).

2.14   Major Purposes of a Business Model

Besides being the basis for an information system, Eriksson and Penker (2000) list five purposes of a business model:

1. To better understand the key mechanisms of an existing business.
2. To act as a basis for improving the current business structure and operations.
3. To show the structure of an innovated business.

4. To experiment with a new business concept or to copy or study a concept used by a competitive company (e.g. benchmarking on the model level).
5. To identify outsourcing opportunities.

2.15 Major Objectives for Investigation on Business Models

Some of the most prominent and often cited objectives for investigation on business models include the following:

1. To understand the key elements and mechanisms in a specific business domain, as well as their relationships (Osterwalder and Pigneur 2002)
2. To communicate and share the understanding of a business model among business or technology stakeholders (Gordijn and Akkermans 2001)
3. To design the information and communication systems supporting the business model (Eriksson and Penker 2000)
4. To experiment with innovative business concepts to determine if current business models can easily adapt to them (Eriksson and Penker 2000) and assess the new, applicable, and feasible business initiatives (Weill and Vitale 2001)
5. To change and improve the current business model (Eriksson and Penker 2000; Osterwalder and Pigneur 2002).

2.16 Functions of a Business Model

According to Henry Chesbrough and Richard Rosenbloom (2002), a business model performs the following functions:

- Articulates the value proposition (i.e., the value created for users by an offering base on technology)
- Identifies a market segment and specifies the revenue generation mechanism (i.e., users to whom technology is useful and for what purpose)
- Defines the structure of value chain required to create and distribute the offering and complementary assets, needed to support position in the chain
- Details the revenue mechanism(s) by which the firm will be paid for the offering
- Estimates the cost structure and profit potential (given value proposition and value chain structure)
- Describes the position of the firm within the value network linking suppliers and customers (incl. identifying potential complementors and competitors)
- Formulates the competitive strategy by which the innovating firm will gain and hold advantage over rivals. (Chesbrough and Rosenbloom 2002).

2.17 Determining Factors of a Business Model's Wealth Potential

To measure the potential of a business model, Hamel (2000) has identified four factors that determine a business model's wealth potential:

- Efficiency. The extent to which the business concept is an efficient way of delivering customer benefits
- Uniqueness. The extent to which the business concept is unique
- Fit. The degree of fit among the elements of the business concept
- Profit Boosters. The degree to which the business concept exploits profit boosters (increasing returns, competitor lockout, strategic economies, strategic flexibility), which have the potential to generate above-average returns.

2.18 Assessing the Economic Feasibility of a Business Model

In a narrower evaluation sense, Gordijn and Akkermans (2001) assess the economic feasibility of a business model, based on assessment of the incoming and outgoing values (benefits vs. costs and risks) for each actor involved. Feasibility of a business model means that all actors involved can make a profit or increase their economic utility. Their evaluation approach is to take into account the net in and out flows of value objects. More specifically, this approach creates profit sheets based on either the actor or activity level. Value objects in the profit sheet are assigned a value expressed in monetary units. Accordingly, the use of "what-if scenarios" can help companies make a sensitivity analysis for the business model under consideration with respect to financial parameters such as customer behavior. In many cases, this sensitivity analysis can potentially be of greater interest than the numbers themselves.

2.19 Measuring the Performance of a Business Model

Afuah and Tucci (2001) define three levels for measuring the performance of a business model:

(a) Measures of profitability that includes comparison of a firm's profitability to that of competitors using profitability measures, such as earnings and cash flows.
(b) Profitability prediction, which is concerned with comparing a firm's profit margins, revenue market share, and revenue growth rate with those of industry competitors.

(c) Business model component attributes, which provide benchmarks for apprais-
     ing each one of the identified components of a business model.

Similarly, Weill and Vitale (2001) refer to three key factors that have an
influence on the profitability and viability of eBusiness models:

1. Level of ownership for the customer relationship, data, and transaction
2. Firm's access to key information about customers, products, markets, and costs
3. Conflicts raising from combination of atomic models to e-business initiatives,
    such as Channel Conflict, Competency Conflict, Infrastructure conflict, and
    Information conflict (Pateli and Giaglis, 2003).

Summarizing, the review has revealed that the evaluation model subdomain is
among the less mature areas of business model research. The majority of the criteria
proposed draws from general theory and is mostly driven by financial indicators
that are very difficult, if possible at all, to measure in all cases.

2.20   The Evaluation and Assessment of Business Models

The last subdomain of the BM field addresses the evaluation and assessment of
business models. From the analysis of contributions in the field, it is evident that the
definition of assessment criteria is naturally dependent on the purpose of evaluation.
Four primary evaluation purposes have been identified:

- Comparison with competitors in Business Model terms
- Assessment of alternative Business Models for implementation by the same firm
- Identification of risks and potential pressure areas for a firm pursuing innovation
- Evaluation of an innovative Business Model in terms of feasibility and
  profitability.

Summarizing, we can observe that the evaluation criteria domain is perhaps the
less mature BM research area. The majority of the criteria proposed in the literature
are derived from generic theory and are mostly driven by financial indicators (for
example, profitability and margins) that are very difficult, if possible at all, to
measure ex ante. However, this result is not surprising. The BM evaluation domain
is inherently complex and to some extent dependent on other domains such as
change methodologies. It is therefore rather expected that knowledge generation
will proceed at a slower pace here, following prerequisite developments of understanding and maturation of other domains.

2.21   The Business Model Logic and Organizational Usage

The BMs' logic includes three different levels: (a) individual organizations (e.g., Venkatraman and Henderson 1998; Linder and Cantrell 2000; Camponovo and Pigneur 2003), or even (b) part of an organization such as business units, products/services, and product/service bundles (e.g., Timmers 1998; Chesbrough and Rosenbloom 2002), and (c) business networks that consists of more than one organization (e.g., Gordijn et al. 2000a; Dubosson-Torbay et al. 2002; Haaker et al. 2006). Moreover, the BM could be used for different purposes within organizations: (a) alignment instrument, (b) mediating construct, and (c) knowledge capital.

2.22   The Positioning of the Business Model Concept Within Organizations

Although the overall goal of conceptual modeling is to support decision-making activities (Gordijn et al. 2000b), business process modeling supports operational decisions, and the process of creating the BM provides support for strategic decision-making.

Nonetheless, the BM is by no means independent; it intersects with the business strategy as well as the business processes, creating a unique strategic, operational, and technological mix. These intersections represent two crucial transitional points to be followed by business organizations.

1. In the first transitional stage from Business strategy to BM, the business model is dependent on and derived from the business strategy.
2. In the second transitional stage from BM to business process model, the business model acts as the base system from which the detailed and operational business process model should be derived.

Moreover, the BM represents a way in which organizations create value (Amit and Zott 2001; Kallio et al. 2006) with two different approaches for the value proposition:

1. The ways in which an organization along with its suppliers and partners (business actors) creates value for its customers (Magretta 2002; Osterwalder et al. 2005; Rajala and Westerlund 2007).
2. The ways in which an organization along with its stakeholders creates value for each party involved (Stähler 2002; Andersson et al. 2006).

Despite the increasing popularity within ICT, telecommunications, and media business companies, the BMs of organizations are rarely articulated or defined explicitly. Most often they represent a tacit knowledge in the minds of one or few key managers within organizations and are seldom communicated to others.

2.23 Two Basic Components of the Business Model

In general a business model consists of two basic components

– Actors which quote organizations having a common understanding of the market produce same products or services, maintain a common set of business processes, etc.
– Relationships referring to the transactions between two or more players.

2.24 Business Model Maturity Stages

The business model maturity stages include six elements:

1. Undifferentiated business model (i.e., commodity; no differentiation)
2. Differentiated business model (i.e., ad hoc processes; hard to sustain)
3. Segmented business model (i.e., can serve multiple segments; more sustainable and profitable; low cost)
4. Externally aware business model (harnesses external sources)
5. Integrated business model
6. Platform leadership business model (Chesbrough 2007a, b)

2.25 The Benefits of Novel Business Model

Zott and Amit (2007) show that novel business models have a positive effect on entrepreneurial firms' performance. Novel business models are radical innovations with the potential to shake whole industries (Demil and Lecocq 2010) and can result in a competitive advantage if they are hard to replicate (Magretta 2002). In addition, business models offer a broader systematic perspective and holistic approach for looking at other forms of innovation.

2.26 The Need for a New Business Model

Teece (2010) argues that "the more radical the innovation, and the more challenging the revenue architecture, the greater the changes likely to be required to traditional business models." Relatedly, business models are required when novel technology is introduced in the market ensuring the customer's value delivery (Chesbrough and Rosenbloom 2002). Correspondingly, the need for business model innovation triggers a pathway to a competitive advantage for firms as well as a form of corporate renewal. Moreover, some organizations may develop dynamic capabilities enabling them to innovate their business models in a systematic manner. That said, the author observes eight strategic circumstances that often require business model change:

1. The consumer has become the driving force in the marketplace, and the standards of acceptable service have been raised.
2. Technology has revolutionized the manner in which information is aggregated, analyzed, managed, and transmitted.
3. The business is consolidating, and new players are entering the market.
4. The opportunity to address through disruptive innovation the needs of large groups of potential customers who are shut out of a market entirely because existing solutions are too expensive or complicated for them. This includes the opportunity to democratize products in emerging markets (or reach the bottom of the pyramid).
5. The opportunity to capitalize on a brand-new technology by wrapping a new business model around it (Apple and MP3 players) or the opportunity to leverage a tested technology by bringing it to a whole new market.
6. The opportunity to bring a job-to-be-done focus where one does not yet exist. That's common in industries where companies focus on products or customer segments, which leads them to refine existing products more and more, increasing commoditization over time.
7. The need to fend off low-end disrupters.
8. The need to respond to a shifting basis of competition. Inevitably, what defines an acceptable solution in a market will change over time, leading core market segments to commoditize (Johnson et al. 2010).

2.27   Main Reasons for Changing Business Model

Changing business model is necessary because:

(a) Customers change their needs
(b) Competitors change their businesses
(c) Corporate technology advances exponentially
(d) Corporations enter into different business cycles.

2.28   Strategies for Reinventing Business Model

The most effective strategies for reinventing generic media business model include offering value proposition substitute and complementary products and services; bundles; reinventing the customer interface (channels) and relationships; inventing new revenue streams, vendor lock-ins, and network externalities; targeting non/-customers, less profitable customers, least satisfied customers, and the chain of buyers; and segmenting customers according to commonalities and circumstances; clusterization.

2.29   Methodology of Business Model design

The author adopts and follows Morris et al.'s (2005) integrated framework of business models design, consisting of six principal and cross-sectional decision modules/stages(questions):

Module 1—Design of value proposition (factors related to the offering): How do we create value?

Module 2—Design of production architecture (market factors): Who do we create value for?

Module 3 (internal capability factors): What is our source of competence?

Module 4 (competitive strategy factors): How do we competitively position ourselves?

Module 5 (economic factors): How we make money?

Module 6 (personal/investor factors): What are our time, scope, and size ambitions?

In addition, the author proposes the implementation and application of presented six principal decision modules/stages as a comprehensive framework providing a substantial and holistic perspective on the dynamics of the Business Model design in order to develop sustainable business models in the new economy. More importantly, these six stages are based and confirmed by numerous studies (e.g., Porter 1996; Fitzsimmons and Fitzsimmons 1998; Jarillo 1995; Barney et al. 2001; Talluri et al. 1999; Lumpkin and Dess 2004; Kim and Mauborgne 2000; Gordijn 2002).

2.30   Conceptual Differences Between Design Rationale of "Business Modeling" and "Process Modeling"

The terms "business modeling" and "process modeling" are often used interchangeably in the information systems literature. However, they serve different purposes.

In the author's view, the main goal of a business model is to answer the question: "who is offering what to whom and expects what in return" (Gordijn et al. 2000a). Therefore, the central notion in any business model should be the concept of value, in order to explain the creation and addition of value in a multi-party stakeholder network, as well as the exchange of value between stakeholders. A business model shows the what aspects: what objects of value are created for whom and by whom in multi-party stakeholder network, whereas a business process model depicts and shows the associated how aspects of business logic (Gordijn et al. 2000a).

Business modeling captures and displays the elements of the business that characterize the economic choices that have been made by the entity. Business modeling depicts the essence of the business and gives the user a clear understanding of the business logic underlying the entity's existence (Gordijn et al. 2000b; Osterwalder et al. 2005). Business modeling is concerned with providing information that reflects the economic and strategic choices that have been made by the entity. It presents views of the business logic underlying the entity's existence that meets the needs of users.

Accordingly, the nature of design decisions to be represented in a business model differs from the decisions being represented in a process model. Consequently, the main design decisions to be represented in a business model are:

1. Who are the value-adding business actors involved?
2. What are the offerings of which actors to which other actors?
3. What are the elements of offerings?
4. What value-creating or adding activities are producing and consuming these offerings?
5. Which value-creating or adding activities are performed by which actors (Gordijn et al. 2000a)?

A business model does not state how value-creating activities are carried out. This is an important goal of business process modeling.

Accordingly, the main goals of business process modeling are:

- Creation of a common approach for work to be carried out
- Incremental improvement of processes (e.g., efficiency)
- Support of processes by workflow management systems
- Analysis of properties of a process (e.g., deadlock free) (Ould 1995; van Hee 1994).

To present the how, a business process model typically shows the following design decisions:

1. Who are the actors involved in the operations?
2. Which operational activities can be distinguished?
3. Which activities are executed by which actors?
4. What are the inputs and outputs of activities?
5. What is the sequence of activities to be carried out for a specific case?
6. Which activities can be carried out in parallel for a specific case (Gordijn et al. 2000a)?

2.31   The Importance of Business Actors' Positioning Within the Dynamic Business Models' Framework

The business model describes both the actors and their roles. The business actors' (such as suppliers, partners, customers, and competitors) role in the dynamic business models is increasingly important because of the functioning of the value network. As a result, every actor has a certain role in the business model that describes their position in the net, and the value that they create in the net (Palo and Tähtinen 2011). Consequently, an actor needs to create considerable value for the chain with its current competences—and an emerging competence can strengthen the value and the business model (Palo and Tähtinen 2011).

2.32 Conclusions

Despite the BM's significance to an organization's success in digital business, there has been little consensus about its basis. The BM concept is relatively young but has been used in various contexts. The lack of consensus is further aggravated/complicated as researchers generally view the concept subjectively, while practitioners perceive it according to their organizations' environment and culture. Consensus about BM compositional aspects is crucial since it represents a framework or a theoretical underpinning on which researchers may apply to different industries within different contexts. It is also fundamental to practitioners since the BM could be utilized as a reference measure for their business performance analysis. To address these issues, this chapter clarifies the BM concept. The author has reviewed the media business, ICT, and telecommunications literature, classified the BM definitions, and extracted a longitudinal, thematic, contextual, and hierarchical taxonomy. Moreover, the taxonomy provides a guideline on which to develop a more profound, articulate, holistic, as well as technologically, economically, and entrepreneurially competitive, applicative, and comprehensive framework.

This chapter also reveals the modeling principles of both the static and dynamic business models. The author believes that this feasible, multifaceted, comprehensive, intact, and unified discussion on the BM framework incorporates new mined knowledge based on the applied, holistic, and systematic literature works as a reference model and enables conceptual consensus on the origin, nature, and application of BMs that has not yet been achieved. In parallel, the success of a business model research design is naturally dependent on addressing holistically numerous interdependent factors such as market conditions, strategic synergies (or conflicts), competencies and assets, financial arrangements (pricing policy, revenue sharing schemes), robust technological infrastructure, effective governance schemes, and so on.

References

Afuah, A. (2004). *Business models: A strategic management approach*. Boston: McGraw-Hill/Irwin.
Afuah, A., & Tucci, C. L. (2000). *Internet business models and strategies: Text and cases*. New York: McGraw-Hill Higher Education.
Afuah, A., & Tucci, C. L. (2001). *Internet business models and strategies: Text and cases* (4th ed.). New York: Irwin/McGraw-Hill.

Afuah, A., & Tucci, C. (2003). *Internet business models and strategies* (2nd ed.). New York: McGraw-Hill.

Agar, M. (1980). *The professional stranger: An informal introduction to ethnography*. New York: Academic. pp. xi, 227.

Al-Debei, M. M., & Avison, D. (2010). Developing a unified framework of the business model concept. *European Journal of Information Systems, 19*(3), 359–376.

Al-Debei, M. M., El-Haddadeh R., & Avison, D. (2008a). Defining the business model in the new world of digital business. In *Proceedings of the 14th Americas conference on information systems AMCIS'08, Toronto, Canada* (pp. 1–11).

Al-Debei, M. M., & Fitzgerald, G. (2010). The design and engineering of mobile data services: Developing an ontology based on business model thinking. In J. Pries-Heje, J. Venable, & J. De Gross (Eds.), *Human benefits through the diffusion of information systems design science research*. IFIP International Federation for Information Processing (IFIP 8.2+8.6). Boston: Springer.

Alt, R., & Zimmermann, H. (2001). Introduction to special section—business models. *Electronic Markets, 11*(1), 3–9.

Amit, R., & Zott, C. (2000). *Value drivers of e-commerce business models (No. 2000–2006)*. Fontainebleau: INSEAD.

Amit, R., & Zott, C. (2001). Value creation in e-business. *Strategic Management Journal, 22*(6–7), 493–520.

Amit, R., & Zott, C. (2012). Creating value through business model innovation. *MIT Sloan Management Review, 53*(3), 41–49.

Andersson, B., Bergholtz, M., Edirisuriya, A., Ilayperuma, I., Johannesson, P., Grégoire, B., et al. (2006, November 6–9). Towards a reference ontology for business models. In *Proceedings of the 25th international conference on conceptual modeling (ER2006), Tucson, AZ, USA* (pp. 1–16).

Applegate, L. M. (2000). E-business models: Making sense of the internet business landscape. In G. Dickson & G. DeSanctis (Eds.), *Information technology and the future enterprise: New models for managers* (pp. 49–101). Englewood Cliffs, NJ: Prentice-Hall.

Applegate, L. M. (2001). *Emerging E-business models: Lessons from the field*. Boston: Harvard Business School.

Applegate, L. M. & Collura, M. (2001). *Ventro: Builder of B2B businesses*. Harvard case study, 9-801-042.

Baden-Fuller, C., & Morgan, M. S. (2010). Business models as models. *Long Range Planning, 43*, 156–171.

Barney, J., Wright, M., & Ketchen, D. J. (2001). The resource-based view of the firm: Ten years after 1991. *Journal of Management, 27*(6), 625–641.

Beattie, V., & Smith, S. J. (2013). Value creation and business models: Refocusing the intellectual capital debate. *The British Accounting Review, 45*(4), 243–254.

Bellman, R., Clark, C. E., Malcolm, D. G., Craft, C. J., & Ricciardi, F. M. (1957). On the construction of a multi-stage, multi-person business game. *Operations Research, 5*(4), 469–503.

Beltramello, A., Haie-Fayle, L., & Pilat, D. (2013, February 26). Why new business models matter for green growth. OECD, France.

Bely, J. (2005). La valeur client, fondation des «business models» gagnants. *L'Expansion Management Review, 3*, 44–53.

Benavent, C., & Verstraete, T. (2000). Entrepreneuriat et NTIC–construction et regénération du business model. Histoire d'entreprendre–les réalités de l'entrepreneuriat, Editions Management et Société, Caen.

Betz, F. (2002). Strategic business models. *Engineering Management Journal, 14*(1), 14–29.

Boons, F., & Lüdeke-Freund, F. (2013). Business models for sustainable innovation: State-of-the-art and steps towards a research agenda. *Journal of Cleaner Production, 45*, 9–19.

Bouwman, H. (2002). The sense and nonsense of business models. In *International workshop on business models, HEC Lausanne 6 p. cat. O, Projectcode: ICT*.

Bouwman, H., De Vos, H., & Haaker, T. (2008). *Mobile service innovation and business models*. Berlin: Springer.

Brandenburger, A. M., & Stuart, H. W. (1996). Value-based business strategy. *Journal of Economics and Management Strategy, 5*(1), 5–24.

Brousseau, E., & Penard, T. (2006). The economics of digital business models: A framework for analyzing the economics of platforms. *Review of Network Economics, 6*(2), 81–110.

Burcham, R. (2000). New pharma business model: Can you survive IT? *Pharmaceutical Executive, 20*(11), 94–100.

Callon, M., Millo, Y., & Muniesa, F. (2007). *Market devices*. Oxford: Blackwell.

Callon, M., & Muniesa, F. (2005). Peripheral vision: Economic markets as calculative collective devices. *Organization Studies, 26*(8), 1229–1250.

Camponovo, G., & Pigneur, Y. (2003, April 23–26). Business model analysis applied to mobile business. In *Proceedings of the 5th international conference on enterprise information systems, Angers* (pp. 1–10).

Casadesus-Masanell, R., & Ricart, J. E. (2007, November). *Competing through business models* (IESE Business School Working Paper No. 713). Boston: Harvard Business School Press.

Casadesus-Masanell, R., & Ricart, J. E. (2010). From strategy to business models and onto tactics. *Long Range Planning, 43*(2–3), 195–215.

Chapman, R. L., Soosay, C., & Kandampully, J. (2003). Innovation in logistic services and the new business model: A conceptual framework. *International Journal of Physical Distribution & Logistics Management, 33*(7), 630–650.

Chesbrough, H. (2003). *Open innovation*. Boston: Harvard Business School Press.

Chesbrough, H. (2006). *Open business models: How to thrive in the new innovation landscape*. Boston: Harvard Business School Press.

Chesbrough, H. (2007a). Business model innovation: It's not just about technology anymore. *Strategy & Leadership, 35*(6), 12–17.

Chesbrough, H. (2007b). Why companies should have open business models. *MIT Sloan Management Review, 48*, 22–28.

Chesbrough, H. (2010). Business model innovation: Opportunities and barriers. *Long Range Planning, 43*(2–3), 354–363.

Chesbrough, H. (2013). *Open business models: How to thrive in the new innovation landscape*. Harvard Business Press.

Chesbrough, H., & Rosenbloom, R. S. (2000). *The role of the business model in capturing value from innovation: Evidence from XEROX Corporation's technology spinoff companies*. Boston, MA: Harvard Business School.

Chesbrough, H., & Rosenbloom, R. S. (2002). The role of the business model in capturing value from innovation: Evidence from Xerox Corporation's technology spin-off companies. *Industrial and Corporate Change, 11*(3), 529–555.

Clancey, W. J. (1984). Classification problem solving. In *Proceedings of the national conference of artificial intelligence* (pp. 49–55). Austin, TX: Morgan Kaufmann.

Dahan, N. M., Doh, J. P., Oetzel, J., & Yaziji, M. (2010). Corporate-NGO collaboration: Co-creating new business models for developing markets. *Long Range Planning, 43*(2), 326–342.

Daidj, N., & Isckia, T. (2009). Entering the economic models of game console manufacturers. *Communications & Strategies,* (73), 23.

DaSilva, C. M., & Trkman, P. (2014). Business model: What it is and what it is not. *Long Range Planning, 47*(6), 379–389.

Demil, B., & Lecocq, X. (2010). Business model evolution: In search of dynamic consistency. *Long Range Planning, 43*, 227–246.

Desmarteau, A. H., & Saives, A. L. (2008, May). Opérationnaliser une définition systémique et dynamique du concept de modèle d'affaires: cas des entreprises de biotechnologie au Québec. In *XVIIe Conférence de l'AIMS* (pp. 28–31).

Doganova, L., & Eyquem-Renault, M. (2009). What do business models do? Innovation devices in technology entrepreneurship. *Research Policy, 38*, 1559–1570.

Dottore, F. A. (1977). Data base provides business model. *Computerworld, 11*(44), 5.

Dubosson-Torbay, M., Osterwalder, A., & Pigneur, Y. (2002). E-business model design, classification, and measurements. *Thunderbird International Business Review, 44*(1), 5–23.

Dunford, R., Palmer, I., & Benveniste, J. (2010). Business model replication for early and rapid internationalization: The ING direct experience. *Long Range Planning, 43*, 655–674.

Edvardsson, B., Kristensson, P., Magnusson, P., & Sundström, E. (2012). Customer integration within service development—A review of methods and an analysis of insitu and exsitu contributions. *Technovation, 32*(7), 419–429.

Elliot, S. (2002a). Research model and theoretical implications. In S. Elliot (Ed.), *Electronic commerce: B2C strategies and models*. Chichester, UK: Wiley.

Elliot, S. (Ed.). (2002b). *Electronic commerce: B2B strategies and models*. Chichester, UK: Wiley.

Eriksson, H., & Penker, M. (2000). *Business modeling with UML—Business patterns at work*. New York: Wiley.

Fielt, E. (2012). *A 'service logic' rationale for business model innovation*. In EURAM Annual Conference 2012, 6–8 June 2012, Erasmus University, Rotterdam (Unpublished).

Fiet, J. O., & Patel, C. (2008). Forgiving business models for new ventures. *Entrepreneurship: Theory & Practice, 32*(4), 749–761.

Fisher, D. H., & Yoo, J. (1993). Categorization, concept learning, and problem solving: A unifying view. In G. Nakamura, R. Taraban, & D. Medin (Eds.), *The psychology of learning and motivation* (Vol. 29, pp. 219–255). San Diego, CA: Academic Press.

Fitzsimmons, J. A., & Fitzsimmons, M. J. (1998). *Service management*. New York: Mac-GrawHill.

Gambardella, A., & McGahan, A. M. (2010). Business-model innovation: General purpose technologies and their implications for industry structure. *Long Range Planning, 43*(2–3), 262–271.

George, G., & Bock, A. J. (2011). The business model in practice and its implications for entrepreneurship research. *Entrepreneurship Theory and Practice, 35*(1), 83–111.

Gershon, R. A. (2015a). *Digital media and innovation: Management strategies for communication industries*. Thousand Oaks, CA: Sage Publications.

Ghaziani, A., & Ventresca, M. J. (2005). Keywords and cultural change: Frame analysis of business model public talk, 1975–2000. *Sociological Forum, 20*(4), 523–559. Kluwer Academic Publishers-Plenum Publishers.

Gordijn, J. (2002). *Value-based requirements engineering—Exploring innovative E-commerce ideas*. PhD thesis, Vrije Universiteit, Amsterdam.

Gordijn, J., & Akkermans, J. M. (2001). Designing and evaluating eBusiness models. *IEEE Intelligent Systems, 16*(4), 11–17.

Gordijn, J., Akkermans, H., & Van Vliet, H. (2000a). What's in an electronic business model? In R. Dieng & O. Corby (Eds.), *Knowledge engineering and knowledge management methods, models, and tools* (pp. 257–273). Berlin: Springer.

Gordijn, J., Akkermans, H., & Van Vliet, H. (2000b). Business modelling is not process modelling. In S. W. Liddle, H. C. Mayr, & B. Thalheim (Eds.), *Conceptual modeling for e-business and the web* (pp. 40–51). Berlin: Springer.

Gordijn, J., Osterwalder, A., & Pigneur, Y. (2005). Comparing two business model ontologies for designing E-business models and value constellations. In D. R. Vogel, P. Walden, J. Gricar & G. Lenart (Eds.), *Proceedings of the 18th Bled electronic commerce conference (Bled 2005)*. Bled, Slovenija: University of Maribor.

Haaker, T., Bouwman, H., & Faber, E. (2004). *Balancing requirements for customer value of mobile services*. BLED 2004 Proceedings, Association for Information Systems.

Haaker, T., Faber, E., & Bouwman, H. (2006). Balancing customer and network value in business models for mobile services. *International Journal of Mobile Communication, 4*(6), 645–661.

Hamel, G. (2000). *Leading the revolution*. Boston: Harvard Business School Press.

Hawkins, R. (2004). Looking beyond the Dot Com bubble: Exploring the form and function of business models in the electronic marketplace. In *E-life after the dot com bust* (pp. 65–81). Physica-Verlag HD.

Hedman, J., & Kalling, T. (2003). The business model concept: Theoretical underpinnings and empirical illustrations. *European Journal of Information Systems, 12*(1), 49–59.

Heikkilä, J., Heikkilä, M., & Tinnilä, M. (2007). The role of business models in developing business networks. In S. A. Becker (Ed.), *Electronic commerce: Concepts, methodologies, tools, and applications*. Hershey, PA: Information Science Reference (an imprint of IGI Global).

Holsti, O. R. (1969). *Content analysis for the social sciences and humanities*. Reading, MA: Addison-Wesley.

Huarng, K.-H. (2013). A two-tier business model and its realization for entrepreneurship. *Journal of Business Research, 66*, 2102–2105.

Itami, H., & Nishino, K. (2010). Killing two birds with one stone: Profit for now and learning for the future. *Long Range Planning, 43*(2), 364–369.

Janssen, M., Kuk, G., & Wagenaar, R. W. (2008). A survey of web-based business models for e-government in the Netherlands. *Government Information Quarterly, 25*(2), 202–220.

Jarillo, J. C. (1995). *Strategic networks*. Oxford: Butterworth-Heinemann.

Javalgi, R. G., Todd, P. R., Johnston, W. J., & Granot, E. (2012). Entrepreneurship, muddling through, and Indian Internet-enabled SMEs. *Journal of Business Research, 65*, 740–744.

Johnson, M. W. (2010). *Seizing the white space: Business model innovation for growth and renewal*. Boston: Harvard Business Press.

Johnson, M. W., Christensen, C. M., & Kagermann, H. (2008). Reinventing your business model. *Harvard Business Review, 86*(12), 57–68.

Johnson, M. W., Christensen, C. M., & Kagermann, H. (2010). *Reinventing your business model*. Boston: Harvard Business School Press.

Joyce, P., & Winch, G. (2004). A framework for codifying business models and process models in e-Business design. In W. L. Currie (Ed.), *E-business models* (pp. 35–64). Butterworth-Heinemann, UK: Elsevier.

Kallio, J., Tinnilä, M., & Tseng, A. (2006). An international comparison of operator-driven business models. *Business Process Management Journal, 12*(3), 281–298.

Kamoun, F. (2008). Rethinking the business model with RFID. *Communications of the AIS, 22*(1), 635–658.

Kim, W. C., & Mauborgne, R. (2000). Knowing a winning business idea when you see one. *Harvard Business Review, 78*(5), 129–138.

Konczal, E. F. (1975). Models are for managers, not mathematicians. *Journal of Systems Management, 26*(165), 12–15.

Kotha, S. (1998). Competing on the Internet: The case of Amazon.com. *European Management Journal, 16*(2), 212–222.

Kraemer, K. L., Dedrick, J., & Yamashiro, S. (2000). Refining and extending the business model with information technology: Dell Computer Corporation. *The Information Society, 16*(1), 5–21.

Lecocq, X., Demil, B., & Warnier, V. (2006). Le business model, un outil d'analyse stratégique. *L'Expansion Management Review, 123*, 96–109.

Leem, C. S., Suh, H. S., & Kim, D. S. (2004). A classification of mobile business models and its applications. *Industrial Management and Data Systems, 104*(1), 78–87.

Linder, J., & Cantrell, S. (2000). *Changing business models: Surveying the landscape* (Working Paper). Accenture Institute for Strategic Change, pp. 1–15.

Lumpkin, G. T., & Dess, G. G. (2004). E-business strategies and internet business models: How the internet adds value. *Organization Dynamics, 33*(2), 161–173.

Magretta, J. (2002). Why business models matter. *Harvard Business Review, 80*(5), 86–92.

Mahadevan, B. (2000). Business models for Internet-based e-commerce: An anatomy. *California Management Review, 42*(4), 55–69.

Maitland, C., & Van de Kar, E. (2002). First BITA case study experiences with regard to complex value systems. In *BITA-B4U symposium business models for innovative mobile services, Delft, The Netherlands.*

Maître, B., & Aladjidi, G. (1999). *Les business models de la nouvelle économie.* Paris: Dunod.

Malmmose, M., Lueg, R., Khusainova, S., Iversen, P. S., & Panti, S. B. (2014). Charging customers or making profit? Business model change in the software industry. *Journal of Business Models, 2*(1), 19–32.

Mansfield, G. M., & Fourie, L. C. H. (2004). Strategy and business models-strange bedfellows? A case for convergence and its evolution into strategic architecture. *South African Journal of Business Management, 35*(1), 35–44.

Markides, C. C., & Charitou, C. D. (2004). Competing with dual business models: A contingency approach. *Academy of Management Executive, 18*, 22–36.

Mason, K. J., & Leek, S. (2008). Learning to build a supply network: An exploration of dynamic business models. *Journal of Management Studies, 45*(4), 774–799.

Mayo, M. C., & Brown, G. S. (1999). Building a competitive business model. *Ivey Business Journal, 63*(3), 18–23.

Miller, D. (1987). The structural and environmental correlates of business strategy. *Strategic Management Journal, 8*(1), 55–76.

Miller, M. C., & Islam, M. A. (1988). *The definition and recognition of assets.* Accounting Theory Monograph NO 7, Melbourne: Australian Accounting Research Foundation.

Mitchell, D. W., & Bruckner Coles, C. (2004a). Business model innovation breakthrough moves. *Journal of Business Strategy, 25*(1), 16–26.

Mitchell, D. W., & Bruckner Coles, C. (2004b). Establishing a continuing business model innovation process. *Journal of Business Strategy, 25*(3), 39–49.

Mitchell, D., & Coles, C. (2003). The ultimate competitive advantage of continuing business model innovation. *Journal of Business Strategy, 24*(5), 15–21.

Morris, L. (2003). *Business model warfare.* White Paper. The Ackoff Center for Advancement of Systems Approaches, The University of Pennsylvania.

Morris, M., Schindehutte, M., & Allen, J. (2005). The entrepreneur's business model: Toward a unified perspective. *Journal of Business Research, 58*(6), 726–735.

Nadler, D., & Tushman, M. (1997). *Competing by design: The power of organizational architecture.* Oxford: Oxford University Press.

Nielsen, C., & Bukh, P. N. (2013). *Communicating Strategy: Using the business model as a platform for investor relations work* (The Business Model Community Working Paper Series, 2013-10).

Osterwalder, A. (2004). *The business model ontology: A proposition in a design science approach.* Doctoral thesis, Présentée à l'Ecole des Hautes Etudes Commerciales de l'Université de Lausanne.

Osterwalder, A., & Pigneur, Y. (2002). *An eBusiness model ontology for modeling eBusiness.* BLED 2002 Proceedings, 2

Osterwalder, A., & Pigneur, Y. (2003). Towards business and information systems fit through a business model ontology. In *Strategic Management Society conference, Baltimore, MD.*

Osterwalder, A., & Pigneur, Y. (2009a). *Business model generation: A handbook for visionaries, game changers, and challengers.* Amsterdam: Modderman Drukwerk.

Osterwalder, A., & Pigneur, Y. (2009b). *Business model generation.* Self Publication.

Osterwalder, A., & Pigneur, Y. (2010). *Business model generation: A handbook for visionaries, game changers, and challengers.* Hoboken, NJ: Wiley.

Osterwalder, A., & Pigneur, Y. (2013). Designing business models and similar strategic objects: The contribution of IS. *Journal AIS, 14*, 237–244.

Osterwalder, A., Pigneur, Y., & Tucci, C. L. (2005). Clarifying business models: Origins, present, and future of the concept. *Communications of the Association for Information Systems, 16*(1), 1.

Ould, M. A. (1995). *Business processes: Modelling and analysis for re-engineering and improvement* (Vol. 598). Chichester: Wiley.

Palo, T., & Tähtinen, J. (2011). A network perspective on business models for emerging technology-based services. *Journal of Business & Industrial Marketing, 26*(5), 377–388.

Parsons, J., & Wand, Y. (2008). Using cognitive principles to guide classification in information systems modeling. *MIS Quarterly, 32*(4), 839–868.

Pateli, A. G., & Giaglis, G. M. (2003). A framework for understanding and analyzing ebusiness models. In *Proceedings of 16th Bled eCommerce conference on eTransformation, Bled, Slovenia* (pp. 329–348).

Pateli, A. G., & Giaglis, G. M. (2004). A research framework for analyzing eBusiness models. *European Journal of Information Systems, 13*(4), 302–314.

Pateli, A. G., & Giaglis, G. M. (2005). Technology innovation-induced business model change: A contingency approach. *Journal of Organizational Change Management, 18*(2), 167–183.

Patzelt, H., zu KnyphausenAufsess, D., & Nikol, P. (2008). Top management teams, business models, and performance of biotechnology ventures: An upper echelon perspective. *British Journal of Management, 19*(3), 205–221.

Petrovic, O., Kittl, C., & Teksten, D. (2001, October 31–November 4). Developing business models for eBusiness. In *Proceedings of the international conference on electronic commerce, Vienna* (pp. 1–6).

Pisano, G., & Verganti, R. (2008). Which kind of collaboration is right for you? *Harvard Business Review, 82*(12), 78–86.

Porter, M. (1996). What is strategy? *Harvard Business Review, 74*(6), 61–78.

Porter, M. E. (2001). Strategy and the internet. *Harvard Business Review, 79*(3), 62–79.

Rajala, R. (2001). *Software business models: A framework for analyzing software industry.* Tekes.

Rajala, R., & Westerlund, M. (2005). Business models: A new perspective on knowledge-intensive services in the software industry. In *18th Bled eCommerce conference eIntegration in action, Bled, Slovenia* (pp. 1–15).

Rajala, R., & Westerlund, M. (2007). Business models—A new perspective on firms' assets and capabilities: Observations from the Finnish software industry. *The International Journal of Entrepreneurship and Innovation, 8*(2), 115–126.

Rasmussen, B. (2007). *Business models and the theory of the firm* (Working Paper). Melbourne: Victoria University of Technology.

Richardson, J. (2008). The business model: An integrative framework for strategy execution. *Strategic Change, 17*(5–6), 133–144.

Saino, L. M., Saarenketo, S., Nummela, N., & Eriksson, T. (2011). Value creation of an internationalizing entrepreneurial firm, the business model perspective. *Journal of Small Business and Enterprise Development, 18*(3), 556–570.

Schweizer, L. (2005). Concept and evolution of business models. *Journal of General Management, 31*(2), 37–56.

Seddon, P. B., & Lewis, G. P. (2003, July 10–13). Strategy and business models: What's the difference? In *7th Pacific Asia conference on information systems, Adelaide, South Australia.*

Seddon, P. B., Lewis, G. P., Freeman, P., & Shanks, G. (2004). The case for viewing business models as abstraction of strategy. *Communications of the Association for Information Systems, 13*, 427–442.

Seelos, C., & Mair, J. (2007). Profitable business models and market creation in the context of deep poverty: A strategic view. *Academy of Management Perspectives, 21*(4), 49–63.

Selz, D. (1999). *Value webs: Emerging forms of fluid and flexible organization.* St. Gallen: University of St. Gallen.

Seppänen, M., & Mäkinen, S. (2007). Assessing business model concepts with taxonomical research criteria. *Management Research News, 30*(10), 735–748.

Shafer, S. M., Smith, H. J., & Linder, J. C. (2005). The power of business models. *Business Horizons, 48*(3), 199–207.

Simmons, O. E., & Gregory, T. A. (2005). Grounded action: Achieving optimal and sustainable change. *Historical Social Research/Historische Sozialforschung, 1*, 140–156.

Slywotzky, A. (1995). *Value migration.* Boston: Harvard Business School Press.

Slywotzky, A., & Linthicum, F. (1997). Capturing value in five moves or less: The new game of business. *Strategy & Leadership, 25*(1), 5–11.

Smith, W. K., Binns, A., & Tushman, M. L. (2010). Complex business models: Managing strategic paradoxes simultaneously. *Long Range Planning, 43*(2), 448–461.

Sosna, M., Trevinyo-Rodríguez, R. N., & Velamuri, S. R. (2010). Business model innovation through trial-and-error learning: The Naturhouse case. *Long Range Planning, 43*(2), 383–407.

Stähler, P. (2001). *Geschäftsmodelle in der digitalen Ökonomie. Merkmale, Strategien und Auswirkungen.* Dissertation, University of St. Gallen HSG.

Stähler, P. (2002). Business models as an unit of analysis for strategizing. In *Proceedings of the 1st international workshop on business models, Lausanne, Suisse.*

Stewart, D. W., & Zhao, Q. J. (2000). Internet marketing, business models, and public policy. *Journal of Public Policy & Marketing, 19*(2), 287–296.

Stone, P. J., Dunphy, D. C., Smith, M. S., & Ogilvie, D. M. (1966). *The general inquirer: A computer approach to content analysis.* Cambridge, MA: MIT Press.

Svejenova, S., Planellas, M., & Vives, L. (2010). An individual business model in the making: A chef's quest for creative freedom. *Long Range Planning, 43*(2), 408–430.

Talluri, S., Baker, R. C., & Sarkis, J. (1999). A framework for designing efficient value chain networks. *International Journal of Production Economics, 62*, 133–144.

Tapscott, D. (2001). Rethinking strategy in a networked world: Or why Michael Porter is wrong about the internet. *Strategy + Business,* (24), 1–8.

Tapscott, D., Ticoll, D., & Lowi, A. (2000). *Digital capital—Harnessing the power of business webs.* Boston: Harvard Business School Press.

Teece, D. (2010). Business model, business strategy, and innovation. *Long Range Planning, 43*(2–3), 172–194.

Tikkanen, H., Lamberg, J. A., Parvinen, P., & Kallunki, J. P. (2005). Managerial cognition, action and the business model of the firm. *Management Decision, 43*, 789–809.

Timmers, P. (1998). Business models for electronic markets. *Journal on Electronic Markets, 8*(2), 3–8.

Trimi, S., & Berbegal-Mirabent, J. (2012). Business model innovation in entrepreneurship. *International Entrepreneurship and Management Journal, 8*(4), 449–465.

van Hee, K. M. (1994). *Information systems engineering: A formal approach.* Cambridge: Cambridge University Press.

Veit, D., Clemons, E., Benlian, A., Buxmann, P., Hess, T., Kundisch, D., et al. (2014). Business models—An information systems research agenda. *Business & Information Systems Engineering—Research, 6*(1), 45–53.

Venkatraman, N., & Henderson, J. C. (1998). Real strategies for virtual organizing. *Sloan Management Review, 40*(3), 33–48.

Verstraete, T., Kremer, F., & Jouison-Laffitte, E. (2012). Le business model: une théorie pour des pratiques. *Entreprendre & innover,* (1), 7–26.

Voelpel, S., Leibold, M., & Tekie, E. (2005). Escaping the red queen effect in competitive strategy: Sense-testing business models. *European Management Journal, 23*(1), 37–49.

Warnier, V., Lecocq, X., & Demil, B. (2004, June). Le business model: l'oublié de la stratégie? In *présenté à la 13ème Conférence Internationale de Management Stratégique* (pp. 2–4).

Weill, P., & Vitale, M. R. (2001). *Place to space: Migrating to eBusiness models.* Boston: Harvard Business School Press.

Wernerfelt, B. (1984). A resource-based view of the firm. *Strategic Management Journal, 5*(2), 171–180.

Winter, S. G., & Szulanski, G. (2001). Replication as strategy. *Organization Science, 12*(6), 730–743.

Wirtz, B. W. (2011). *Business model management: Design—Instruments—Success factors.* Wiesbaden: Gabler.

Wirtz, B. W., & Lihotzky, N. (2003). Customer retention management in the B2C electronic business. *Long Range Planning, 36*(6), 517–532.

Yuan, Y., & Zhang, J. J. (2003). Towards an appropriate business model for m-commerce. *International Journal of Mobile Communications, 1*(1–2), 35–56.

Yunus, M., Moingeon, B., & Lehmann-Ortega, L. (2010). Building social business models: Lessons from the Grameen experience. *Long Range Planning, 43*(2), 308–325.

Zhifang, M. (1988). Theoretical clustering and a scheme of its implementation. In *Proceedings of the ACM sixteenth annual conference on Computer science Atlanta, GA* (pp. 663–666).

Zott, C., & Amit, R. (2002). *Measuring the performance implications of business model design: Evidence from emerging growth public firms.* Indsead working papers, Fontainebleau: Insead.

Zott, C., & Amit, R. (2007). Business model design and the performance of entrepreneurial firms. *Organization Science, 18*(2), 181–199.

Zott, C., & Amit, R. (2008). The fit between product market strategy and business model: Implications for firm performance. *Strategic Management Journal, 29*(1), 1–26.

Zott, C., & Amit, R. (2010). Business model design: An activity system perspective. *Long Range Planning, 43*(2–3), 216–226.

Zott, C., Amit, R., & Massa, L. (2011). The business model: Recent developments and future research. *Journal of Management, 37*(4), 1019–1042.

Internet Sources—Webography

BMWi. (2012). Rösler: IKT sind Treiber für Innovation und Wachstum. http://www.bmwi.de/DE/Presse/pressemitteilungen,did=505772.html. Accessed 2012-11-02.

Jean-Pierre Ubuad MBA Course Outline—MANAGEMT 7234—Managing various business models across borders, The University of Adelaide, 2014. http://www.adelaide.edu.au/course-outlines/106173/1/summer/2014/

Rappa, M. (2000). Managing the digital enterprise: Business models on the web. Retrieved February 18, 2000, from http://ecommerce.ncsu.edu/business_models.html

Rappa, M. (2008). Managing the digital enterprise [wwwdocument]. http://digitalenterprise.org/index.html

Chapter 3
Framing Current Business Model Innovation Research Agenda

3.1 Introduction

Research on business model innovation (BMI) is in its infancy and the cradle is mainly located in the fields of strategy and innovation (Zott et al. 2011). Despite the various attempts to classify the growing literature on BMI (for a review, see, for example, Spieth et al. 2014), the phenomenon is still fuzzy.

Business model innovation is the unique and sustainable invention of using core competencies in doing business, with the aim to provide more scalable as well as interoperable and new and/or increased added value network for the customers, the corporation itself, and its stakeholders. Moreover, business model innovation refers to organizations rethinking their dominant value logic and coming up with new ways of creating value principles for their customers and themselves (Fielt 2012). It offers a transformational approach, via the business model's addressing the change and focus on innovation, either in the organization or in the business model itself (Demil and Lecocq 2010). BMI can be defined as the "discovery of a fundamentally different business model in an existing business" (Markides 2006) or as "the search for new business logics of the firm and new ways to create and capture value for its stakeholders" (Casadesus-Masanell and Zhu 2013).

3.2 The Main Functions of Business Model Innovation

Business model innovation is critical to assist corporate executives and entrepreneurs. Accordingly, the corporate and entrepreneurial function of the business model includes:

(a) Building entrepreneurial processes and capabilities for innovation
(b) Enabling to stay customer/consumer relevant
(c) Adapting how corporation creates, delivers, and captures value

© Springer International Publishing Switzerland 2016   67
Z. Vukanović, *Foreign Direct Investment Inflows Into the South East European Media Market*, Media Business and Innovation, DOI 10.1007/978-3-319-30512-7_3

(d) Creating a framework which delivers incremental, adjacent, adaptive, and transformative value.

3.3 The Importance of Business Model Innovation

The importance of business model innovation has increased in recent years, since companies no longer regard product innovation as the only source of competitive advantage. The glut of market choice in products and services means that often innovative business models are what differentiate global competitors (Amit and Zott 2012). But there is more to it than that: business model innovation is relevant for both start-ups trying to attain significant size and profitability (e.g., Zott and Amit 2007) and incumbents trying to adapt to change or seize opportunities outside their core operating space (e.g., Johnson 2010). Business model innovation is important because it is a form of innovation in itself; it can complement other forms of innovation, and it is often required to commercialize new technologies (Amit and Zott 2001). Radical business model innovations have the potential to shake whole industries (Demil and Lecocq 2010; Steenkamp and Arnoldi-Van der Walt 2004) and can result in a competitive advantage if they are hard to replicate (Magretta 2002).

Business model innovation has become increasingly important both in academic literature and in practice given the increasing number of opportunities for business model configurations enabled by technological progress, increasing global competitiveness, new customer preferences, and deregulation (Casadesus-Masanell and Zhu 2010). At root, business model innovation refers to the search for new logics of the firm and new ways to create and capture value for its stakeholders and focuses primarily on finding new ways to generate revenues and define value propositions for customers, suppliers, and partners (Amit and Zott 2001; Magretta 2002; Zott and Amit 2007, 2008; Baden-Fuller et al. 2010; Casadesus-Masanell and Ricart 2010; Gambardella and McGahan 2010; Teece 2010). As a result, business model innovation often affects the whole enterprise (Amit and Zott 2001). However, few executives know how to apply it to their businesses (Johnson 2010).

Amit and Zott (2012) argue that business model innovation matters to managers, entrepreneurs, and academic researchers for at least three important reasons: "First, it represents an often underutilized source of future value. Second, competitors might find it more difficult to imitate or replicate an entire novel activity system than a single novel product or process. Since it is often relatively easier to undermine and erode the returns of product or process innovation, innovation at the level of the business model can sometimes translate into a sustainable performance advantage. Third, because business model innovation can be such a potentially powerful competitive tool, managers must predict and counter competitors' moves and reactions. Competitive threats often come from outside their traditional industry boundaries."

Moreover, in terms of specific market and entrepreneurial importance, the business model innovation is:

(a) Major element of differentiation and sustainable competitive advantage
(b) Key to the commercialization of new technologies
(c) Fundamental to more adaptable performance and seizing of opportunities in an increasingly changing business climate
(d) A form of innovation itself complementing other forms of innovation, and often requiring commercialization of new technologies.

In addition, business model innovation is relevant for young companies trying to attain significant size and profitability (Zott and Amit 2007) and for established companies trying to seize opportunities outside their core operating space (Johnson 2010). Relatedly, the business model innovation is increasingly popular within ICT, telecommunications, media management, and strategy literature.

In summary, business model innovation is the key to unlocking/achieving transformational growth by fulfilling unmet customer needs in their current markets, serving entirely new customers and creating new markets, and responding to tectonic shifts in market demand, government policy, and technologies that affect entire industries. More importantly, business model innovation is vital to sustaining open innovation.

3.4 Degrees of Business Model Innovation

Business model innovation covers changes from incremental adjustments to more dynamic changes. Mitchell and Coles (2003) propose a classification of business model innovations which distinguishes improvement, catch-up, replacement, and actual innovation. As all of these steps of improvement are somehow related to (more or less incremental or radical) innovation, different notions are proposed here to match the purpose of creating business cases for sustainability (Schaltegger et al. 2012). Four stages—adjustment, adoption, improvement, and redesign—are differentiated in the following:

- Business model adjustment refers to changes of only one (or a minor number of) business model element(s), excluding the value proposition; i.e., modifications of customer relationships, business infrastructure, or the financial pillar alone constitute improvements (Schaltegger et al. 2012).
- Business model adoption similar to the "catch-up" stage proposed by Mitchell and Coles (2003) refers to changes that mainly focus on matching competitors' value propositions. The goal is to not fall behind market standards and competitors. This requires adoptions of products and/or services, but sometimes also parts of the customer relationship pillar and the business infrastructure as these elements can be part of the value proposition as well (Osterwalder 2004).

- Business model improvement takes place when substantial parts of the business model elements are changed. Mitchell and Coles (2003) call this "replacement," even though the value proposition is not replaced. That is, simultaneous changes of a major number of elements, such as customer relationship approaches, infrastructure elements such as the business network, and the financial logic, are required to replace an existing model. The value proposition, however, stays unaltered (Schaltegger et al. 2012).
- Business model redesign exists in a focused sense when an improvement leads to a completely new value proposition. While a business model might be improved without changing the value proposition to the market (e.g., shifting from own production to purchasing), a real redesign replaces the underlying business logic and offers new products, services, or product-service systems (Devisscher and Mont 2008).

The strategic leverage effect of business model innovation increases the effectiveness of business strategies (Schaltegger et al. 2012).

3.5 The Elements of a Successful Business Model Innovation

A successful business model innovation aligns profitably innovative and disruptive value capture, as well as value delivery with the user value by finding customer lock-in points, corporate clusterization, possible vicious cycles, and the efficient configuration of the value architecture (value delivery business system—ecosystem). In other words, BMI operationalizes and executes the delivery of new value forms and therefore is facilitator as well as epicenter of its own added value network. Thus, to create the sustainable business model, it is necessary to attain an equilibrium between maximum value for the user and maximum value for the company. The successful business model should be made in line with the current Zeitgeist (i.e., spirit of the age or spirit of the time) (Valtysson 2012).

Moreover, successful companies thoroughly understand their business models via:

(a) Knowing how the building blocks relate to each other
(b) Constantly rethinking and redesigning these blocks and their relationship to innovate before the competition copies them (Osterwalder and Pigneur 2010).

3.6   The Impact of Long Tail Effects on the Business Model Innovation Revenue Model

Although, for centuries, the long tail phenomenon has seen described by statisticians and given names such as Pareto Law, Pareto Principle, and 80/20 rule, it was Chris Anderson, Editor-in-Chief of Wired magazine and former correspondent for The Economist, who used the term long tail to explain why, by taking advantage of the Internet's properties—such as its near-infinite shelf space—a firm could make money by selling small quantities of very many one-of-a-kind products rather than selling many units each of a small number of hits.

The following instances of long tail distribution are effective in improving the firm's chances of profiting by aggregating the niches of the tails of the distributions:

- A significant fraction of eBay's revenues come from selling small volumes of many hard-to-find (one-of-a-kind) items.
- A large number of the DVD titles that Netflix rents out are nonblockbusters that are not found in brick-and-mortar stores.
- Most of Google's revenues come from the many obscure customers who spend small amounts on advertising rather than from a few large advertisers who spent huge amounts, as bricks-and-mortar advertisers.
- Apple used a razor-and-blade revenue model in which it made very little from music sales—9 cents out of 99 per song—but made a lot of money from the iPod (Afuah 2014).

3.7   The Relation Between Intra-firm Network Configurations and Business Model Innovation

Bonakdar et al.'s (2014) research confirms positive and linear relation on intra-firm network configurations and business model innovation. Moreover, their research suggests that the solidarity benefits of cohesive networks outweigh the information benefits of sparse networks in order to develop novelty-centered business models. Thus, dense networks with few structural holes can play an important role to reshape, interpret, and integrate the distant information obtained outside the company. Since the benefits of close networks result from reducing uncertainty and uncertainty increases with the degree of novelty of the respective business model innovation, the benefits of close networks to develop novelty-centered business models will also increase. Concurrently, the value network is continuously interrupted. Moreover, a company can innovate along any of 12 different dimensions with respect to its (1) offerings, (2) platform, (3) solutions, (4) customers, (5) customer experience, (6) value capture, (7) processes, (8) organization, (9) supply chain, (10) presence, (11) networking, and (12) brand.

3.8   Current Perspectives on Business Model Innovation

Previous reviews of the literature on business models have attempted to categorize business model innovation research into different ways. Among those, Morris et al. (2005) define three general categories—economic, operational, and strategic—to cluster the various definitions in accordance with their major emphasis. Zott et al. (2011) classify the existing literature in accordance with their main focus area of explanation: e-business and use of information technology, strategic issues, and innovation and technology management. Perkmann and Spicer (2010) identify transactional structures, value extracting devices, and mechanisms for organizational structuring as dominant business model conceptions. Demil and Lecocq (2010) differentiate between static and transformational approaches of the business model concept. George and Bock (2011) distinguish six broad themes that business models commonly reflect: organizational design, the resource-based view, narrative and sensemaking, the nature of innovation, the nature of opportunity, and transactive structures. Schneider and Spieth (2013) categorize existing literature on business model innovation into three streams of research: (1) prerequisites of conducting business model innovation, (2) elements and process of business model innovation, and (3) effects achieved through business model innovation. While all of these classifications contribute to achieve a better understanding of the business model concept, the author argues that in order to further develop and unite the various understandings of a business model, it is essential to focus on the roles and functions assigned to the concept. As the interest in the concept of business models arose in response to a variety of different and partly unrelated challenges (e.g., new ways of doing business, rapid technological developments, and new forms of value creation), the interest in the concept is naturally based on distinct motivations.

3.9   Main Barriers for Business Model Innovation

Chesbrough (2010) analyzed two main types of barriers for business model innovation in organizations. One results from inability of the firm to adjust existing resources to complex change and the other from the constraining effect of the current business model upon potential new ideas. The dominant logic trap and the identity trap (Tripsas and Gavetti 2000) are similar phenomena, and according to different authors, experimentation is the key to finding suitable business models, pointing to the need for hypotheses, tests, and revisions (Magretta 2002; Chesbrough 2010; McGrath 2010). In a similar vein, other authors emphasize the importance of trial-and-error learning during the process of business model innovation (Santos et al. 2009). Trial-and-error learning and/or experimentation are nonlinear, non-orderly, non-predictable processes and are proposed by literature to be applied in situations of great uncertainty (e.g., Thomke et al. 1998).

Clearly, separate business model innovation processes can even be harmful, if they are not linked to other efforts, since this can disrupt the business model logic. Many changes in the business model building blocks were of a disruptive nature to the dominant business model and undermined the value capture flow as they were not coupled with other innovation process outcomes. This observation strongly favors a coordination of the different business model innovation processes. The process of business model innovation always needs to be related to the business model logic to ensure the value of each innovation step. The multifaceted structure of business model innovation requires its own set of resources and capabilities. This calls for a purposeful inter- and intra-organizational process of strategic goal development and dissemination conducted by top-level management. The dynamic management of relational capabilities, as well as individual and organizational learning, becomes a cornerstone to successfully managing and developing the business model.

3.10   Major Challenges and Constraints in Understanding, Studying, and Adopting Business Model Innovations

Understanding and studying business model innovation is challenging because (a) the concepts "business model" and "business model innovation" lack conceptual clarity and theoretical underpinning and (b) it is a form of innovation that is mostly not explicitly recognized and studied so far and presents significant challenges for organizations. As a result of its complex structure, business model innovation challenges different types of innovation, high risk and uncertainty, and individual and team models/cognitive maps. "When executives think of innovation, they all too often neglect the proper analysis and development of business models which can translate technical success into commercial success" (Teece 2010). Unsurprisingly, the multinational corporations have created unique business models and intangible assets that competitors can't easily replicate. Such business models now have a greater impact developing a pioneering, innovative, novel, and applicative business model and its performance metrics. Analyzing the literature on business model innovation, as well as on innovation processes in firms, Hülsmann and Pfeffermann (2011) argue that a main challenge to business model innovation is the organizational challenge. The organizational challenges are threefold: challenges based on the resources, values, and the team.

In sum, business model innovation barriers include a cognitive inability by managers to see the value of a new business model as well as resistance in the form of established configurations of resources and processes within the firm, which could lead to a state of inertia (Chesbrough 2010). Taken together, the born global firms need certain capabilities to manage a balance between existing business models and business model innovation over time and reshape strategic choices according to different and changing market demands and fluctuating business cycles (Johansson and Abrahamsson 2014).

References

Afuah, A. (2014). *Business model innovation: Concepts, analysis, and cases*. New York: Routledge.

Amit, R., & Zott, C. (2001). Value creation in e-business. *Strategic Management Journal, 22*(6–7), 493–520.

Amit, R., & Zott, C. (2012). Creating value through business model innovation. *MIT Sloan Management Review, 53*(3), 41–49.

Baden-Fuller, C., MacMillan, I., Demil, B., & Lecocq, X. (2010). Special issue call for papers: Business models. *Long Range Planning*, pp. 143–145.

Bonakdar, A., Frankenberger, K., & Gassmann, O. (2014). Intra-firm networks and novelty-centered business models. In ACAD MANAGE PROC.

Casadesus-Masanell, R., & Ricart, J. E. (2010). From strategy to business models and onto tactics. *Long Range Planning, 43*(2-3), 195–215.

Casadesus-Masanell, R., & Zhu, F. (2010). Strategies to fight ad-sponsored rivals. *Management Science, 56*(9), 1484–1499.

Casadesus-Masanell, R., & Zhu, F. (2013). Business model innovation and competitive imitation: The case of sponsor-based business models. *Strategic Management Journal, 34*(4), 464–482.

Chesbrough, H. (2010). Business model innovation: Opportunities and barriers. *Long Range Planning, 43*(2–3), 354–363.

Demil, B., & Lecocq, X. (2010). Business model evolution: In search of dynamic consistency. *Long Range Planning, 43*, 227–246.

Devisscher, T., & Mont, O. (2008). An analysis of a product service system in Bolivia: Coffee in Yunga. *International Journal of Innovation and Sustainable Development, 3*(3/4), 262–284.

Fielt, E. (2012). A 'service logic' rationale for business model innovation. In EURAM annual conference 2012, 6–8 June 2012, Erasmus University, Rotterdam.

Gambardella, A., & McGahan, A. M. (2010). Business-model innovation: General purpose technologies and their implications for industry structure. *Long Range Planning, 43*(2-3), 262–271.

George, G., & Bock, A. J. (2011). The business model in practice and its implications for entrepreneurship research. *Entrepreneurship: Theory and Practice, 35*(1), 83–111.

Hülsmann, M., & Pfeffermann, N. (2011). *Strategies and communications for innovations: An integrative management view for companies and networks*. New York: Springer.

Johansson, M. & Abrahamsson, J. T. (2014). Competing with the useful business model innovation: An exploratory case study of the journey of born global firms, *2*(1), pp. 33–55.

Johnson, M. W. (2010). *Seizing the white space: Business model innovation for growth and renewal*. Cambridge, MA: Harvard Business Press.

Magretta, J. (2002). Why business models matter. *Harvard Business Review, 80*(5), 86–92.

Markides, C. (2006). Disruptive innovation: In need of better theory. *Journal of Product Innovation Management, 23*(1), 19–25.

McGrath, R. G. (2010). Business models: A discovery driven approach. *Long Range Planning, 43*(2), 247–261.

Mitchell, D., & Coles, C. (2003). The ultimate competitive advantage of continuing business model innovation. *Journal of Business Strategy, 24*(5), 15–21.

Morris, M., Schindehutte, M., & Allen, J. (2005). The entrepreneur's business model: Toward a unified perspective. *Journal of Business Research, 58*(6), 726–735.

Osterwalder, A. (2004). *The business model ontology: A proposition in a design science approach*. Doctoral thesis, Présentée à l'Ecole des Hautes Etudes Commerciales de l'Université de Lausanne.

Osterwalder, A., & Pigneur, Y. (2010). *Business model generation: A handbook for visionaries, game changers, and challengers*. Hoboken, NJ: Wiley.

Perkmann, M., & Spicer, A. (2010). What are business models? Developing a theory of performative representations. *Research in the Sociology of Organizations, 29*, 269–279.

Santos, J., Spector, B., & Van Der Heyden, L. (2009). *Toward a theory of business model innovation within incumbent firms* (Working paper no. 2009/16/EFE/ST/TOM). Fontainebleau, France: INSEAD.

Schaltegger, S., Lüdeke-Freund, F., & Hansen, E. G. (2012). Business cases for sustainability: The role of business model innovation for corporate sustainability. *International Journal of Innovation and Sustainable Development, 6*(2), 95–119.

Schneider, S., & Spieth, P. (2013). Business model innovation: Towards an integrated future research agenda. *International Journal of Innovation Management, 17*(01), 1340001.

Spieth, P., Schneckenberg, D., & Ricart, J. E. (2014). Business model innovation—State of the art and future challenges for the field. *R&D Management, 44*(3), 237–247.

Steenkamp, C. J. H., & Arnoldi-Van der Walt, S. E. (2004). Web phenomenon applied as ICT platform in support of business model innovation. *South African Journal of Information Management, 6*(1).

Teece, D. (2010). Business model, business strategy, and innovation. *Long Range Planning, 43* (2–3), 172–194.

Thomke, S. H. (1998). Managing experimentation in the design of new products. *Management Science, 44*(6), 743–762.

Tripsas, M., & Gavetti, G. (2000). Capabilities, cognition, and inertia: Evidence from digital imaging. *Strategic Management Journal, 21*(10–11), 1147–1161.

Valtysson, B. (2012). Facebook as a digital public sphere: Processes of colonization and emancipation. *tripleC, 10*(1), 77–91.

Zott, C., & Amit, R. (2007). Business model design and the performance of entrepreneurial firms. *Organization Science, 18*(2), 181–199.

Zott, C., & Amit, R. (2008). The fit between product market strategy and business model: Implications for firm performance. *Strategic Management Journal, 29*(1), 1–26.

Zott, C., Amit, R., & Massa, L. (2011). The business model: Recent developments and future research. *Journal of Management, 37*(4), 1019–1042.

Chapter 4
The Paradigm Shift: From Static to Evolutionary/Dynamic/Transformational/ Networked/Modular/Dynamic Business Model Concept

4.1 The Core, Constitutive, and Complementary Semantics and Concepts of the Static and Dynamic Business Model Comparison

In this modern digital world as opposed to the traditional one, translating business strategy into business processes has become much more of a challenge. Business processes are now mainly digitized and ICT enabled. Consequently, today's ICT-based businesses' environment and management are more dynamic, characterized by ongoing fast changes and severe stakeholders' pressure. Therefore, the dynamic BM has risen to prominence as a conceptual and contextual tool of "alignment" to fill the gap between corporate strategy and business processes including their web, Internet, and digital infrastructure, providing crucial harmonization among these organizational layers. A successful business should treat the business strategy, BM, and business processes along with their IS, as a harmonized package. Furthermore, the author argues that the BM is an essential conceptual tool of alignment in digital business. More specifically, it represents an intermediate layer between business strategy and ICT-enabled business processes, fulfilling the missing link created by the complex and digitized environment.

Broadly, two major and different conceptual types/approaches and applicative uses of business models can be identified. The first refers to a static approach. The second use of the concept represents a static/transformational approach. The static view [of a business model] allows us to build typologies and study [its] relationship with performance (Demil and Lecocq 2010). The dynamic/transformational view deals with the major managerial question of how to change [it]. The static model captures the target business and the key components of a business plan (Morris et al. 2005), while the dynamic/evolutionary model describes how a business evolves via four approaches, including enhancing, extending, expanding, and exiting (Applegate et al. 2003). Moreover, transformational model addresses change and innovation in the organization, or in the model itself (Demil and Lecocq

© Springer International Publishing Switzerland 2016   77
Z. Vukanović, *Foreign Direct Investment Inflows Into the South East European Media Market*, Media Business and Innovation, DOI 10.1007/978-3-319-30512-7_4

2010). Static business models ignore dynamics and change (Palo and Tähtinen 2011). Such models may not help companies to demonstrate their business in uncertain contexts (Doganova and Eyquem-Renault 2009). Likewise, dynamics, a modular component inherent in digital media, ICT, and telecommunications-related products and services, is missing from the models.

The author notes that the ICT and media businesses must adopt the digital media into the center of their business operations and incorporate their digital divisions such as efficient interoperability, better scalability, and effective innovation into the main enterprise.

4.2   The Benefits of a Dynamic/Transformational Business Model

Transformational/dynamic business models must be designed around ways to improve the customer experience, not around ways to improve the performance of the current business model. Dynamic business model will help target benefits in three key areas:

- Higher profitability—by reducing operational costs through common platforms and integrated business processes, enabling the enterprise to leverage identifiable unique content and consumer experience assets across multiple platforms.
- Better scalability—through digital workflows, rights, and royalties solutions that can support millions of digital transactions, and digital consolidation of physical format archives to reduce costs and boost commercial exploitation.
- More effective and continual innovation—through integration and automation, freeing up time for staff to collaborate and generate new ideas.

Repositioning digital as the engine of the business enables it to rebalance its skills and capabilities around control, data, and to drive new services. Furthermore, the move from the physical world to the digital world is more than simply replicating physical goods in digital forms, or even creating new digital products. The move to digital also requires a major shift in a business' revenue model (Macnamara 2010).

In an era of hypercompetitive and volatile markets, a successful dynamic business model disrupts not only channels, operations, and products but established revenue models as well. The dynamic business model is a catalyst as well as harbinger of the new digital mediascape. The dynamic business model should be regarded as the evolutionary/longitudinal/causal strategy process and dynamics. Accordingly, digital models are constantly evolving as consumer, business technologies, and customer preferences are changing rapidly (Macnamara 2010).

One of the most contentious and pressing issues concerning media in the early twenty-first century is identifying viable business models, with widespread reports that twentieth-century business models underpinning press, radio, and television are collapsing because of "audience fragmentation" driven by an ever-widening range of choice in media content and sources on the Internet (Macnamara 2010). Increasing demand on technological innovation in media industry drives paradigmatic changes in FDI business models (Macnamara 2010). Moreover, in today's increasingly global and competitive market business models in media and ICT industry shift from incremental to disruptive and transformational business model innovation (Macnamara 2010). Thus, identification of sustainable media business models is an urgent priority, as continuing decline in audiences and collapse of media organizations pose a major threat to journalism and society, with scholars agreeing that further erosion of quality journalism threatens democracy. Future media business models also have major implications for the advertising industry and a wide range of content producers (Macnamara 2010).

At this stage, no consensus or even widespread agreement has emerged on any alternative business model, and many of those proposed require further development and analysis. In that process, economic feasibility and market acceptance need to be balanced sensitively. However, the diversity of types of media content and media users' needs and preferences indicates that a "one-size-fits-all approach" is unlikely to ensure media survival—or, better, reform and renewal. As David Carr (2010) suggests, the best way forward may be a hybrid model involving diversification to create multiple revenue streams developed to suit each medium and its operations.

4.3   The Impact of Exponential Growth of ICT Network, Traffic, and Web/Multimedia/Hypermedia Content on the Formation of Dynamic Business Model

Economic growth and technology are inextricably linked. Viewed longitudinally, technology is probably the most powerful influence on business models in the media sector, and the quality of an organization's response to changes in this domain is probably one of the most important determinants of strategic outcomes. Also viewed longitudinally, the pattern of technology development for the sector is consistent: Technology gives and technology takes away, but it seldom takes everything away. Technological innovations supplement, rather than replace, previous technologies. The previous medium is not destroyed but progressively undermined (Küng 2011). Additionally, businesses are, like media technologies in general, always already remediated: When new models emerge, old models are supplemented and only rarely displaced (Deuze 2011).

Current economic conditions are fostering investment in technology as emerging markets ramp up their demand for technology to fuel growth, and advanced markets seek new ways to cut costs and drive innovation. This becomes a virtuous circle as digital technologies drive consumer income and demand, education and training, and efficient use of capital and resources—leading to increased economic growth, particularly in emerging markets. Executives must be aware of the new challenges facing their firms as market momentum accelerates. Moreover, the 2007 recession and financial crisis caused a seismic shift reshaping the global business landscape and producing a sluggish growth in the West, as well as a shift in power to the East, and value-driven customers and rising risks everywhere. At the same time, the downturn has accelerated the adoption of the cutting-edge technologies (IOT, cloud computing, broadband internet, smart phones, etc).

A leitmotif throughout this monograph is the fast-changing context of the media industry. While current global markets are subject to greater turbulence and complexity at higher velocities, the urgency to respond and adapt depends on media multinationals' tailored strategies of mass customization, multimedia optimization, downstream production, and adaptive and innovative business models. Accordingly, media corporations should adapt to the fast, tectonic, unparalleled, unprecedented, and seismic technological, market and demand developments, building a competitive as well as sustainable advantage because market dynamics make existing capabilities obsolete tomorrow (van Kranenburg and Ziggers 2013).

Instead of trying to create stability, media corporations must actively work to disrupt their own advantages and the advantages of competitors by continuously challenging existing capabilities. It involves continuous search for improvement along a fixed production function, while the latter requires discontinuous shifts from one production function to another that is more profitable. Consequently, a media firm only incrementally adapts its existing business model emphasizing process efficiency and effectiveness. The challenge for media corporations is to develop and to incorporate new business models, such as the innovation-centered business model, to fulfill the new requirements and demands. This approach enables the media corporations to be really innovative and to develop new capabilities and resources to sustain their competitive position (van Kranenburg and Ziggers 2013).

The accelerating growth of digital media and eBusiness has raised the interest in transforming traditional business models via developing new ones that better exploit the opportunities enabled by disruptive technological innovations. One of the major impacts of eBusiness on traditional business practices has been the multiplication of possible business configurations (networked multi-platforms), which increases consumers' choices as well as the architectural implementation of business models and managerial decisions. Thus, the four key technologies (digital megatrends) that are bringing the new digital economy into adulthood include mobility, cloud computing, business intelligence, and social media.

4.4   The Influence of ICT Exponential Development on Digital Business Model

After the commercial usage of Internet, the average number of published academic articles increased approximately 4000 %. Businesses and consumers will add approximately 40 exaflops of computing capacity in 2014, up from 5 in 2008 and less than 1 in 2005 (Dobbs et al. 2014). These extraordinary advances in capacity, power, and speed are fueling the rise of artificial intelligence, reshaping global manufacturing (George et al. 2014), and turbocharging advances in connectivity. This will be further dynamized with the current and future development and application of the Internet of Things or Industry 4.0—the physical world, becoming a type of information system—through sensors and actuators embedded in physical objects and linked through wired and wireless networks via the Internet Protocol. Moreover, advances in wireless networking technology and the greater standardization of communications protocols make it possible to collect data from these sensors almost anywhere at any time.

4.5   Trends of Global IP Traffic Growth

The Cisco® Visual Networking Index (VNI) document "The Zettabyte Era—Trends and Analysis" presents some of the main findings of Cisco's global IP traffic forecast and explores the implications of IP traffic growth for service providers. Moreover, the document reveals that the global IP traffic has increased fivefold over the past 5 years and will increase threefold over the next 5 years. Overall, IP traffic will grow at a compound annual growth rate (CAGR) of 23 % from 2014 to 2019. Two-thirds of all IP traffic will originate with non-PC devices by 2019. In 2014, only 40 % of total IP traffic originated with non-PC devices, but by 2019 the non-PC share of total IP traffic will grow to 67 %. PC-originated traffic will grow at a CAGR of 9 %, and TVs, tablets, smartphones, and machine-to-machine (M2M) modules will have traffic growth rates of 17 %, 65 %, 62 %, and 71 %, respectively. Traffic from wireless and mobile devices will exceed traffic from wired devices by 2016. By 2016, wired devices will account for 47 % of IP traffic, and Wi-Fi and mobile devices will account for 53 % of IP traffic. In 2014, wired devices accounted for the majority of IP traffic, at 54 %. Global Internet traffic in 2019 will be equivalent to 66 times the volume of the entire global Internet in 2005. Globally, Internet traffic will reach 37 gigabytes (GB) per capita by 2019, up from 15.5 GB per capita in 2014.

The number of devices connected to IP networks will be more than three times the global population by 2019. There will be more than three networked devices per capita by 2019, up from nearly two networked devices per capita in 2014. Accelerated in part by the increase in devices and the capabilities of those devices, IP traffic per capita will reach 22 GB per capita by 2019, up from 8 GB per capita in

2014. Broadband speeds will more than double by 2019. By 2019, global fixed broadband speeds will reach 42.5 Mbps, up from 20.3 Mbps in 2014. Globally, IP video traffic will be 80 % of all IP traffic (both business and consumer) by 2019, up from 67 % in 2014. This percentage does not include the amount of video exchanged through peer-to-peer (P2P) file sharing.

Internet video to TV grew 47 % in 2014. This traffic will continue to grow at a rapid pace, increasing fourfold by 2019. Internet video to TV will be 17 % of consumer Internet video traffic in 2019, up from 16 % in 2014. Consumer VoD traffic will nearly double by 2019. The amount of VoD traffic in 2019 will be equivalent to 7 billion DVDs per month. Globally, mobile data traffic will increase 10-fold between 2014 and 2019. Mobile data traffic will grow at a CAGR of 57 % between 2014 and 2019, reaching 24.3 exabytes per month by 2019. Global mobile data traffic will grow three times faster than fixed IP traffic from 2014 to 2019. Global mobile data traffic was 4 % of total IP traffic in 2014 and will be 14 % of total IP traffic by 2019.

IP traffic is growing fastest in the Middle East and Africa, followed by Asia Pacific and Central and Eastern Europe. Total Internet traffic has experienced dramatic growth in the past two decades. More than 20 years ago, in 1992, global Internet networks carried approximately 100 GB of traffic per day. In 2014, global Internet traffic reached 16,144 GBps. By 2019, it is projected that the global internet traffic will amount to 51,794 GBps. Globally, IP traffic will reach 22 GB per capita by 2019, up from 8 GB per capita in 2014, and Internet traffic will reach 18 GB per capita by 2019, up from 6 GB per capita in 2014. Importantly, the global average broadband speed continues to grow and will more than double from 2014 to 2019, from 20.3 to 42.5 Mbps. Globally, the average mobile network connection speed in 2014 was 1.7 Mbps. The average speed will double and will be nearly 4 Mbps by 2019. Moreover, global Wi-Fi connection speeds originated from dual-mode mobile devices will nearly double by 2019. The average Wi-Fi network connection speed (10.6 Mbps in 2014) will exceed 18.5 Mbps in 2019. Globally, there will be nearly 341 million public Wi-Fi hotspots by 2018, up from 48 million hotspots in 2014, a sevenfold increase (iPass Inc. and Maravedis and Rethink Study, 2014). Wi-Fi is also on the move, becoming available on 60 % of planes and 11 % of trains by 2018. This compares to only 16 % of planes and 3 % of trains equipped with Wi-Fi in 2014. Community "homespot" public Wi-Fi hotspots will see the most explosive growth, rising from just under 40 million in 2014 to over 325 million in 2018. Accordingly, between 2000 and May 2016, the web has grown 60-fold from 17.08 million to 1.03 billion users.

4.6   Anticipation of Global Market Shifts in Real Time

Industries most affected by digital transformation include IT (72 %), telecommunications (66 %), entertainment, media, and publishing (65 %), retail (48 %), and banking (47 %) (Oxford Economics White Paper 2011). Itami and Nishino (2010) consider that a business model contains what the business does and how the business makes profit. The business model describes conceptually corporate innovation, resource, market, and value. In addition, the business model may derive from the analysis of market opportunity, product and services, competitive dynamics, or strategies (Applegate et al. 2003).

The overall essence, and the ultimate goal and objective of a firm's business model, is to exploit a business opportunity by creating value for its customers/stakeholders, enticing them to pay for the value, and converts those payments to profit (Zott and Amit 2010; Afuah and Tucci 2001; Applegate 2001; Huarng and Yu 2011; Petrovic et al. 2001; Teece 2010).

A business model should reflect financial conditions in a business (Dubosson-Torbay et al. 2002). In other words, a business model should translate the conceptual model into numbers (Meyer and Crane 2010). Thus, a financial model, consisting of cost, revenue, and profit, serves as the second tier of the two-tier business model. To become sustainable, businesses may need to adapt their business models as time goes by (Dahan et al. 2010).

The digital revolution is the most challenging transformation shaking the traditional-conservative business models (analog) and establishing new online/emerging networked multi-platforms. The digital design evolves into digital architecture, network, architectural multi-platform and consequently to ecosystem. From the analogue axiomatic principle/ground rule: The content/distribution is the king—the discussion evolves into: choice/access/apps is the king. Moreover, the digital media business paradigm is further emphasized via different media content consumption and distribution patterns: access vs. content, franchises over networked and multi-platform distribution channel, free vs. pay/premium, broadcast/printed journalism-drone journalism/online journalism/web journalism/, user vs. prosumer, producer vs. produser, traditional social media networks (Facebook, Twitter, YouTube) vs. temporary social media networks (Snapchat, WhatsApp), etc. Additionally, Internet of things creates more synergetic and convergent added value network. More specifically, it personalizes the business context and value exchange creating more effective network effects between potential prosumers and applications/services/products.

4.7 The Dynamic Business Model

Characterizing the BM as dynamic (Hedman and Kalling 2003; MacInnes 2005) is essential mainly because many industries today, such as media, ICT, and telecommunications, are undergoing continuing revolutions driven by innovative technologies, globalization including deregulations, and market changes. Indeed, the business environment has been greatly transformed. Unlike the traditional world of business which is characterized by stability and low levels of competition, the world of digital business is complex, granular, networked, modular, and dynamic displaying high levels of uncertainty and competition. As a result, in the more complex and sometimes unique digital business, the BM needs to be explicit and more flexible.

An evolving dynamic/networked/modular business model consists of strategic objectives, missions, and structures (Hambrick and Fredrickson 2001; Porter 1996); target markets (scope and market segment) and business value chain/network/ proposition (alliances, partnerships, product/service offering) (Achrol and Kotler 1999; Anderson et al. 1994); key intra- and inter-organizational operational processes and resources (capabilities and assets) (Bartlett and Ghoshal 1995; Barney 1991; Nelson and Winter 1982); finance and accounting system; and cost and revenue model (cost and revenue streams, pricing policy) (Norton and Kaplan 1992). Moreover, in Table 4.1, the author outlines the key building blocks of dynamic and static business models.

The advent of the Internet represents a crucial landmark in the digital media evolution. Accordingly, new media global landscapes demand new business model maps. Media companies are trying to face up the challenges of this emerging scenario, as new consumers and new markets are transforming traditional business models into dynamic media business markets. As a consequence, the media corporate players are moving strategically and the whole audiovisual product's value chain will be readjusted (Guerrero et al. 2013).

The multi-platform audiovisual model influence on production is inextricably bound up with the question of the business models that may enable a recouping of the costs involved. A key aspect of the design of any business model is the identification of revenue streams. These network-based, symbiotic, market-driven relationships among the various entities and social media are the genesis of sustainable business models for the emerging social media industry. The dynamic business model is actively co-created between the various actors/platforms involved.

4.8   Main Paradigm Shifts in New/Social Media Over Old/Traditional Media

Although both the old/traditional and new/social media can reach small or large audiences, there are many fundamental differences in terms of the competitive advantage in distribution, production, technology, and market targeting that favor new/social media over old/traditional media. In Table 4.1, these marking differences are exposed in order to more effectively outline the major conceptual differences between new and old media.

Table 4.1 The common denominators of major paradigmatic shifts from the static to dynamic/transformational media business model building blocks

Static Media Business Model Building Blocks	Dynamic/Transformational/Networked/Modular Media Business Model Building Blocks
Analog Media	Digital Media
Organizational design	Organizational Architecture evolving to organizational ecosystem and smart grid networks
One-sided market	Two-sided/Multi Platform/Network/market
Upstream supply chain (Push marketing, low-cost producers)	downstream supply chain (customization, targetization, high margins)
Top-down content production/distribution	Bottom-up content production/distribution
One to many content distribution	Many to many content distribution
Linear, One-way communication	Interactive communication evolving to Immersive communication
Reaching the audience	Connecting the audience
Passive users/consumers	Active users - produsers and prosumers
Mass Audience	Audience Fragmentation or Disaggregation
Less available and accessible consumption to the public	On-demand access
Low level of collaborative content sharing	High level of collaborative content sharing – UGC - User Generated Content; P2P; tagging; folksonomy; big data analytics; IOT – Internet of Thing; Social networks; WOT – Web of Things; Wearable technology; Locative/Mobile media
Bundling	Complementarities and Vendor Lock-in strategies
Broadcasting	Broadband, Narrowcasting, Microcasting and Egocasting
Content & Distribution is the king	Choice, Share, Access, Application is the king
Competition	Co-opetition
Freemium	Premium
Industrial, Tangible Economy - Economies of scale	Information, Intangible Economy - Economies of Scope, Long Tail Economics, Digital Economics, Network Economics, Information Economics, Experience Economics
Push Market Revenue Model	Pull Market Revenue Model - 'behavioural targeting', 'advergaming', 'gamification', 'product placement', micro-payment, paywall, content repurposing, sale of data and 'asynchronous ads'
Two-dimensional media	3D media
Web 1.0 and Web 2.0	Web 3.0 (semantic web) and Web 4.0 (symbiotic web)
Symmetric information flow	Asymmetric information flow
First build a marketplace, than a community.	First build a community, than a marketplace.
Attention span is longer	Attention span is shorter
Owning the accessed content	Sharing the accessed content
Searching the data	Searching the metadata
Hardware based media	Software (cloud) based media
Demand is the king	Choice is the king
Connect individual with the information/content/product	Share content and experience among groups
Information based service	Conversation/Communication based service
Place bounded media	Space bounded media
Individual/one screen media	Multi-screen media
Value is contained in transaction	Value is contained in relationship
Information based service	Conversation/Communication based service
Usage-based pricing	Access-based pricing

Important notice: The static media business model building block is highlighted in blue, while the dynamic/transformational media business model building block is highlighted in red

4.9   The Positioning Modeling Principles of Dynamic Business Model

The digital era has meant that the availability of appropriate levels of information and knowledge has become critical to the success of the business. Organizations need to adapt in order to survive and succeed as their business domains, processes, and technologies change in a world of increasing environmental complexity. Enhancing their competitive positions by improving their ability to respond quickly to rapid environmental changes with high-quality business decisions can be supported by adopting suitable BMs for this new world of digital business.

However, the main reason behind this confusion is the shift that the business world experienced from the traditional ways of doing business to the new ways of digital business, which feature a high level of complexity and rapid change. This transformation has created a gap between strategy and processes which calls for new ways of thinking about BMs.

The modern media, telecommunications, and ICT-based world of business imposes a vital need for BMs with high levels of adaptability to accommodate the ongoing changes more efficiently. Within today's business environment, the BM should also be enjoying dynamicity to cope successfully with the continuous changes.

The granularity and modularity of the dynamic business model implies flexibility in its related functions such as design, architecture, management, evaluation, and change and also facilitates the reusability of the components for new BMs. This highlights the concept as an efficient and effective framework essential to digital organizations. This subfield of research is still unexplored; therefore, theoretical as well as practical investigation and delineation of this particular area would be very useful.

4.9.1   The Evolution and Position of the Business Model Within the New World of Digital Business

Business model researchers are attempting to determine its meaning, boundaries, components, and relationships with other business aspects, such as business processes and business strategy. There is already some consensus regarding the differences between the business model and the process model (Pateli and Giaglis 2003; Morris et al. 2005). However, the debate on the difference between the business model and business strategy has not been resolved (Porter 2001; Stähler 2002; Pateli and Giaglis 2004). Some researchers see them as identical and use the terms interchangeably: Kallio et al. (2006) depict business model components as a set of business strategies. Other researchers suggest that even though both concepts are related, they represent different levels of information, useful for different purposes. They see the business model as an interface or an intermediate theoretical layer between the business strategy and the business processes (Osterwalder 2004; Tikkanen et al. 2005; Rajala and Westerlund 2005; Morris et al. 2005). Magretta (2002) argues that the business strategy explains how business organizations hope to do better than their rivals, while the business model describes how the pieces of a business all fit together.

The main reason behind this confusion is the shift that the business world experienced from the traditional way of doing business to the new way of digital (e)business, which is engulfed with high level of complexity and rapid change. This new world of digital business has created a gap between the business strategy and business processes. In this context, translating business strategy into business process has become much more of a challenge. Accordingly, the business model has risen to prominence as a conceptual tool of alignment to fill the gap that has been created in this world of digital business.

The business model facilitates the fit and an interface or an intermediate layer between business strategy and business processes. Furthermore, the business model enhances digital business managers' control over their business and enables them to compete better due to the appropriate and necessary level of information that the business model provides. This level of information also extends digital business managers' knowledge of how the business organization will adapt their strategy, business model, and business processes to cope with the complex, uncertain, and rapidly changing digitalized environment. Thus, there are improvements in the organizations' abilities in achieving their strategic goals and objectives. This is because the information that the business model offers is neither highly aggregated, which it is in the case of business strategy, nor highly detailed, which it is in the case of the operational business process model. The business model is by no means independent; it intersects with the business strategy as well as the business processes.

4.10 Digital Business Model Perspectives: From Place to Space

Before the Internet, business operated primarily in a physical world of "place": It was a world that was tangible, product based, and oriented toward customer transactions. Today, many industries—all moving at different rates—are shifting toward a digital world of "space": more intangible, more service based and application based, and oriented toward customer experience. In the world of "space," the components of content, packaging, and infrastructure have morphed (e.g., converged) and split (e.g., diverged). Content has mushroomed and is no longer strictly proprietary. The packaging has transformed into a consistent digital customer experience on many different devices. Infrastructure has morphed into a powerful combination of internal and external digital platforms—some controlled by media content producers and some not.

The concept of a digital business model draws on previous research on business models, much of which focused on eBusiness (for example, Dubosson-Torbay et al. 2002; Mahadevan 2000; Gordijn et al. 2005; Gordijn and Akkermans 2001; Hedman and Kalling 2002; Menasce 2000; Swatman et al. 2006; Gordijn 2004; Osterwalder and Pigneur 2002; Shin and Park 2009; Chen and Ching 2002; Pigneur 2000; Currie 2004a, b; Gordijn et al. 2000; Faber et al. 2003); Damanpour and Damanpour 2001; Argoneto and Renna 2010; Gordijn 2003; Jarvenpaa and Tiller 1999; Papakiriakopoulos et al. 2001; Lambert 2006a, b; Pateli and Giaglis 2005). eBusiness models can be regarded as a subset of business models (Vermolen 2010).

In a highly globalized and competitive market, media and ICT enterprise needs to strengthen its digital business model. However, digital business models can crash quickly, because switching costs in the digital world are often lower than in the physical world.

4.11   Main Components of a Digital Business Model

A digital business model has three components: content (What is consumed?), customer experience (How is it packaged?), and platform (How is it delivered?) These three components work together to create a compelling customer value proposition. The digital content includes digital products (e.g., includes software, movies, e-books) as well as information about price and use details, etc.

The customer experience embodies what it is like to be a digital customer of the organization. The platform consists of a coherent set of digitized business process, data, and infrastructure. The platform has internal and external components and may both deliver digital content to the customer and manage physical product delivery to the customer. Amazon's internal platforms include customer data and all the business processes that don't touch the customer, such as customer analytics, human resources, finance, and merchandising. External platforms include the phones, tablets, or computers that consumers use to research and purchase the products, along with telecommunications networks and Amazon's partnerships with delivery companies like UPS that deliver physical products and generate text messages on delivery; all of these external platforms neatly integrate with Amazon's internal platforms. To achieve economies of scale with digital business models requires the development and reuse of digitized platforms across the enterprise (Weill and Ross 2009). Without such shared platforms, the IT units in companies implement a new solution in response to every business need, creating a spaghetti-like arrangement of systems that do meet specific customer needs but are expensive and fragile—and don't scale enterprise wide. Worse still, the customer experience suffers as the customer gets a fragmented product-based experience rather than a unified multiproduct experience.

4.12   Measuring Effectiveness of Digital Business Models' Content, Experience, and Platform

To better understand digital business models by industry, the author surveyed companies to assess the effectiveness of their content, experience, and platform. For each of the three aspects of a digital business model (content, experience, and platform), the author aggregated the answers to eight or nine survey questions to get a broad base for assessing effectiveness. The industry with the strongest effectiveness scores overall was IT software and services, while energy and mining and health care were among the poorest. Interestingly, the top financial performers in each industry also had better digital business model effectiveness. For example in the financial services industry, companies in the top third of financial performers had 29 %, 35 %, and 26 % better content, experience, and platform scores, respectively, than those in the bottom third.

4.13   eBusiness Model

The eBusiness is experiencing an unprecedented paradigm shift in terms of not being able to fully predict corporate sales, customer interaction, value added network, etc. Therefore, corporations have to put a tremendous emphasis on quick response instead of traditional planning. The eBusiness model as opposed to the old industrial is marked by fundamental not incremental change. Thus, it is impossible to plan eBusiness model for the long term; instead, they must shift to a more flexible, predefined, and anticipative model of planning (Malhotra 2000).

4.14   The Research Dynamics of Transformational BMs

The majority of research into dynamic BMs has been concerned with eBusiness and eCommerce, and there have been some attempts to develop convenient classification schemas. For example, definitions, components, and classifications into eBusiness models have been suggested (Alt and Zimmermann 2001; Afuah and Tucci 2003). Researchers have also looked at the BM concept in the context of different domains. Accordingly, Linder and Cantrell (2000) and Magretta (2002) have applied the BM concept in the domains of business management and strategy (Bouwman et al. 2008; Al-Debei and Fitzgerald 2010), software, the telecom sector including mobile technology along with its services industry (Rajala and Westerlund 2007), and eGoverment (Janssen et al. 2008).

Weill and Woerner (2013) define three converging trends in raising the stakes for the effectiveness of the enterprise's digital business model. "The first is the continued march toward the digitization of ever-increasing aspects of business—incorporating more of your customers' experience, executing more of your business processes and working together with partners in your value chain. The second trend is the increasing number of "digital natives"—young current and future customers and employees—who expect a brilliant digital experience in all of their interactions with companies. The third trend is the dawning of the age of the customer voice, in which customers have a much stronger impact on enterprises via ratings of their services (such as the customer rating stars on Amazon and customer experience surveys) through Twitter and other social media comments."

In addition, Weill and Vitale (2001) define eight finite eBusiness models (direct customer, full-service provider, intermediary, whole of enterprise, shared infrastructure, virtual community, value net integrator, and content provider) based on a systematic and practical analysis of several case studies.

As business models are moving towards maturity, corporate and academic interests shift to the investigation of opportunities for more effective and efficient market exploitation of innovative and specifically topical business models. However, there is an alarming lack of empirical strategic models in the literature to structure, categorize, and systematically codify knowledge in the area. This chapter draws on an extensive review of the literature to propose the incremental/gradual evolution of business models from static to dynamic/networked/modular architecture framework.

The literature on business models recognizes its applicative and market importance and influence on business environment dynamics and corporate strategy. Thus, the difference between success and failure of transformative activities boils down to the firm's ability to change its business model effectively and in rhythm with the dynamics of the external business environment (Burgelman 1994; Siggelkow 2001). Moreover, there is a lack of studies that would focus on the competition preceding radical business model changes.

While many researchers have concentrated on conceptualizing various generic components of the business model concept (Morris et al. 2005; Siggelkow 2001; Amit and Zott 2001), managers' conceptualizations of business models and their links to paradigmatic business model evolution have mostly escaped from researchers' attention so far. Academic research (for a review, see e.g. Tikkanen et al. 2005), in turn, has referred to business models particularly when dealing with the novel and systemic mechanisms and architectures through which business will be done vis-à-vis the greater business environment and industry networks (Zott and Amit 2008; Chesbrough and Rosenbloom 2002).

References

Achrol, R. S., & Kotler, P. (1999). Marketing in the network economy. *The Journal of Marketing, 63*, 146–163.

Afuah, A., & Tucci, C. L. (2001). *Internet business models and strategies: Text and cases* (4th ed.). New York: Irwin/McGraw-Hill.

Afuah, A., & Tucci, C. (2003). *Internet business models and strategies* (2nd ed.). New York: McGraw-Hill.

Al-Debei, M. M., & Fitzgerald, G. (2010). The design and engineering of mobile data services: Developing an ontology based on business model thinking. In J. Pries-Heje, J. Venable & J. De Gross (Eds.), *Human benefits through the diffusion of information systems design science research*. IFIP International Federation for Information Processing (IFIP 8.2+8.6). Boston: Springer.

Alt, R., & Zimmermann, H. (2001). Introduction to special section—business models. *Electronic Markets, 11*(1), 3–9.

Amit, R., & Zott, C. (2001). Value creation in e-business. *Strategic Management Journal, 22*(6–7), 493–520.

Anderson, J. C., Håkansson, H., & Johanson, J. (1994). Dyadic business relationships within a business network context. *The Journal of Marketing, 58*(4), 1–15.

Applegate, L. M. (2001). *Emerging E-business models: Lessons from the field.* Boston: Harvard Business School.

Applegate, L. M., Austin, R. D., & McFarlan, F. W. (2003). *Corporate information strategy and management* (6th ed.). New York: McGraw Hill.

Argoneto, P., & Renna, P. (2010). Production planning, negotiation and coalition integration: A new tool for an innovative e-business model. *Robotics and Computer-Integrated Manufacturing, 26*(1), 1–12.

Barney, J. (1991). Firm resources and sustained competitive advantage. *Journal of Management, 17*(1), 99–120.

Bartlett, C. A., & Ghoshal, S. (1995). Changing the role of top management: Beyond systems to people. *Long Range Planning, 28*(4), 126.

Bouwman, H., De Vos, H., & Haaker, T. (2008). *Mobile service innovation and business models.* Berlin: Springer.

Burgelman, R. A. (1994). Fading memories: A process theory of strategic business exit in dynamic environments. *Administrative Science Quarterly, 39,* 24–56.

Carr, D. (2010). Government funding cannot save journalism. *The Nation,* 19 April, www. thenation.com/doc/20100419/carr_video.

Chen, J. S., & Ching, R. K. (2002). A proposed framework for transitioning to an e-business model. *Quarterly Journal of Electronic Commerce, 3*(4), 375–389.

Chesbrough, H., & Rosenbloom, R. S. (2002). The role of the business model in capturing value from innovation: Evidence from Xerox Corporation's technology spin-off companies. *Industrial and Corporate Change, 11*(3), 529–555.

Currie, W. L. (2004a). Value creation from the application service provider e-business model: The experience of four firms. *Journal of Enterprise Information Management, 17*(2), 117–130.

Currie, W. (2004b). *Value creation from E-business models.* Oxford: Butterworth-Heinemann.

Dahan, N. M., Doh, J. P., Oetzel, J., & Yaziji, M. (2010). Corporate-NGO collaboration: Co-creating new business models for developing markets. *Long Range Planning, 43*(2), 326–342.

Damanpour, F., & Damanpour, J. A. (2001). E-business e-commerce evolution: Perspective and strategy. *Managerial Finance, 27*(7), 16–33.

Demil, B., & Lecocq, X. (2010). Business model evolution: In search of dynamic consistency. *Long Range Planning, 43,* 227–246.

Deuze, M. (2011). *Managing media work.* Thousand Oaks, CA: Sage.

Dobbs, R., Ramaswamy, S., Stephenson, E., & Viguerie, S. P. (2014). Management intuition for the next 50 years. *McKinsey Quarterly,* September.

Doganova, L., & Eyquem-Renault, M. (2009). What do business models do? Innovation devices in technology entrepreneurship. *Research Policy, 38,* 1559–1570.

Dubosson-Torbay, M., Osterwalder, A., & Pigneur, Y. (2002). E-business model design, classification, and measurements. *Thunderbird International Business Review, 44*(1), 5–23.

Faber, E., Ballon, P., Bouwman, H., Haaker, T., Rietkerk, O., & Steen, M. (2003). Designing business models for mobile ICT services. In *Workshop on concepts, metrics & visualization, at the 16th Bled electronic commerce conference eTransformation, Bled, Slovenia.*

George, K., Ramaswamy, S., & Rassey, L. (2014). Next-shoring: A CEO's guide. *McKinsey Quarterly.*

Gordijn, J. (2003). Why visualization of e-business models matters. In *16th eCommerce conference eTransformation panel business models & the mobile industry: Concepts, metrics, visualization and cases* (pp. 878–883).

Gordijn, J. (2004). E-business model ontologies. In W. Curry (Ed.), *e-Business modelling using the e3value ontology* (pp. 98–128).

Gordijn, J., & Akkermans, J. M. (2001). Designing and evaluating eBusiness models. *IEEE Intelligent Systems, 16*(4), 11–17.

Gordijn, J., Akkermans H., & Vliet H. V. (2000). What's in an electronic business model? In *12th International conference on knowledge engineering and knowledge management, Juan-les-Pins, France.*

Gordijn, J., Osterwalder, A., & Pigneur, Y. (2005). Comparing two business model ontologies for designing e-business models and value constellations. In *BLED 2005 Proceedings, 15.*

Guerrero, E., Diego, P., & Pardo, A. (2013). Distributing audiovisual contents in the new digital scenario: Multiplatform strategies of the main Spanish TV networks. In M. Friedrichsen & W. Mühl-Benninghaus (Eds.), *Handbook of social media management: Value chain and business models in changing media markets.* Berlin: Springer.

Hambrick, D. C., & Fredrickson, J. W. (2001). Are you sure you have a strategy? *The Academy of Management Executive, 15*(4), 48–59.

Hedman, J., & Kalling, T. (2002). *IT and business models: Concepts and theories.* Malmö: Liber Ekonomi.

Hedman, J., & Kalling, T. (2003). The business model concept: Theoretical underpinnings and empirical illustrations. *European Journal of Information Systems, 12*(1), 49–59.

Huarng, K. H., & Yu, T. H. K. (2011). Entrepreneurship, process innovation and value creation by a non-profit SME. *Management Decision, 49*(2), 284–296.

Itami, H., & Nishino, K. (2010). Killing two birds with one stone: Profit for now and learning for the future. *Long Range Planning, 43,* 364–369.

Janssen, M., Kuk, G., & Wagenaar, R. W. (2008). A survey of web-based business models for e-government in the Netherlands. *Government Information Quarterly, 25*(2), 202–220.

Jarvenpaa, S. L., & Tiller, E. H. (1999). Integrating market, technology, and policy opportunities in e-business strategy. *The Journal of Strategic Information Systems, 8*(3), 235–249.

Kallio, J., Tinnilä, M., & Tseng, A. (2006). An international comparison of operator-driven business models. *Business Process Management Journal, 12*(3), 281–298.

Küng, L. (2011). Managing strategy and maximizing innovation in media organisations. Managing media work. In M. Deuze (Ed.), *Managing media work* (pp. 249–262). Thousand Oaks, CA: Sage.

Lambert, S. (2006a). A business model research schema. In *18th Bled eConference, 06–08 June, Bled, Slovenia.*

Lambert, S. (2006b). Do we need a 'real' taxonomy of E-business models? School of Commerce research paper series: 06-6, School of Commerce, Flinders University.

Linder, J., & Cantrell, S. (2000) *Changing business models: Surveying the landscape* (Working Paper). Accenture Institute for Strategic Change, pp. 1–15.

MacInnes, I. (2005). Dynamic business model framework for emerging technologies. *International Journal of Service Technology and Management, 6*(1), 3–19.

Macnamara, J. (2010). Remodelling media: The urgent search for new media business models. *Media International Australia, 137,* 20–35.

Magretta, J. (2002). Why business models matter. *Harvard Business Review, 80*(5), 86–92.

Mahadevan, B. (2000). Business models for internet-based e-commerce: An anatomy. *California Management Review, 42*(4), 55–69.

Malhotra, Y. (2000). Knowledge management for e-business performance: Advancing information strategy to "internet time". *Information Strategy: The Executive's Journal, 16*(4), 5–16.

Menasce, D. (2000). Scaling for e-business. In *Proceedings of the 8th international symposium on modeling, analysis and simulation of computer and telecommunication systems* (pp. 511–513). IEEE.

Meyer, M. H., & Crane, F. G. (2010). *Entrepreneurship: An innovator's guide to startups and corporate ventures.* Thousand Oaks, CA: Sage.

Morris, M., Schindehutte, M., & Allen, J. (2005). The entrepreneur's business model: Toward a unified perspective. *Journal of Business Research, 58*(6), 726–735.

Nelson, R. R., & Winter, S. G. (1982). The Schumpeterian tradeoff revisited. *The American Economic Review, 72*, 114–132.

Norton, D., & Kaplan, R. (1992). The balanced scorecard: Measures that drive performance. *Harvard Business Review, 70*(1), 52–58.

Osterwalder, A. (2004). *The business model ontology: A proposition in a design science approach.* Doctoral thesis, Présentée à l'Ecole des Hautes Etudes Commerciales de l'Université de Lausanne.

Osterwalder, A., & Pigneur, Y. (2002, June 17–19). An e-business model ontology for modeling e-business. In C. Loebbecke, R. T. Wigard, J. Gricar, A. Pucihar & G. Lenart (Eds.), *Proceedings of the 15th Bled electronic commerce conference—eReality: Constructing the eEconomy, Bled, Slovenia* (pp. 75–91).

Palo, T., & Tähtinen, J. (2011). A network perspective on business models for emerging technology-based services. *Journal of Business & Industrial Marketing, 26*(5), 377–388.

Papakiriakopoulos, D., Poylumenakou, A. K., & Doukidis, G. J. (2001). Building e-business models: An analytical framework and development guidelines. In *Proceedings of the 14th Bled electronic commerce conference* (Vol. 25, p. 26).

Pateli, A. G., & Giaglis, G. M. (2003). A framework for understanding and analyzing ebusiness models. In *Proceedings of 16th Bled eCommerce conference on eTransformation, Bled, Slovenia* (pp. 329–348).

Pateli, A. G., & Giaglis, G. M. (2004). A research framework for analyzing eBusiness models. *European Journal of Information Systems, 13*(4), 302–314.

Pateli, A. G., & Giaglis, G. M. (2005). Technology innovation-induced business model change: A contingency approach. *Journal of Organizational Change Management, 18*(2), 167–183.

Petrovic, O., Kittl, C., & Teksten, D. (2001). Developing business models for eBusiness. In *Proceedings of the international conference on electronic commerce, Vienna* (pp. 1–6), 31 October–4 November.

Pigneur, Y. (2000). *The e-business model handbook.* École des HEC–Université de Lausanne.

Porter, M. (1996). What is strategy? *Harvard Business Review, 74*(6), 61–78.

Porter, M. E. (2001). Strategy and the internet. *Harvard Business Review, 79*(3), 62–79.

Rajala, R., & Westerlund, M. (2005). Business models: A new perspective on knowledge-intensive services in the software industry. In *BLED 2005 proceedings, 10*.

Rajala, R., & Westerlund, M. (2007). Business models—a new perspective on firms' assets and capabilities: Observations from the Finnish software industry. *The International Journal of Entrepreneurship and Innovation, 8*(2), 115–126.

Shin, J., & Park, Y. (2009). On the creation and evaluation of e-business model variants: The case of auction. *Industrial Marketing Management, 38*(3), 324–337.

Siggelkow, N. (2001). Change in the presence of fit: The rise, the fall, and the renaissance of Liz Claiborne. *Academy of Management Journal, 44*(4), 838–857.

Stähler, P. (2002). Business models as an unit of analysis for strategizing. In *Proceedings of the 1st International workshop on business models, Lausanne, Suisse.*

Swatman, P. M., Krueger, C., & van der Beek, K. (2006). The changing digital content landscape: An evaluation of e-business model development in European online news and music. *Internet Research, 16*(1), 53–80.

Teece, D. (2010). Business model, business strategy, and innovation. *Long Range Planning, 43*(2–3), 172–194.

The new digital economy: How it will transform business: A white research paper produced in collaboration with AT&T, Cisco, Citi, PwC & SAP, Oxford Economics, June 2011.

Tikkanen, H., Lamberg, J. A., Parvinen, P., & Kallunki, J. P. (2005). Managerial cognition, action and the business model of the firm. *Management Decision, 43*, 789–809.

van Kranenburg, H., & Ziggers, G. W. (2013). How media companies should create value: Innovation centered business models and dynamic capabilities. In M. Friedrichsen & W. Mühl-Benninghaus (Eds.), *Handbook of social media management: Value chain and business models in changing media markets* (pp. 239–267). Berlin: Springer.

Vermolen, R. (2010). Reflecting on IS business model research: Current gaps and future directions. In *Proceedings of the 13th Twente student conference on IT, University of Twente, Enschede, Netherlands* (pp. 291–299).

Weill, P., & Ross, J. W. (2009). *IT savvy: What top executives must know to go from pain to gain.* Boston: Harvard Business School Press.

Weill, P., & Vitale, M. R. (2001). *Place to space: Migrating to eBusiness models.* Boston: Harvard Business School Press.

Weill, P., & Woerner, S. L. (2013). Optimizing your digital business model. *MIT Sloan Management Review, 54*(3), 71–78.

Zott, C., & Amit, R. (2008). The fit between product market strategy and business model: Implications for firm performance. *Strategic Management Journal, 29*(1), 1–26.

Zott, C., & Amit, R. (2010). Business model design: An activity system perspective. *Long Range Planning, 43*(2–3), 216–226.

Chapter 5
The Conceptual Foundation, Common Motivation, Major Benefits/Disadvantages, and Importance of FDI on Economic Growth and Development

5.1 The Conceptual Foundation of the FDI Flows

FDI is defined by as inflows of investment to acquire a lasting management interest (10 % or more of voting stock) in an enterprise operating in an economy other than that of the investor. In addition to mergers and acquisitions, FDI would also include greenfield investments, such as the setting up of new factories or subsidiaries by foreign investors or multinational corporations (MNCs) in a country different from that of the source of capital.

FDI flows come in at least four separate forms: (a) FDI in extractive industries, (b) FDI in infrastructure, (c) FDI in manufacturing, and (d) the under-researched field of FDI in Services. Foreign direct investment in media industry belongs to the category of FDI in the sector of Services. Each form of FDI flows presents such distinctive economic challenges and generates such diverse impacts for MNCs as well as for developing-country host authorities/economy, undermining the usefulness of any research that does not simultaneously aggregate and disaggregate the FDI flows.

5.2 The Most Common Motivation for FDI

It is well known that the growth of multinational enterprise (MNE) activity in the form of foreign direct investment (FDI) has grown at a faster rate than most other international transactions, particularly trade flows between countries. Correspondingly, these real-world trends have led to substantial recent interest by the international and empirical economics literature investigating the fundamental factors driving FDI trends and behavior.

Since Markusen (1984) and Helpman (1984), MNE general equilibrium theory has suggested two very distinct motivations for FDI: to access markets in the face of trade frictions (horizontal FDI) or to access low wages for part of the production process (vertical FDI). More recently, a number of papers have begun to sketch out more complicated patterns of FDI. For example, an important possibility is export platform FDI (Ekholm et al. 2003; Bergstrand and Egger 2004) where an MNE places FDI into a host country to serve as a production platform for exports to a group of (neighboring) host countries. Another important example is a more complicated vertical interaction (or fragmentation) result where affiliates of an MNE in a variety of hosts are shipping intermediate goods between them for further processing before shipping a (more) finished product back to the parent (see e.g., Baltagi et al. 2004).

Perhaps the most commonly cited motivation for FDI is as a substitute for exports to a host country. As laid out by the model of Buckley and Casson (1981), one can think of exports as involving lower fixed costs but higher variable costs of transportation and trade barriers. Servicing the same market with affiliate sales from FDI allows one to substantially lower these variable costs, but likely involves higher fixed costs than exports. This suggests a natural progression from exports to FDI once the foreign market's demand for the MNE's products reaches a large enough scale (size).

According to the capital-market approach, the important reason for FDI inflows is motivated by interest rate differentials and MNCs' capital tendency to flow the region where capital gets highest return (Jadhav 2012). According to product life cycle theory, firms set up production facilities abroad for products that had already been standardized and matured in the home markets (Vernon 1966). The OLI paradigm (Dunning 1980, 1993) provides an ownership, location, and internalization advantage-based framework to analyze why, where, and how MNCs would invest abroad. According to Dunning, this investment could be natural resource seeking, market seeking, efficiency seeking, and strategic asset seeking. According to new theories of FDI which used general equilibrium model, increasing returns to scale, imperfect competition, and MNCs' firm-specific advantages are primarily based on knowledge capital consisting of intangible assets such as patents, human capital, trademarks, and brand name (Markusen 1995).

5.3 Drawbacks and Disadvantages of the FDI

A number of recent empirical studies, which find mixed evidence of technology transfer from FDI, have prompted many observers to conclude that enthusiasm for FDI is not warranted (Blalock and Gertler 2002). Rodrik (1999), in a summary of the evidence, comments, "today's policy literature is filled with extravagant claims about positive spillovers from FDI, [but] the hard evidence is sobering." More specifically, multinationals will attempt to minimize technology leakage to competitors by limiting the mechanisms, such as labor mobility and imitation, through which spillover occurs (Blalock and Gertler 2002). Further, multinationals with non-protectable technology will likely choose not to enter overseas markets at all (Blalock and Gertler 2002). Accordingly, FDI can be a mixed blessing.

In small economies, large foreign companies can—and often do—abuse their dominant market positions and, especially in developing countries, attempt to monopolize and take over the highly profitable sectors as well as influence the domestic political process. Large investors are sometimes able to coax concessions from country governments in return for locating investment there and aggressively use transfer pricing to minimize their tax obligations. FDI can also give rise to potentially volatile balance of payment flows (Demekas et al. 2005). The long-run balance of payment position of the host economy may be potentially jeopardized when the investor manages to recover its initial outlay. Once the initial investment starts to turn profitable, it is inevitable that capital returns from the host country to where it originated from, that is, the home country. The investors can sell off unprofitable portions of the company to local, less sophisticated investors. In addition, companies often engage in round-tripping—using subsidiaries to borrow in local capital markets and then lending back to the parent company. This adds to high private sector leverage and is likely to flow out rapidly in the event of a financial crisis, acting more like portfolio investment than FDI as it is commonly understood (Loungani and Razin 2001). As it focuses its resources elsewhere other than the investor's home country, foreign direct investment can sometimes hinder domestic investment. Because political issues in other countries can instantly change, foreign direct investment is very risky. Correspondingly, political changes can also lead to expropriation, which is a scenario where the government will have control over investors' property and assets.

5.4 The Aggregate Conditions, Variables, Effects, and Impacts of the Macroeconomic Importance and Benefits of FDI on Economic Growth and Development

FDI is commonly seen as a main indicator and force of globalization, with FDI growing faster than trade in goods and services, as well as faster than world output through the last decade. Technological advance and liberalization process have increased the competition between firms, and FDI is perhaps the most efficient way of increasing market share and obtaining market power. From a macroeconomic perspective, FDI is a crucial medium through which national economies become interconnected on a global basis.

There are also more substantial macroeconomic arguments in favor of public support to FDI than globalization and the wish to increase local employment and growth rates in cyclical downturns. The strongest ones are based on the prospect for knowledge spillovers. Since the technology and knowledge employed by foreign firms are to some extent public goods, foreign investment can result in benefits for their host countries even if the MNCs carry out their foreign operations in wholly owned affiliates (Blomström et al. 2003). These benefits take the form of various types of externalities or spillovers. For instance, local firms may be able to improve their productivity as a result of forward or backward linkages with MNC affiliates; they may imitate MNC technologies or hire workers trained by MNCs. The increase in competition that occurs as a result of foreign entry may also be considered a benefit, in particular if it forces local firms to introduce new technology and work harder (Blomström et al. 2003).

Foreign direct investment (FDI) can potentially benefit domestic firms. The benefits arise from foreign firms demonstrating new technologies, providing technological assistance to their local suppliers and customers, and training workers who may subsequently move to local firms. Local firms can also learn by watching. Moreover, case studies showed that MNCs' FDI may (a) contribute to efficiency by breaking supply bottlenecks (but that the effect may become less important as the technology of the host country advances); (b) introduce new know-how by demonstrating new technologies and training workers who later take employment in local firms; (c) either break down monopolies and stimulate competition and efficiency or create a more monopolistic industry structure, depending on the strength and responses of the local firms; (d) transfer techniques for inventory and quality control and standardization to their local suppliers and distribution channels; (e) force local firms to increase their managerial efforts, or to adopt some of the marketing techniques used by MNCs, either on the local market or internationally (Blomström et al. 2003); (f) determine the potentially volatile balance of payment flows (Popescu 2014); (g) establish producer-driven networks significantly (Galgóczi 2009); (h) advance the performance of production networks (i.e., Real GDP Growth, Real Domestic Demand Growth, Real Exports Growth, and Real Private Consumption Growth) (Fung et al. 2009); (i) entail a transfer of knowledge from the MNC to its subsidiary or foreign affiliate, affecting the behavior of local companies as well as other elements of the business environment; (j) assist in boosting capital stock in the host country, advancing productivity and the pace of economic growth; (k) allow host economies to increase capital formation and to augment the quality of the capital stock, shifting to up-to-date technology and innovation; and (l) assist in boosting capital stock in the host country, advancing productivity and the pace of economic growth.

There are various empirical studies showing a positive relationship between FDI and Economic Growth and trying to create favorable conditions to attract more FDI inflow into their economies (Adhikary 2011; Thangamani et al. 2011; Azam 2010; Schneider and Frey 1985; Ancharaz 2000; Hassan 2000; Chakrabarti 2001; Yusop and Choong 2002; Chowdury and Mavrotas 2005). More specifically, the empirical results in the study of Hansen and Rand (2006) indicate that a one percentage point increase in the mean of the FDI ratio, on average, causes a 2.25 % increase in the GDP level. Borensztein et al. (1998) find that FDI raises growth, but only in countries where the labor force has achieved a certain level of education. Moreover, FDI, as sound long-term capital inflow, reinforces insufficient domestic funds to finance both ownership alteration and capital composition as well as introduces technology, managerial know-how, and skills required for restructuring companies (Popescu 2014).

Dutta and Roy (2008) confirm that FDI is instrumental in economic growth by means of stimulating technological progress. Technological progress leads to knowledge spillovers through the channels of imitation, competition, linkages, and/or training (Lensink and Morrissey 2001; Barry et al. 2004; Hermes and Lensink 2003). In addition, the impacts of FDI on trade, i.e., exports and imports, are ambiguous (Dutta and Roy 2008). A horizontal FDI, for instance, theoretically induces a decrease in the host country's imports and, ceteris paribus, an improvement of its trade balance. This prediction may not hold true if the inputs used by the foreign-owned firm are imported from abroad. Furthermore, an FDI consisting of selling in the host country goods manufactured abroad, that is, a vertical integration forward, will have the effect of increasing the home country's imports. MNCs are also capable of setting up their own corporate governance systems in the sense of imposing new company policies, internal reporting systems, and rules about information disclosures and employment of foreign managers (Dutta and Roy 2008). This may boost corporate efficiency.

FDI has increasingly been viewed by policymakers in developing and emerging market economies (EMEs) as a tool to finance development, increase productivity, and import new technologies (Arbatli 2011). In addition, the relative stability of FDI inflows constitutes a buffer against sharp reversals in portfolio inflows during periods of crisis, such as the one experienced in 2009 (Arbatli 2011).

Among other capital flows, foreign direct investment (FDI) is often considered a superior alternative due to the attributed benefits it brings to the host economy: permanence in the long run; enhanced competition; increased employment; improved access for exports abroad, notably in the source country; knowledge productivity, technology—R & D transfer and spillover to domestic firms and the labor force; and other positive externalities (Sánchez-Martín et al. 2015). Moreover, since FDI flows are non-debt-creating, they are a preferred method of financing external current account deficits, especially in developing countries, where these deficits can be large and sustained. Lipsey (2001) shows that FDI flows are much more stable than other capital flows during severe exchange rate crises. In turn, other capital flows, such as portfolio debt flows, including portfolio bond flows and commercial bank loans, are short term, volatile, and pro-cyclical, accentuating macroeconomic volatility in some developing countries.

Due to its long-term nature, FDI is considered to be a preferred source of international capital, economic stability, and development. Correspondingly, governments around the globe try to attract it for multiple reasons, including compensating current account deficits, signaling macroeconomic stability, generating employment, and allowing for externalities and technological upgrading. Governments often use special economic zones, tax breaks, and improvements in the business environment in order to appeal to the interest of the foreign investor.

Recent evidence suggests that developing economies with a higher exposure to portfolio investments and foreign loans suffered more severe liquidity crunches than those more dependent on FDI (Tong and Wei 2011). FDI not only raises the level of investment or capital stock but increases employment by creating new production capacity and jobs, transfers intangible assets such as technology and managerial skills to the host country, and provides a source of new technologies, processes, products, organizational technologies and management skills, and Backward and Forward linkages with the rest of the economy (Ho and Rashid 2011).

Horizontal FDI tends to be established when trade costs are moderate to high, the origin and host countries are similar in size as well as relative factor endowments, and total demand is significant (large market). Conversely, vertical multinationals dominate production when the countries differ significantly in relative factor endowment but are somewhat similar in size. Horizontal FDI (HFDI) is market-seeking investment, focused mainly on the domestic market in the host economy, whereas vertical FDI (VFDI) is cost-minimizing investment (market magnitude, trade limitations, and transport expenditures can have various impacts on HFDI and VFDI) (Popescu 2014). Shatz and Venables (2000) argue that FDI in developed economies is mainly horizontal, whereas in developing economies it tends to be vertical. Venables (2003) considers that horizontal FDI is likely to be a substitute for trade, as firms use FDI to supply the market instead of imports and wind up competing with local firms. By contrast, vertical FDI is a complement to trade and may even create trade flows. It is export oriented, so it does not usually compete with local companies. There is a rise at the international level in the proportion of vertical FDI, attracted by low production expenditures (Popescu 2014). These different characteristics are relevant since they imply that economic integration will have a varied impact depending on the type and motivations of FDI. Today, it is generally accepted that FDI and international trade are complements rather than substitutes.

The increase in productivity from FDI could go beyond the subsidiaries of MNCs and spill over onto other firms in the host economy. But it would be difficult for technological transfers to take place intra-industry (horizontal) since local firms may lack absorptive capacity, MNCs might be export oriented and local firms domestically oriented, and MNCs would try to minimize technology leakages to competitors (Blalock and Gertler 2008). Moreover, as some firms have stated in surveys, the arrival of MNCs is often accompanied by increased competition and a loss of market share by the local firms.

From a macroeconomic perspective FDI is often regarded as generator of employment, high productivity, competiveness, and technology spillovers. Especially for the least developed countries, FDI means higher exports and access to international markets and international currencies, being an important source of financing, substituting bank loans. There is some evidence to support the idea that FDI promotes the competitiveness of local firms. Caves (1996) considers that the efforts made by various countries in attracting foreign direct investments are due to the potential positive effects that this would have on economy. FDI would increase productivity, technology transfer, managerial skills, know-how, international production networks, reducing unemployment, and access to external markets. The result confirms that FDI enhances productivity growth; however, the impact is much larger when R-D-intensive developed countries invest in the emerging economies than the other way round. Country-specific bilateral elasticities also support this outcome (Neuhaus 2006). Borensztein et al. (1998) supports these ideas, considering FDI as ways of achieving technology spillovers, with greater contribution to the economic growth than would have national investments. The importance of technology transfer is highlighted also by Findlay who believes that FDI leads to a spillover of advanced technologies to local firms (Findlay 1978). The potential positive or negative effects on the economy may also depend on the nature of the sector in which investment takes place, according to Hirschman (1958) who stated the positive effects of agriculture and mining are limited. Hymer (1976) recognized that FDI is a firm-level strategy decision rather than a capital-market financial decision. FDI has particularly positive effect in specific industrial sectors such as ICT, Semiconductor industry, and manufacturing.

The motivation for, or type of, FDI is not per se a channel for FDI externalities. But it is expected to influence the intensity of the channels for spillovers. Altenburg (2000) argues that domestic-market-oriented foreign subsidiaries (horizontal FDI) are more likely to purchase inputs locally than export oriented (vertical FDI), thus presenting more backward linkages. In general, market-seeking (horizontal) FDI seems to be more likely to provide higher spillover potential as it tends to present higher linkages with the rest of the economy (Farole and Winkler 2012).

On the other hand, the export-oriented (vertical) FDI tends to rely less on domestic suppliers than market-seeking (horizontal) FDI. Thus, in general, export-oriented firms tend to depend less on domestic suppliers. In addition, affiliates with a lower degree of foreign ownership (joint ventures) normally use a higher percentage of inputs of domestic origin. This may be due to domestic shareholders of foreign affiliates being more knowledgeable about local markets and reliable suppliers in upstream industries than, say, the foreign manager of a wholly owned branch of a MNC working in the host country for the first time.

There is strong empirical evidence that FDI flows are less volatile than other capital flows (e.g., IMF—World Economic Outlook 2007) and a widespread impression that FDI is somehow better for growth and development than other capital flows. While empirical support for FDI being better for growth is mixed, there is evidence that given certain country prerequisites, FDI does in fact lead to better growth outcomes (e.g., Borensztein et al. 1995). These qualities of FDI have led to substantial interest among policymakers on the factors that might attract FDI flows.

There is a long-standing impression among policymakers that foreign direct investment is more conducive to long-run growth and development than other forms of capital inflows. Arguments for this hypothesis have been diverse, but most often based on the idea that FDI brings with it foreign technology and management skills, which can then be adapted by the host country in other contexts.

However, Navaretti and Venables (2004) find the mixed evidence about the impact of the relationship between FDI and growth, investment, and productivity. In general, economic growth is found to be positively associated with FDI but only under certain conditions: for example, when countries are sufficiently rich (Blomström et al. 1994), have a minimum threshold stock of human capital (Borensztein et al. 1998), or are financially developed. These positive findings are not, however, corroborated in Carkovic and Levine (2005) who take into account the problem of reverse causality and do not find evidence in support of a relationship between FDI and growth. The micro-literature instead investigates the effects of FDI on firms and industries (Aitken and Harrison 1999) identifying productivity spillovers to domestic both horizontal firms (Haskell et al. 2007) and vertical firms, (Javorcik 2004). Görg and Greenaway (2004) who survey some 40 studies conclude that the evidence for positive productivity spillovers is weak. The meta-analyses of Meyer and Sinani (2009) indicate that the scale and direction of the FDI impact on the host economy are conditional on factors such as the level of development or minimum levels of human capital, financial market development, and market linkages (Bruno and Campos 2013). The empirical evidence to date on spillovers from FDI into transition economies is also mixed. Meyer and Sinani (2009) identify five studies covering the transition region. In three studies [Liu (2002) on China, Yudaeva et al. (2003) on Russia, and Sinani and Meyer (2004) on Estonia], positive spillovers are identified, but in two others the effects are found to be negative [Konings (2001) on Bulgaria and Romania and Djankov and Hoekman (2000) on Czech Republic]. Even so, it is widely argued that FDI played an extremely important role throughout most of the transition region, as a supplement to domestic savings and frequently as a major driver of enterprise restructuring during privatizations (Estrin et al. 2009).

In sum, four main points emerge from this section analysis: (1) FDI is preferred among other capital flows because it is expected to result in greater macroeconomic stability, it helps finance current account gaps, and it is long term in nature; (2) the motivations for FDI vary (horizontal, vertical, or asset seeking), implying that not all types of subsidiaries may be equally beneficial for the host economy or create the same potential for externalities; (3) both the theoretical and empirical literature highlight a series of channels of spillover effects through which FDI could influence productivity and, indirectly, economic growth; and (4) the empirical evidence to date on spillovers from FDI into transition economies is mixed.

References

Adhikary, B. K. (2011). FDI, trade openness, capital formation, and economic growth in Bangladesh: A linkage analysis. *International Journal of Business and Management, 6*(1), 16–28.

Aitken, B. J., & Harrison, A. E. (1999). Do domestic firms benefit from direct foreign investment? Evidence from Venezuela. *American Economic Review, 89*(3), 605–618.

Altenburg, T. (2000). *Linkages and spillovers between transnational corporations and small and medium-sized enterprises in developing countries* (DIE Working Papers, issue 5). Bonn: German Development Institute (DIE).

Ancharaz, V. D. (2000). *Trade liberalization and foreign direct investment in sub-Saharan Africa: A comparative perspective.* PhD dissertation, Brandeis University, USA.

Arbatli, E. C. (2011). *Economic policies and FDI inflows to emerging market economies* (IMF Working Papers). pp. 1–25.

Azam, M. (2010). An empirical analysis of the impacts of exports and foreign direct investment on economic growth in South Asia. *Interdisciplinary Journal of Contemporary Research in Business, 2*(7), 249.

Baltagi, B. H., Egger, P., & Pfaffermayr, M. (2004). Estimating models of complex FDI: Are there third-country effects? Mimeo.

Barry, F., Görg, H., & Strobl, E. (2004). Foreign direct investment, agglomerations, and demonstration effects: An empirical investigation. *Review of World Economics, 127*(3), 583–600.

Bergstrand, J. H., & Egger, P. (2004). A theoretical and empirical model of international trade and foreign direct investment with outsourcing: Part I, developed countries. Mimeo.

Blalock, G., & Gertler, P. (2002). *Technology diffusion from foreign direct investment through supply chain* (Working paper). Haas School of Business, UC Berkeley.

Blalock, G., & Gertler, P. (2008). Welfare gains from foreign direct investment through technology transfer to local suppliers. *Journal of International Economics, 74*(2), 402–421.

Blomström, M., Kokko, A., & Mucchielli, J. L. (2003). *The economics of foreign direct investment incentives* (pp. 37–60). Berlin: Springer.

Blomström, M., Lipsey, R. E., & Zejan, M. (1994). What explains developing country growth? National Bureau of Economic Research, no. w4132.

Borensztein, E., De Gregorio, J., & Lee, J. W. (1995). *How does foreign direct investment affect economic growth?* (NBER Working Paper No. 5057) Cambridge, MA: National Bureau of Economic Research.

Borensztein, E., De Gregorio, J., & Lee, J. W. (1998). How does foreign direct investment affect economic growth? *Journal of International Economics, 45*(1), 115–135.

Bruno, R. L., & Campos, N. (2013). *Reexamining the conditional effect of foreign direct investment* (IZA Discussion Paper no. 7458).

Buckley, P. J., & Casson, M. (1981). The optimal timing of foreign direct investment. *Economic Journal, 91*(361), 75–87.

Carkovic, M., & Levine, R. (2005). Does foreign direct investment accelerate economic growth? In T. H. Moran, E. M. Graham, & M. Blomstrom (Eds.), *Does foreign direct investment promote development?* Washington, DC: Center for Global Development.

Caves, R. E. (1996). *Multinational enterprise and economic analysis* (2nd ed.). Cambridge: Cambridge University Press.

Chakrabarti, A. (2001). The determinants of foreign direct investment: Sensitivity analysis of cross-country regressions. *Kyklos, 54,* 89–114.

Chowdury, A., & Mavrotas, G. (2005). *FDI and growth: A causal relationship* (Research Paper No. 2005/25). UNU-WIDER.

Demekas, D. G., Horváth, B., Ribakova, E., & Wu, Y. (2005). *Foreign direct investment in Southeastern Europe: How (and how much) can policies help?* (IMF Working Paper, WP/05/110).

Djankov, S., & Hoekman, B. (2000). Foreign investment and productivity growth in Czech enterprises. *World Bank Economic Review, 14*(1), 49–64.

Dunning, J. H. (1980). Toward an eclectic theory of international production: Some empirical tests. *Journal of International Business Studies, 11*(1), 9–31.

Dunning, J. H. (1993). *Multinational enterprises and the global economy.* Reading, MA: Addison-Wesley.

Dutta, N., & Roy, S. (2008). *The role of foreign direct investment on press freedom* (MPRA Paper No. 10185).

Ekholm, K., Forslid, R., & Markusen, J. R. (2003). *Export-platform foreign direct investment* (NBER Working Paper No. 9517).

Estrin, S., Hanousek, J., Kocenda, E., & Svejnar, J. (2009). The effects of privatization and ownership in transition economies. *Journal of Economic Literature, 47*(3), 699–728.

Farole, T., & Winkler, D. E. (2012). *Foreign firm characteristics, absorptive capacity and the institutional framework: The role of mediating factors for FDI spillovers in low- and middle-income countries* (Policy Research Working Paper Series 6265). World Bank.

Findlay, R. (1978). Relative backwardness, direct foreign investment and transfer of technology. *Quarterly Journal of Economics, 92*, 1–16.

Fung, K. C., Korhonen, I., Li, K., & Ng, F. (2009). China and Central and Eastern European countries: Regional networks, global supply chain or international competitors? *Journal of Economic Integration, 24*, 476–504.

Galgóczi, B. (2009). Boom and bust in Central and Eastern Europe: Lessons on the sustainability of an externally financed growth model. *Journal of Contemporary European Research, 5*, 614–625.

Görg, H., & Greenaway, D. (2004). Much ado about nothing? Do domestic firms really benefit from foreign direct investment? *The World Bank Research Observer, 19*(2), 171–197.

Hansen, H., & Rand, J. (2006). On the causal links between FDI and growth in developing countries. *The World Economy, 29*(1), 21–41.

Haskell, J., Pereira, S., & Slaughter, M. (2007). Does inward investment boost the productivity of domestic firms? *Review of Economics and Statistics, 89*(3), 482–496.

Hassan, M. (2000). *Trade balances, economic growth and linkages to multinational foreign direct investment*. PhD dissertation, Nova Southeastern University, USA.

Helpman, E. (1984). A simple theory of international trade with multinational corporations. *Journal of Political Economy, 92*(3), 451–471.

Hermes, N., & Lensink, R. (2003). Foreign direct investment, financial development and economic growth. *Journal of Development Studies, 40*(1), 142–163.

Hirschman, A. O. (1958). *The strategy of economic development* (Vol. 10). New Haven, CT: Yale University Press.

Ho, C. S., & Rashid, H. A. (2011). Macroeconomic and country specific determinants of FDI. *The Business Review, 18*(1), 219–226.

Hymer, S. H. (1976). *The international operations of national firms: A study of direct foreign investment* (Vol. 14, pp. 139–155). Cambridge, MA: MIT Press.

Jadhav, P. (2012). Determinants of foreign direct investment in BRICS economies: Analysis of economic, institutional and political factor. *Procedia-Social and Behavioral Sciences, 37*, 5–14.

Javorcik, B. S. (2004). Does foreign direct investment increase the productivity of domestic firms? In search of spillovers through backward linkages. *American Economic Review, 94*, 605–627.

Konings, J. (2001). The effects of foreign direct investment on domestic firms: Evidence from firm-level panel data in emerging economies. *The Economics of Transition, 9*(3), 619–633.

Lensink, R., & Morrissey, O. (2001). *FDI flows, volatility and growth* (CREDIT Research Paper 01/06). University of Nottingham.

Lipsey, R. E. (2001). *Foreign direct investors in three financial crises* (NBER Working Paper No. 8084).

Liu, Z. (2002). Foreign direct investment and technology spillover: Evidence from China. *Journal of Comparative Economics, 30*(3), 579–602.

Loungani, P., & Razin, A. (2001). How beneficial is foreign direct investment for developing countries? *Finance and Development, 38*(2), 6–9.

Markusen, J. R. (1984). Multinationals, multi-plant economies, and the gains from trade. *Journal of International Economics, 16*(3–4), 205–226.

Markusen, J. R. (1995). The boundaries of multinational enterprises and the theory of international trade. *The Journal of Economic Perspectives, 9*(2), 169–189.

Meyer, K., & Sinani, E. (2009). When and where does foreign direct investment generate positive spillovers? A meta-analysis. *Journal of International Business Studies, 40*, 1075–1094.

Navaretti, G. B., & Venables, A. J. (2004). *Multinational firms in the world economy*. Princeton, NJ: Princeton University Press.

Neuhaus, M. (2006). *The impact of FDI on economic growth: An analysis for the transition countries of Central and Eastern Europe*. Heidelberg: Springer.

Popescu, G. H. (2014). FDI and economic growth in Central and Eastern Europe. *Sustainability, 6*(11), 8149–8163.

Rodrik, D. (1999). The new global economy and developing countries: Making openness work, Policy essay no. 24. Overseas Development Council; Distributed by Johns Hopkins University Press, Washington, DC

Sánchez-Martín, M. E., De Piniés, J., & Antoine, K. (2015). *Measuring the determinants of backward linkages from FDI in developing economies: Is it a matter of size?* (World Bank Policy Research Working Paper, 7185).

Schneider, F., & Frey, B. (1985). Economic and political determinants of foreign direct investment. *World Development, 13*, 161–175.

Shatz, H. J., & Venables, A. (2000). *The geography of international investment* (Vol. 2338). Washington, DC: World Bank.

Sinani, E., & Meyer, K. E. (2004). Spillovers from technology transfer: The case of Estonia. *Journal of Comparative Economics, 32*(3), 445–466.

Thangamani, B., Xu, C., & Zhong, C. (2011). Determinants and growth effect of FDI in South Asian economies: Evidence from a panel data analysis. *International Business Research, 4*(1), 43.

Tong, H., & Wei, S. J. (2011). The composition matters: Capital inflows and liquidity crunch during a global economic crisis, review of financial studies. *Oxford University Press for Society for Financial Studies, 24*(6), 2023–2052.

Venables, A. J. (2003). Winners and losers from regional integration agreements. *The Economic Journal, 113*(490), 747–761.

Vernon, R. (1966). International investment and international trade in the product cycle. *Quarterly Journal of Economics, 80*, 190–207.

World Economic Outlook. (2007). International Monetary Fund—IMF, Washington, DC.

Yudaeva, K., Kozlov, K., Melentieva, N., & Ponomareva, N. (2003). Does foreign ownership matter? Russian experience. *The Economics of Transition, 11*(3), 383–410.

Yusop, Z., & Choong, C. K. (2002, October 2–4). Foreign direct investment determinants in the Malaysian manufacturing sector. In *Proceedings of Asia Pacific economics and business conference 2002* (pp. 356–364).

Chapter 6
An Evolutionary Conceptual and Multidisciplinary Frameworks, Principles, and Criteria for FDI Inflows Determinants

6.1 Introduction

The globalization has led to a reconfiguration of the ways in which MNEs pursue their resource-seeking, market-seeking, and efficiency-seeking objectives (Nunnenkamp 2002). The opening of markets to trade, FDI, and technology flows has offered MNEs a wider range of choices on how to serve international markets, gain access to immobile resources, and improve the efficiency of production systems (Dunning 1999). Reportedly, MNEs are increasingly pursuing complex integration strategies where they can combine their own mobile assets most efficiently with the immobile resources they need to produce goods and services for the markets they want to serve (Nunnenkamp 2002). This is expected to have two related consequences regarding the determinants of FDI:

- Host countries are evaluated by MNEs on the basis of a broader set of policies than before. The number of policies constituting a favorable investment climate increases, in particular with regard to the creation of location-specific assets sought by MNEs.
- The relative importance of FDI determinants changes. Even though traditional determinants and the types of FDI associated with them have not disappeared with globalization, their importance is said to be on the decline. More specifically, "one of the most important traditional FDI determinants, the size of national markets, has decreased in importance. At the same time, cost differences between locations, the quality of infrastructure, the ease of doing business and the availability of skills have become more important" (UNCTAD 1996a, UNCTAD 1996b).

Asymmetric information between the firm's insiders and outsiders is an important factor contributing to preference for FDI compared with other sources of financing (Razin et al. 1998; Kinoshita and Mody 1999). This is even more so in the transition economies characterized by a general lack of transparency, low standards of business conduct, and inadequate protection of creditor and minority

© Springer International Publishing Switzerland 2016
Z. Vukanović, *Foreign Direct Investment Inflows Into the South East European Media Market*, Media Business and Innovation, DOI 10.1007/978-3-319-30512-7_6

shareholder rights. As a result, companies in transition economies rely primarily on FDI, and in particular with the foreign strategic investor taking majority control of the firm (Buiter et al. 1998).

6.2   The Vertical and Horizontal FDI Determining Factors

Proximity-concentration trade-off theory states that MNCs compare trade costs to the costs of producing at different locations in the world. If the trade cost is higher, MNCs will undertake the Horizontal FDI. When MNCs exploit differences in factor cost between different geographical locations, then it leads to Vertical FDI (Helpman 1984). Export-Platform FDI explains MNC production in a host economy when the output is sold in third markets and not in the parent or host country market (Ekholm et al. 2007). Christie (2003) examines whether horizontal or vertical FDI is predominant in the region and reports that in Central European economies HFDI is prevalent, but that the evidence for Southeastern European countries is inconclusive.

Trade policies and, more broadly, trade costs (tariffs, nontariff barriers, and transportation costs) are generally found to have a significant impact on FDI flows, but in aggregate regressions their sign is ambiguous (Demekas et al. 2005). This is probably due to the different effect barriers to trade can be expected to have on horizontal and vertical FDI: they tend to attract HFDI, which aims at penetrating the domestic market, but repel VFDI (Demekas et al. 2005). At the aggregate level, the trade barrier to VFDI and HFDI would thus depend on which kind of FDI is prevalent in the particular host country. Empirical studies that look separately at horizontal and vertical FDI tend to support this hypothesis: Brainard (1997) finds that freight costs and tariffs have a positive effect on HFDI; Barrell and Pain (1999) report a similar result for protectionist measures, and Markusen and Maskus (1999), decomposing the sales of foreign-owned firms in the host country, find that higher trade costs stimulate HFDI and deter VFDI.

There is evidence that regional integration reduces HFDI—certainly flows within the area where integration takes place—and stimulates VFDI (Demekas et al. 2005). In the context of transition economies, studies generally find that steps toward integration with the EU have a positive effect on FDI flows (Braconier and Ekholm 2002; Bevan, Estrin and Grabbe 2001). These results, however, need to be interpreted with caution: it is not clear that they capture the effect on FDI of increasing regional integration rather than the prospect of greater political and institutional stability expected to accompany accession to the European Union (Demekas et al. 2005).

6.3 The Consensus on the Key Drivers, Roles, Links, and Effects of Endogenous and Exogenous Macroeconomic Determining Factors of FDI Inflows

This chapter looks at the relationship and multicolinearity of FDI into SEECs markets with following macroeconomic variables/factors: Agglomeration (cluster of firms) effects, The host market size and growth potential, The gravity approach, The macroeconomic stability, The Trade barriers(protections)/openness of the host economy, Tariff jumping, Political stability/risk, Infrastructure, Institutions (Institutional framework), Business/investment climate, Fiscal/Tax Incentives, Exchange Rate Effects, Human capital, Indebtedness, Democracy, Gross Capital Formation, Labor and production factor costs, Transport costs, EU accession and regional membership status, Economic privatization, and International Investment Incentives. These factors are based on their relative importance from prior systematic literature.

There are, of course, other variables with particular importance for transition economies. "Intangible assets" such as the business culture may have a potential impact on FDI inflows. The method and the level of privatization can catch such an effect because they are closely related to the effectiveness of corporate governance. More specifically, Holland and Pain (1998) and Bevan and Estrin (2000) take the private sector share of GDP as a proxy for the level of privatization and expect this variable to influence positively FDI.

In emerging economies, the analysis of empirical data indicates that economics factors are more significant in attracting FDI inflows than institutional and political factors. The success of the developing countries in attracting FDI is likely to be associated with an investment climate characterized by growing markets and increasingly liberal policy frameworks (Jun and Singh 1996).

Although clarifying the drivers of FDI is important for comprehending their economic change (Popescu 2014), there is a lack of consensus on the effect of macroeconomic determinants on FDI except for market size and gravity approach. Measured by GDP or GDP per capita, market size seems to be the most robust FDI determinant (e.g., among many others, Kravis and Lipsey 1982; Wheeler and Mody 1992; Billington 1999). The effects of vertical FDI (VFDI) determinants are even more debated (Artige and Nicolini 2006).

The literature is large enough that a comprehensive review is not possible. Instead, this chapter highlights only more important and novel papers in the high-impact international per-reviewed empirical literature on FDI determinants. Studies of FDI flows are considerably behind the parallel trade literature, but face even more daunting issues. In fact, intuition and academic research suggest that MNE and FDI behavior is likely much more complicated to model than trade flows.

As a result, the great variety of FDI determinants observed in investor surveys (e.g., A.T. Kearney 2003) emerges in the form of a lack of consensus in the econometric studies. This can be explained by the lack of aggregate data, on the different variables of FDI determinants in the empirical literature. In principle, the existing empirical literature on the determinants of FDI can be categorized into two groups: studies focusing on aggregate, economy-wide FDI flows and microeconomic (firm- or sector-level) studies, building on the work of R. Vernon (1966). In this section, the author concentrates on both, with emphasis on research covering transition economies. The author includes 16 Southeastern European countries: Albania, Bosnia and Herzegovina, Croatia, Slovenia, Kosovo, the former Yugoslav Republic of Macedonia (hereinafter referred to as FYR of Macedonia), Serbia, Montenegro, Bulgaria, Cyprus, Hungary, Greece, Malta, Moldova, Romania, and Turkey.

The choice of FDI determining variables is, on the one hand, based on FDI theories which stress the difference between market-related (e.g., market size) and efficiency-related (e.g., factor endowment) location factors (see, for instance, Markusen and Maskus 2002; Bellak et al. 2010a, Bellak et al. 2010b). On the other hand, variables are derived from existing, partly gravity-model based, empirical studies on the determinants of FDI (e.g., Devereux and Griffith 1998; Markusen and Maskus 2002; Yeaple 2003; Clausing and Dorobantu 2005; Bénassy-Quéré et al. 2007a, b; Demekas et al. 2007; Buch and Lipponer 2007; Bellak et al. 2010a, Bellak et al. 2010b).

To interpret the findings of the literature on the determinants of FDI, it is useful to keep in mind the distinction between two types of FDI identified in theory—although in real life this distinction is often blurred. Horizontal FDI (HFDI) is market-seeking investment, aimed primarily at the domestic market in the host country, when local production is seen as a more efficient way to penetrate this market than exports from the source country. Vertical FDI (VFDI) is cost-minimizing investment, when a multinational corporation chooses the location of each link of its production chain to minimize global costs. As a result of these differences in motivation, a number of host country factors, such as market size, trade restrictions, and transport costs, can have different effects on HFDI and VFDI. There is broad agreement that HFDI is more prevalent (Navaretti and Venables 2004). However, there is also evidence that the recent surge in FDI flows to developing countries, in particular, was mainly VFDI (Hanson et al. 2001; Markusen and Maskus 1999). Both types of FDI are, in principle, subject to "agglomeration," that is, clustering in certain locations—where the existing business infrastructure is set up to serve a particular industry or the presence of other investors provides positive externalities through network effects or backward and forward linkages—and "herding," where investors tend to follow a leader that establishes operations in a particular country (Demekas et al. 2005).

Horizontal FDI will arise when there is similarity in market size and relative factor endowment (factor costs) between FDI home and host country, and when the transport costs are high (Markusen and Venables 1998). Vertical FDI occurs when countries are of a different size and with production facilities located in a country with a large domestic market that makes it possible to achieve plant-level economies of scale; headquarters services are performed by a country relatively endowed with skilled labor (Derado 2013). An improvement of this model is offered by Bergstrand and Egger (2007), who demonstrated a complementarity between FDI and trade even between identical countries and found out that trade, FDI, and foreign affiliate sales can increase (on aggregate level) as GDP size and similarity between countries grow.

6.3.1 Agglomeration (Cluster of Firms) Effects

Agglomeration (cluster of firms) effects signal high quality of infrastructure, human capital, specialization, and also higher competition (Artige and Nicolini 2006). These affect both horizontal- and vertical-type FDI. By clustering with other firms, new investors benefit from positive spillovers from existing investors in the host country (Walsh and Yu 2010). Evidence for these effects is widespread, with Wheeler and Mody (1992) in the case of US firms, Barrell and Pain (1999) in the Western European context, and Campos and Kinoshita (2003) in the transition economies, all finding empirical evidence of agglomeration effects.

Although some studies find agglomeration and herding to be important (Barrell and Pain 1999; Campos and Kinoshita 2003), a further research is needed to separate spurious from real correlation. Agglomeration effects are most commonly proxied by the quality of infrastructure, degree of development, and lagged stock of FDI, but these variables may influence FDI through other channels as well (Demekas et al. 2005). Finally, Bevan and Estrin (2000) report some evidence of feedback effects (FDI contributing to changes in the host environment that, in turn, stimulate more FDI) that might explain the emergence of leaders and laggards among host countries.

6.3.2 The Host Market Size and Growth Potential

Among more traditional FDI determinants, the host market size-related factors as measured by GDP or GDP per capita seem to be the most robust FDI determinant in econometric studies. This is the main determinant for horizontal FDI. It is irrelevant for vertical FDI (Shatz and Venables 2000; Billington 1999; Brainard 1997; Wheeler and Mody 1992; Kravis and Lipsey 1982). Larger host countries' markets may be associated with higher foreign direct investment due to larger potential demand and lower costs due to scale economies (Resmini 2000; Bevan and Estrin 2000).

Suder and Sohn (2010) are among the many authors who find the GDP level of CEE countries strongly influencing the attractiveness for foreign investors, as the host market size is positively and strongly correlated with the FDI inflows. In a frequently quoted survey of the earlier literature on FDI determinants, Agarwal (1980) found the size of host country markets to be the most popular explanation of a country's propensity to attract FDI, especially when FDI flows to developing countries are considered. Shamsuddin (1994) reiterated Agarwal's finding some 15 years later: "Most empirical studies support the market size hypothesis."

Subsequent empirical studies corroborated this finding. Addison and Heshmati (2003) found the pair-wise correlation coefficient between net FDI inflow and size of the country to be positive.

A large domestic/host country market size promotes ICT investment but reduces openness and GDP growth. Even authors who dismissed earlier studies as seriously flawed came up with results supporting the relevance of market-related variables such as GDP, population, GDP per capita, and GDP growth; examples are Schneider and Frey (1985), Wheeler and Mody (1992), Tsai (1994), Jackson and Markowski (1995), and, more recently, Driffield and Taylor (2000). Chakrabarti (2001), while questioning the robustness of various other FDI determinants, finds the correlation between FDI and market size to be robust to changes in the conditioning information set.

Analysis of empirical data indicates that coefficients of market size measured by real GDP, return on investment, and trade openness are significant determinates of total inward FDI which implies that most of the investment in emerging economies is motivated by market-seeking purpose (Schneider and Frey 1985; Ancharaz 2000; Chakrabarti 2001; Asiedu 2002; Eicher 2002; Ismail and Yussof 2003; Choong and Lim 2007). As international consumption and international production have been shifted to emerging economies, MNCs are increasingly investing in both efficiency-seeking and market-seeking projects in these emerging countries.

The growth of domestic/host country market size/magnitude has been widely accepted as a significant determinant of FDI flows; nearly all empirical studies explain determinants of FDI (Bhavan et al. 2011; Aw and Tang 2010; Leitão and Faustino 2010; Leitão 2010; Hailu 2010; Schneider and Matei 2010; Mohamed and Sidiropoulos 2010; Estrin and Uvalic 2014).

Several Studies used Real Gross Domestic Product per capita or real gross national product per capita for the market size of a country or income within the country. Real GDP used as a proxy to market size shows higher purchasing power, where firms can potentially receive higher returns on investment on their capital and gain higher profit from their investment. Thus, the author expects positive relationship between Market Size and FDI (Jadhav 2012).

6.3.3   The Gravity Approach

Gravity models have been used extensively in recent years trying to quantify potential trade levels, particularly with transition countries (Christie 2002). Virtually all empirical studies (Lankes and Venables 1996; Lim 2001; Singh and Jun 1996; Estrin et al. 1997; Claessens et al. 1998; Brenton et al. 1999; Bevan and Estrin 2000; Resmini 2000; Carstensen and Toubal 2004; Demekas et al. 2007; Janicki and Wunnava 2004) find that gravity factors (market size/magnitude and proximity/vicinity to the source country economy) are the most important determinants of FDI in emerging and transition economies. Just as with trade flows (Breuss and Egger 1999; Di Mauro 2000; Feenstra et al. 2001), the gravity model (the distance between host and home economy) consistently explains about 60 % of aggregate FDI flows, regardless of the region.

More specifically, Bevan and Estrin (2004) find that FDI is related positively to both source and host country GDP. Moreover, it is related inversely to the distance between the countries and to unit labor costs. A multinational's decision to locate in a foreign market depends on the trade-off between the incremental fixed costs of investing in production capacity abroad and the costs of exporting output from the domestic source country. The gravity approach suggests that these elements are captured by the relative market sizes of the two economies and their distance from each other. Distance can be viewed as a measure of the transaction costs of undertaking foreign activities. For example, the costs of transport and communications, the costs of dealing with cultural and language differences, the costs of sending personnel abroad, and the informational costs of institutional and legal factors, e.g., local property rights, regulations, and tax systems, are all assumed to increase with distance.

Since gravity factors are exogenous, the prevalence of its variables among the drivers of FDI indicates that governmental and policymakers' trade, FDI promotion strategies, and policies can have a rather restricted effect.

6.3.4 The Macroeconomic Stability

Studies of FDI in emerging markets stress the importance of a sound and stable institutional macroeconomic environment, typified by the variance in growth rates, low inflation, exchange rate stability, and low economic and political risk, e.g., Henisz (2000), and reflected in policies towards FDI, tax regimes, the transparency and effectiveness of the commercial legal code, and the extent of corruption and political stability, represented by measures of political freedom. The author considers these factors to be correlated to FDI. The overall macroeconomic, financial, and institutional condition (Nica 2014) of the host country is a significant driver of FDI inflows. Specifically, the impact of FDI is positively correlated with credit rating alterations (Popescu 2014).

6.3.5 The Trade Barriers (Protections)/Openness (Liberalization) of the Host Economy

Global trade liberalization has made it easier for MNCs to set up international production networks, so that a larger share of output is shipped to international customers or affiliated companies in other countries rather than sold to local customers. This has reduced the impact of market size and allowed smaller countries to compete for investments that would automatically have been directed to the major markets some decades ago (Blomström et al. 2003). Nevertheless, the trade barriers/openness is somewhat an uncertain determinant. The effect of trade barriers is found to be positive by Lunn (1980), negative by Kravis and Lipsey (1982) and Culem (1988), and insignificant by Wheeler and Mody (1992) and Blonigen and Feenstra (1996). Openness to trade proxied by the proportion of exports in GDP has economically a chief, significant, and outstanding positive influence on the net inflows of FDI (Inglehart et al. 2014). Moreover, it is likely to further global trade and support FDI flows. The positive impacts of FDI on trade are more numerous than the negative ones (Popescu 2014).

A weak openness tends to favor horizontal FDI and deter vertical FDI. Moreover, the positive correlation between trade openness and FDI is restricted to the manufacturing sector, whereas the correlation is insignificant for FDI in the services sector (Nunnenkamp 2002). Considering that the recent boom of FDI in developing countries is largely because of FDI in non-traded services, the relevance of openness even may have declined. FDI is stimulated if the trade policy of the host country is liberal and because multinational companies have a more substantial tendency to export (Popescu 2014).

The positive relationship between FDI and trade volumes implies that countries wishing more FDI should increase trade (Jadhav 2012). Most of the studies find that trade openness is positively related to FDI in host country, but the impact of openness on FDI depends on whether the investment is market seeking or export oriented. According to "tariff-jumping" hypothesis less open economy with trade restrictions can have a positive effect on FDI (Market-Seeking). Export-oriented MNCs prefer to locate to a more open economy because trade protection generally states higher transaction cost associated with exporting. Most of the FDI literature used share of trade in GDP as a proxy for openness (Bhavan et al. 2011; Aw and Tang 2010; Leitão and Faustino 2010; Leitão 2010).

The hypothesized link between FDI and trade protection is seen as fairly clear by most trade economists—higher trade protection should make firms more likely to substitute affiliate production for exports to avoid the costs of trade production. This is commonly termed tariff-jumping FDI. There is a sizeable empirical literature interpreting the high levels of foreign direct investment (FDI) in a number of economies resulting in "tariff jumping": since tariffs increase the cost of exporting, foreign firms prefer to jump the tariff and take up production within the protected market. Hwang and Mai (2002) state that a foreign firm has an incentive to jump over the tariff wall in order to locate in a foreign territory and thereby escape tariffs. Contrary to the conventional wisdom tariff-jumping FDI may well be beneficial, rather than harmful, to a small receiving country (Dehejia and Weichenrieder 2001). An increase in FDI into a specific market increases consumer's likelihood to favor further trade protection.

6.3.6   Tariff Jumping

Gastanaga et al. (1998) address the tariff-jumping hypothesis in the context of a panel analysis on the effects of host country reforms on FDI. Cross-section results suggest that FDI flows are motivated more strongly by tariff jumping than by potential exports. These authors conclude that "over time in individual countries trade liberalization has become the more important motive for FDI." According to the sensitivity analysis of Chakrabarti (2001), openness to trade (proxied by exports plus imports to GDP) has the highest likelihood of being correlated (positively) with FDI among all explanatory variables classified as fragile.

Tariff-jumping FDI allows a foreign firm to avoid a trade barrier by locating production within the destination market. Such activities can thereby substantially mitigate welfare consequences of the original trade protection policy. Theoretically, the likelihood of tariff-jumping FDI for a given trade barrier and the magnitude of its effect on welfare of various agents depend on a number of factors, including differential production costs, relocation costs, other entry barriers, and demand conditions. Surprisingly, trade economists ignore tariff jumping in the academic literature, particularly in the case of strategic trade policy (Blonigen et al. 2004).

6.3.7   Political Stability/Risk

Political stability and risk generally affect the decision whether to invest or not in a particular location (Dunning 1993; Moosa 2002). Political risk indicates the political actions interrupting sales or causing harm to property or personnel including, riots, operational restrictions impeding their abilities to undertake certain actions, and governmental takeover of property (Trevino, Daniels & Arbelaez 2002). Political risk factors generally affect negatively the investment decisions of MNCs in that particular country (Dunning 1993; Dupasquier and Osajwe 2006; Li 2008). Correspondingly, FDI flows and military conflicts are inversely related.

Moreover, various empirical research works argue that political instability, inefficient institutions, and corruption discourage foreign investment (Gastanaga et al. 1998; Campos et al. 1999; Asiedu and Villamil 2000; Wei 2000; Asiedu 2005; Aw and Tang 2010; Hines 1995a, b; Eicher 2002; Smarzynska and Wei 2002). However, most of the political and corruption risk factors and determinants are less important and statistically significant in determining the FDI inflows into a certain region than the size of the market and low-cost labor. This supports the results of Cuervo-Cazurra (2006) who states that investors from countries with high corruption and the lack of enforcement of anticorruption laws select similar countries when they internationalize in order to exploit their familiarity with corrupt environments and also because they face lower costs of operating as opposed to other investors. Endeavors to upgrade governance and withstand corruption may not influence FDI directly, but could encourage foreign investment indirectly via their positive impacts on the economy (Popescu 2014).

6.3.8 Infrastructure

There are different proxies used in the literature for measuring the impact of infrastructure on FDI. For Gramlich (1994), the relevant infrastructure includes transport, communication, and electricity production facilities, as well as transmission facilities for electricity, gas, and water. Bellak, Leibrecht & Römisch (2007) also utilize variables including telecommunication, electricity, and transport production facilities in order to determine the impact of overall infrastructure. Although the study finds a strong link between infrastructure endowments and FDI, the results also indicate that information and telecommunication infrastructure, followed by the transport infrastructure, are more significant in attracting FDI than electricity generation capacity (Bellak, Leibrecht & Römisch 2007).

In explaining FDI, Goodspeed et al. (2009) use a composite infrastructure index comprehending transport, telecommunication, energy, and environment infrastructures and find a positive impact upon FDI. Of great significance is their observation indicating that FDI is more sensitive to host country infrastructure quality in developing host countries than in developed ones (Goodspeed et al. 2009).

In examining infrastructure impact on country attractiveness, Bellak, Leibrecht & Römisch (2007) establish a composite indicator expressing infrastructure endowment based on the principal component analysis, focusing on telecommunication, electricity, and transport production facilities. The variables used to analyze the infrastructure endowment are per capita data on penetration with telephone mainlines, mobile phones, personal computers, broadband connections to the Internet, and the number of Internet users (for measuring the telecommunications infrastructure), the density of railways, motorways, non-motorway roads, and waterways, as well as the number of major air- and seaports (for transport infrastructure) and the annual electricity generation capacity per capita in GWh (for measuring the electricity supply capacity). The author finds a positive impact of infrastructure endowment growth on inward FDI.

These findings are consistent with those obtained by Leibrecht and Riedl (2010), who use the same variables expressing infrastructure endowment but in an empirical model encompassing spatial interdependencies. A faster method for assessing infrastructure is used by Bellak et al. (2010a) with the same positive relation regarding FDI. Here, the infrastructure is represented by the sum of telephone mainlines, mobile phone subscribers, and Internet connections per 1000 inhabitants, referring overall to the information and communication infrastructure endowment.

The relevant quality of infrastructure does not influence the attractiveness of FDI in the SEECs (Popescu 2014). Specifically, Botrić and Škuflić (2006) investigate the determinants of FDI in South Eastern European countries. One of the variables used is the ICT, defined as the number of telephone lines per 100 inhabitants or the number of Internet connections. The countries on the top positions of FDI attractiveness are those with a better infrastructure for ICT. The sector not only has an increasing importance in the foreign investors' decision, but is also a resource for diversifying economies. It helps to reduce the dependence on the natural resource endowment and to reduce the disadvantages of a landlocked country. The ICT infrastructure endowment leads to an increase in FDI by about 0.73 % (Bellak et al. 2008). Addison and Heshmati (2003) investigate the determinants of FDI inflows to developing countries and establish that the spread of ICT increases FDI inflows to developing countries. In their study, the ICT variable is defined as the sum of total spending on information technology plus communications equipment and services as a percentage of the gross domestic product (Addison and Heshmati 2003).

6.3.9 Institutions (Institutional Framework)

Estimating the magnitude of the effect of institutions on FDI is difficult because there are no accurate measurements of institutions. Thus, comparability of the multidisciplinary composite index of a country's political, legal, and economic institutions, developed from business survey responses, is questionable when survey respondents vary across the countries (Blonigen 2005).

Wilhelms and Witter (1998) develop the theory of institutional fitness pointing to the fact that inward FDI is mostly depending on the institutional variables (such as the policies, laws, and the ways of enforcing them) than on the intransigent fundamentals, including the size of the population or sociocultural characteristics. Although less mentioned in the literature, the main contribution of the theory is that it strongly emphasizes that not the most powerful or big countries are successful in attracting FDI, but the most adaptable ones, suggesting the strong influence of institutions in the host countries for inward FDI (Wilhelms and Witter 1998).

For this reason, the institutional capacity to adapt at the global changes is considered an advantage and makes a country more attractive than others. For Dixit (2009), good economic governance is equivalent with property rights protection and contracts enforcement. Dunning (2004) states that the quality of institutions is becoming increasingly important for attracting FDI and meeting the needs of investors.

For SEECs, the actual institutional environment remains a barrier for FDI attractiveness. The lack of the capacity to develop and make the institutional context more flexible is a weak point for these countries. In the literature, the impact of state regulations on FDI is mostly assessed for the developing or transition economies. Institutional variables affect FDI inflows in the SEECs economies, besides GDP magnitude and trade openness (Tintin 2013). Goodspeed et al. (2009) indicate that, compared with the developed countries, FDI in developing countries is sensitive to the levels of corruption in the host country. In measuring corruption, the authors use the Corruption Perception Index from Transparency International (Goodspeed et al. 2009).

6.3.10   Business/Investment Climate

Business/investment climate relates to the institutional framework. Regulatory, bureaucratic, and judicial environments are now considered as very important criteria for investment and development. In addition, foreign entrepreneurs seem to be more predisposed to invest in countries with a higher degree of government stability and protection for investors (Sánchez-Martín et al. 2014).

6.3.11   Fiscal/Tax Incentives

While countries with an above average infrastructure endowment can finance their infrastructure by taxing corporations, countries with an inferior infrastructure endowment are forced to cut corporate income taxes for increasing attractiveness in order to receive FDI in the short run (Bellak and Leibrecht 2009a). Correspondingly, the smaller the host country market, the more important influences of tax rates on FDI. The usual behavior of companies is to search for attractive environments, seeking opportunities that enable them to obtain various types of competitive advantages (Morgan and Katsikeas 1997). The role of taxation is therefore significantly important.

The evidence on the impact of tax policies on FDI is evolving. Earlier studies found only a negligible effect (Brainard 1997). But more recent work shows increasing evidence that a low tax burden attracts FDI (Hines 1999). The responsiveness to tax policies may have increased in recent years if VFDI, which is mainly driven by the relative cost of production, is becoming more prominent. The evidence on tax incentives is inconclusive, but there are some indications that transparent and simple tax systems tend to be most attractive for FDI (Hassett and Hubbard 1997; OECD 2003).

The effect of taxes on FDI has been the subject of many papers with contradictory results. Hartman (1984) found a negative relationship between retained earnings FDI and the host country tax rate. Billington (1999) confirms the negative effect, while Swenson (1994) found a positive effect and Wheeler and Mody (1992) concluded this determinant insignificant.

Gordon and Hines (2002) argue that econometric studies of the past 15 years show that both the level and location of FDI are highly sensitive to the treatment of taxes. Madies and Dethier (2010) conclude that the result of most empirical studies shows that FDI flows into developing countries are sensitive in varying degrees to the taxation of corporate income and fiscal incentives. Goodspeed et al. (2009) deal with the taxation issue in the developing and developed countries. The results show that FDI stock is more sensitive and pronounced to the host country taxation in developed countries and not in developing ones. However, tax incentives are not sufficient to overcome the structural inefficiencies encountered in infrastructure or bureaucracy. Bellack et al. (2007) identify that the location decisions made by MNEs are influenced by both taxes and infrastructure. Moreover, taxrate elasticity of FDI is a decreasing function of infrastructure endowment. In most countries, the existent infrastructure can be taxed without a loss of FDI. While countries with an above average infrastructure endowment can finance their infrastructure by taxing corporations, countries with an inferior infrastructure endowment are forced to cut corporate income taxes for increasing attractiveness in order to receive FDI in the short run.

Although the empirical evidence concerning FDI and taxation in the Central and East European Countries (CEECs) has consistently not found evidence that taxes matter for location decisions, Bellak and Leibrecht (2009b) study indicates that tax-lowering strategies of SEECs governments seem to have an important impact on foreign firms' location decisions. Bellak and Leibrecht's paper differs from previous studies by including a theoretically well-founded measure of the tax burden, namely forward-looking effective tax rates derived by Devereux and Griffith (1999), rather than the statutory tax rate, which has various shortcomings in explaining FDI.

In addition to the underlying empirical concepts, empirical studies on FDI and taxation vary widely with respect to specification, sample size, and so on (Feld and Heckemeyer 2011). One very important aspect in which they differ is the dependent variable. Since FDI in its broad definition does not only comprise real investments but also financial flows due to mergers or acquisitions of already existing capital, some authors prefer to use a dependent variable which better reflects real economic activity. They therefore rely on investments in stocks of property, plant, and equipment (PPE) which are undertaken or held by foreign affiliates in a particular host country.

The central explanatory variable, i.e., the tax variable, also varies on the basis of different alternative concepts. Besides the use of statutory tax rates at the country or regional level, many empirical studies rely on average tax rates. In contrast to statutory tax rates, average tax rates reflect the tax base to which statutory tax rates apply. They are computed on the basis of previous microeconomic or macroeconomic data and are therefore also known as backward-looking tax measures (Feld and Heckemeyer 2011). One special feature of backward-looking tax measures is that they capture the "true" tax burden on investments or companies. Since they are based on actual tax payments they reflect the outcome of tax planning and discretionary tax provisions. However, one of their major caveats also lies in this backward orientation. As Devereux (2006) points out, average tax measures might introduce an endogeneity bias into empirical analyses. Since they are based on previous data, average tax rates might be influenced by recent investments (e.g., through depreciation allowances). The direction of causation between the dependent FDI variable and the average tax rate thus might be ambiguous.

From a theoretical point of view, it is preferable to use forward-looking tax measures as they better reflect the FDI entry. Forward-looking tax measures are differentiated into effective marginal and effective average tax rates. Effective marginal tax rates measure the tax-induced relative wedge between pre- and posttax returns on marginal investment. They are mainly calculated using neoclassical investment models developed by King and Fullerton (1984) or Devereux and Griffith (1998, 1999). Devereux and Griffith (1999) also calculate effective average tax rates, which measure relative tax-induced reductions of the net present value of inframarginal, i.e., profitable, investments. More importantly, these measures reflect the major provisions of the considered tax system in a transparent and compact way corresponding to the forward-looking nature of investment decisions being taken on the basis of future taxes and triggered by the respective projects (Feld and Heckemeyer 2011).

FDI from worldwide taxation countries that offer their parent firms credits is relatively insensitive to tax rates. This is best represented by Hines (1996), which creatively brought the issue of the territorial versus worldwide-tax treatment issue to the preexisting literature by examining whether state-level taxes affect location of US inward FDI. Previous studies examining the effect of state taxes on state location of FDI found insignificant results (Coughlin et al. 1991). Like federal taxes, MNEs facing state-level taxes may differ in their responses based on whether they face a territorial-tax or worldwide-tax system in their parent country. Hines (1996) finds that higher tax rates of 1 % are associated with a 9 % larger FDI decrease by the noncredit-system investors relative to the credit-system investors.

MNEs face tax rates at a variety of levels in both the host and parent country, and policies to deal with double taxation can substantially alter the effects of these taxes on an MNE's incentive to invest (Blonigen 2005). In summary, the literature empirical approaches and data samples have differed a fair amount, so that there are still significant questions about how much taxes affect FDI. The literature has also only recently begun to examine other related taxes beyond corporate income taxes. For example, a working paper by Desai et al. (2004) finds evidence that indirect business taxes have an effect on FDI that is in the same range as corporate income taxes. Nevertheless, the effect of bilateral international tax treaties on FDI activity has been an unexplored issue empirically until just recently. There are thousands of such tax treaties which negotiate reductions in countries withholding rates among other things. Hallward-Dreimeier (2003) and Blonigen and Davies (2004) find little evidence that these treaties affect FDI activity in any significant fashion. Blonigen et al. (2005) suggest that these treaties are more about uncovering tax evasion by MNEs.

6.3.12 Exchange Rate Effects

An early empirical paper by Cushman (1985) finds evidence that an expected real appreciation of the home currency increases FDI, whereas the current level of the exchange rate has no consistently significant impact. Correspondingly, Froot and Stein's (1991) study finds empirical evidence through simple regressions that a currency appreciation in an imperfect capital market increases foreign investment by a firm. Klein and Rosengren (1994), however, confirm that exchange rate depreciation increases US FDI using various samples of US FDI disaggregated by country source and type of FDI.

Other studies have generally found consistent evidence that short-run movements in exchange rates lead to increased inward FDI, including Grubert and Mutti (1991), Swenson (1994), Blonigen (1997), and Kogut and Chang (1996), with limited evidence that the effect is larger for merger and acquisition FDI (Klein and Rosengren 1994). Thus, the evidence has largely been consistent with the Froot and Stein (1991) hypotheses. Campa (1993) finds evidence that greater exchange rate uncertainty increases the option for firms to wait until investing in a market, depressing current FDI.

A related paper by Goldberg and Kolstad (1995) alternatively hypothesizes that exchange rate uncertainty will increase FDI by risk-averse MNEs if such uncertainty is correlated with export demand shocks in the markets they intend to serve. They confirm this hypothesis with empirical analysis relying on quarterly bilateral data on US FDI with Canada, Japan, and the United Kingdom.

In summary, the literature has derived important and interesting firm-level models of how exchange rate uncertainty can affect FDI flows, depending on firm characteristics, expected exchange rate levels, uncertainty, or even volatility.

6.3.13 Human Capital

Noorbakhsh et al.'s (2001) study focuses on human capital as a determinant of FDI. Their study is suggestive of an increasing importance of human capital through time. Consequently, the estimated coefficients of the variables used as proxies for human capital as well as their *t*-ratios increase in magnitude across the consecutive sample periods. Moreover, a low degree of skilled labor curbs FDI inflows, indicating the relevance of labor quality in affecting SEECs economies' FDI inflows (Popescu 2014). Accordingly, labor skills have usually positive consequences on FDI, skill-rich economies attracting high-skill industries.

6.3.14 Indebtedness

Indebtedness has negative impacts on foreign direct investment. This is to be expected for the reasons of potential foreign investors steering clear of countries with high debt, fearing both macroeconomic instability and potential devaluation (which cuts the dollar value of any remitted profit) (Addison and Heshmati 2003).

6.3.15 Democracy

Democracy has a positive effect on FDI, especially for Latin America. This is one of the most important results, emphasizing the hypothesis that foreign investors increasingly take note of whether or not a society is a democracy, in part because of the trend toward corporate social responsibility, and also because of indications that well-functioning democracies pursue better economic policies (Addison and Heshmati 2003).

6.3.16 Gross Capital Formation

In a transition economy, improvements in the investment climate help to attract higher FDI inflows. It translates into higher Gross capital formation which in turn leads to greater economic growth. Vijayakumar et al. (2010) find little evidence of FDI having an impact on capital formation in developed countries and observe that the most important aspect of FDI in the selected sample of countries is related to ownership change. The relationship between FDI and Capital Formation is not simple (Vijayakumar et al. 2010). In the case of certain privatization, it may not lead to increase at all or even result in reduction. Thus, the unclear relation between FDI and capital formation may also hold in a transition economy. Although a significant positive or negative relationship between FDI and Capital Formation is expected, the overall and long-term focus FDI/GCF ratio "isolates" the knowledge and composition effects of FDI inflows as we condition on gross capital formation (Vijayakumar et al. 2010).

6.3.17 Labor and Production Factor Costs

Labor cost and production factor costs also play a significant role and are found to be positively related to FDI by Wheeler and Mody (1992) and Feenstra and Hanson (1997). However, the effect is negative for Culem (1988) and insignificant for Lucas (1993). The unit labor cost proxied by the modification in competitiveness impacts notably the entry of FDI (Popescu 2014). Relatively low unit labor costs have a notable effect on GDP growth and are the chief motivator of MNCs vertical FDI (Kornecki and Raghavan 2011). FDI flows are more substantial for settings with lower unit labor expenditures, irrespective of distance or host country magnitude (Popescu 2014).

Conversely, a higher wage corresponds to a lower level of FDI both at home and in foreign markets (Jadhav 2012). Moreover, dependency hypothesis and modernization hypothesis agreed the importance of low-cost labor in attracting FDI (International Division of labor). This is the main criterion motivating vertical

FDI. Lower cost is also favorable to horizontal FDI. Feenstra and Hanson (1997) find that labor cost is positive and significant for US FDI in Mexico. A similar result is obtained by Wheeler and Mody (1992) for US FDI in electronics.

6.3.18   Transport Costs

Transport costs will be determinant for horizontal FDI. However, it can also be decisive for vertical FDI since this is often an investment with the objective to export the goods produced. Brainard (1997) finds a positive correlation between FDI and transport costs.

6.3.19   EU Accession and Regional Membership Status

The Eurozone business cycle has a positive and statistically important impact on FDI inflows. In the long term, both the wide-ranging privatization index and the banking reform index have a positive and considerable consequence on net FDI inflows in SEECs economies (Jimborean and Kelber 2014). In this context, the chances of integration with the EU have driven reform and transition processes in SEECs economies. Thus, potential European Union (EU) membership may be a substantial generating driver of FDI mode and entry (Estrin and Uvalic 2014). Relatedly, the EU admission enhances degrees of FDI to the possible members. Correspondingly, substantial integration with the EU has influenced SEECs with respect to huge capital inflows (Popescu 2014). In addition, FDI into and from the SEECs is influenced by the process and chance of EU integration. Accordingly, EU membership further accelerates FDI consequently generating more growth and development (Bevan and Estrin 2004). In contrast, countries that are less successful in implementing transition policies are given longer timetables to EU accession, which may discourage FDI inflows (Bevan and Estrin 2004).

Consequently, a factual or prospective EU accession for the transition economies would entail membership of the Single European Market providing EU firms with the opportunity to relocate production in areas of lower labor cost as well as determining additional regional FDI inflows (Te Velde and Bezemer 2006; Bevan and Estrin 2000). Moreover, the prospect of EU membership might be viewed by potential investors as reducing country risk, both because meeting the requirements for EU admission represents an external validation of progress in transition and because ultimate EU membership implies guarantees of macroeconomic, political, institutional and legal environment stability (Bevan and Estrin 2000).

Regional integration diminishes HFDI and encourages VFDI (Popescu 2014).

6.3.20   Economic Privatization

Throughout the precrisis period, SEECs attracted substantial capital inflows, augmented by privatization and expectations of EU accession (Popescu 2014). Accordingly, for most transition nations, the process of privatization has constituted a separate incentive for FDI. SEECs that advanced quickest in privatization could attract more FDI. Moreover, effective governmental policies to accomplish substantial scale privatization are related to enhanced FDI in the transition economy region (Estrin and Uvalic 2014). In those SEECs market economies characterized by entering a final stage of economic restructuring privatization, transition, and reform of formerly state-owned media enterprises, the growth of inward FDI is declining.

6.3.21   International Investment Incentives

The main question in this subsection is whether the host country's costs for providing the incentives—in terms of grants, subsidies, and other expenses—are justified. Are investment incentives likely to yield benefits that are at least as large as the costs?

The arguments for international investment incentives are justified on the ground of positive or increasing of externalities, or spillovers of FDI resulting from an investment, such as the diffusion of new knowledge/technology upgrading of the workforce's skills or investment in R&D (Ricupero 2000). When the costs of operating in them are higher than the benefits, there are incentives for the MNC to develop its own internal organizational structure to achieve internal coordination of activities. International FDI incentives are justified if the foreign firms differ from local companies in that they possess some firm-specific intangible asset that can spill over to local firms (Blomström et al. 2003). Incentives have also become increasingly important for national policymakers who are trying to promote local production, employment, and welfare. Considering that market integration has reached further at the regional rather than global level, it is also clear that the effects of incentives are likely to be particularly strong in the competition for FDI within regions (or even countries), when the initial investment decision has been taken and the investor is choosing between alternative locations in a given region (e.g., Coughlin et al. 1991; Grubert and Mutti 1991; Hines 1996; Neven and Siotis 1993; Swenson 1998). For instance, if a firm has two more or less similar location alternatives for its investment, incentives can tilt the investment decision. This is particularly the case for financial incentives like grants and other types of subsidies, since they reduce the initial costs of the investment and lower the risk of the FDI project.

Nevertheless, empirical research shows that international investment incentives play either a limited or marginal role in determining the international pattern of foreign direct investment (see e.g. Blomström et al. 2000; Blomstrom and Kokko 2002). Factors like market characteristics, relative production costs, and resource availability explain most of the cross-country variation in FDI inflows.

However, recent econometric studies on the effects of FDI incentives, in particular fiscal preferences, suggest that they have become more significant determinants of international direct investment flows (e.g., Taylor 2000). The main reason for the increasing prominence of FDI incentives is arguably the internationalization, globalization, and regionalization of the world economy making FDI incentives more interesting and important for national governments. The scope for active national trade and exchange rate policy has diminished most clearly for present and potential EU members, who are largely bound by decisions taken by the EU Commission and the European Central Bank and shifted attention to industrial policy, including measures such as investment incentives (Blomström et al. 2003). Relatedly, the views on the importance of incentives have begun to change in recent years as a result of the proliferation of international investment incentives across the world and intensifying global competition as well as increasing number of host governments providing various forms of investment incentives to encourage foreign-owned companies to invest in their jurisdiction (Blomström et al. 2003). As a result, the incentives provided by many countries have become more generous over the years, and decisions that would not have been influenced by a mere 2-year tax holiday may well be swayed by a 10-year holiday (Easson 2001). Most clearly, governments keep promoting the competitiveness and welfare and are likely to put more emphasis on those policy instruments remaining at their disposal, including FDI incentives. The fact that most others subsidize foreign investment is another important reason why more and more countries are drawn into the subsidy game. More specifically, more than 100 countries provided various FDI incentives already in the mid-1990s, and dozens more have introduced such incentives; since then, few countries compete for foreign investment without any form of subsidies today (UNCTAD 1996a, UNCTAD 1996b). Correspondingly, these incentives take a variety of forms including fiscal incentives such as lower taxes for foreign investors, financial incentives such as grants and preferential loans to MNCs, as well as other incentives like market preferences and monopoly rights. Thus, even a small country may now compete for FDI, given that it can provide a sufficiently attractive incentive package.

On one hand, it is hard to justify investment incentives focusing on foreign MNCs that do not differ fundamentally from local companies. On the other hand, Neven and Siotis (1993) provide arguments for investment subsidies in cases with imperfect labor markets, where the likelihood that unemployed workers find new jobs in the absence of FDI incentives is very low.

Moreover, competition among governments (national or local) to attract FDI may create problems (Oman 2000). When governments compete to attract FDI, there is a tendency to overbid and the subsidies may very well surpass the level of the spillover benefits, with welfare losses as a result (Blomström and Kokko 2003). These problems may be particularly severe if the incentives discriminate against local firms and cause losses of local market shares and employment. The most important argument against investment incentives focusing exclusively on foreign firms is that spillovers are not automatic, but depend crucially on the conditions for local firms (Herrmann and Lipsey 2003). Given their broad scope, the investment incentives in question should be considered part of the economy's innovation and growth policies rather than a policy area that is only of relevance for foreign investors. Consequently, aiming to increase the potential for investment incentives, spillovers may be inefficient unless they are complemented with measures to improve the local firms' capability and motivation to learn from foreign MNCs as well as to maintain a competitive local business environment, and to invest in new technology (Blomström and Kokko 2002). To motivate subsidization of foreign investment, it is therefore necessary, at the same time, to support learning and investment in local firms as well (Blomström and Kokko 2002). Thus, the investment incentive packages as part of the country's overall FDI policy should focus particularly on those activities creating the strongest potential for spillovers, including linkages between foreign and local firms, education, training, and R&D.

At the same time, there are good reasons to remain cautious in granting incentives focusing exclusively on foreign investors. We have seen that in the global media and ICT volatile market, it is not easy to determine where and how spillovers will occur, which creates problems of "picking winners, i.e., identifying firms that are likely to yield spillover benefits" (Herrmann and Lipsey 2003). It is also difficult to calculate the value of these externalities, which is important, since national welfare will increase only if the investment incentive is smaller than the value of the externality. If the subsidies are larger than what is motivated by the externalities, the host country will not only lose public revenue, but the incentives will also discriminate against local firms that may lose jobs and market shares. Some of the main problems in this context are related to tax holidays and tax breaks, which may appear to be simple and innocuous forms of incentives.

However, they are likely to lead to transfer pricing and other distortions as firms try to shift as many transactions as possible to the sector or activity with low or no taxes or set up new firms as the tax preferences of existing firms expire (McLure 1999). Another reason is that some of the perceived benefits (in particular, the jobs created by FDI) are easily observable while some of the costs (particularly related to tax breaks and other fiscal incentives) are distributed over long periods of time and hard to measure. Consequently, there is a tendency to overbid and the subsidies may very well surpass the level of spillover benefits, with welfare losses as a result (Herrmann and Lipsey 2003).

FDI spillovers are not automatic, but depend crucially on the conditions for local firms. The potential for spillovers is not likely to be realized unless local firms have the ability and motivation to learn from foreign MNCs as well as to maintain competitive local business environment and to invest in new technology. Moreover, the incentives should ideally not be of an ex ante type being granted and paid out prior to the investment, but should instead promote those activities creating a potential for spillovers (Herrmann and Lipsey 2003). In particular, these include education, training, and R&D activities, as well as linkages between foreign and local firms.

In this subchapter, the author argued that the use of investment incentives focusing exclusively on foreign firms, although motivated in some cases from a theoretical point of view (and in even more cases from political considerations), is generally not an efficient way to raise national welfare. On one hand, the main reason is that the strongest theoretical motive for financial subsidies to inward FDI spillovers of foreign technology and skills to local industry is not an automatic consequence of foreign investment. On the other hand, the potential spillover benefits are realized only if local firms have the ability and motivation to invest in absorbing foreign technologies and skills (Blomström and Kokko 2003). By enhancing the local supply of human capital and modern infrastructure and by improving other fundamentals for economic growth, a country does not only become a more attractive site for multinational firms, but there is increased likelihood that its private sector benefits from the foreign participation through spillover benefits.

In sum, investment incentives may be politically attractive in the short run, but costly in the long run; protectionism may also promote local employment and production in the short run at a high long run cost.

References

Addison, T., & Heshmati, A. (2003). The new global determinants of FDI flows to developing countries: The importance of ICT and democratization (No. 2003/45). WIDER Discussion Papers/World Institute for Development Economics (UNU-WIDER).

Agarwal, J. P. (1980). Determinants of foreign direct investment: A Survey. *Weltwirtschaftliches Archiv, 116*(4), 739–773.

Aitken, B. J., & Harrison, A. E. (1999). Do domestic firms benefit from direct foreign investment? Evidence from Venezuela. *American Economic Review, 89*(3), 605–618.

Aizenman, J., & Spiegel, M. M. (2002). *Institutional efficiency, monitoring costs, and the investment share of FDI* (NBER Working Paper No. 9324).

Ancharaz, V. D. (2000). *Trade liberalization and foreign direct investment in sub-Saharan Africa: A comparative perspective.* PhD dissertation, Brandeis University, USA.

Anderson, J. E., & van Wincoop, E. (2003). Gravity with gravitas: A solution to the border puzzle. *American Economic Review, 93*(1), 170–192.

Artige, L., & Nicolini, R. (2006). Evidence on the determinants of foreign direct investment. The case of three european regions (No. 0607). Centre de Recherche en Economie Publique et de la Population (CREPP) (Research Center on Public and Population Economics) HEC-Management School, University of Liège.

Asiedu, E. (2002). On the determinants of foreign direct investment to developing countries: Is Africa different? *World Development, 30,* 107–119.

Asiedu, E. (2005). *Foreign direct investment in Africa: The role of natural resources, market size, government policy, institutions and political instability* (Working paper). United Nations University.

Asiedu, E., & Villamil, A. (2000). Discount factors and thresholds: Foreign investment when enforcement is imperfect. *Macroeconomic Dynamics, 4*(1), 1–21.

A.T. Kearney. (2003, September). FDI confidence index. Global Business Policy Council. Vol. 6.

Aw, Y. T., & Tang, T. C. (2010). The determinants of inward foreign direct investment: The case of Malaysia. *International Journal of Business and Society, 11*(1), 59–76.

Barrell, R., & Pain, N. (1999). Domestic institutions, agglomeration and foreign direct investment in Europe. *European Economic Review, 43*, 925–934.

Bellak, C., & Leibrecht, M. (2009a). Improving infrastructure or lowering taxes to attract foreign direct investment? in Columbia FDI Perspectives on topical foreign direct investment issues, The Vale Columbia Center on Sustainable International Investment, No. 6, June 3.

Bellak, C., & Leibrecht, M. (2009b). Do low corporate income tax rates attract FDI?—Evidence from Central-and East European countries. *Applied Economics, 41*(21), 2691–2703.

Bellak, C., Leibrecht, M., & Liebensteiner, M. (2010a). Attracting foreign direct investment: The public policy scope for South East European countries. *Eastern Journal of European Studies, 1* (2), 37–53.

Bellak, C., Leibrecht, M., & Römisch, R. (2007). On the appropriate measure of tax burden on foreign direct investment to the CEECs. *Applied Economics Letters, 14*(8), 603–606.

Bellak, C., Leibrecht, M., & Stehrer, R. (2008). *The role of public policy in closing foreign direct investment gaps: An empirical analysis* (Working Paper No. 48). Vienna: The Vienna Institute for International Economic Studies.

Bellak, C., Leibrecht, M., & Stehrer, R. (2010b). The role of public policy in closing Foreign Direct Investment gaps: An empirical analysis. *Empirica, 37*(1), 19–46.

Bénassy-Quéré, A., Coupet, M., & Mayer, T. (2007a). Institutional determinants of foreign direct investment. *The World Economy, 30*(5), 764–782.

Bénassy-Quéré, A., Gobalraja, N., & Trannoy, A. (2007b). Tax and public input competition, *Economic Policy,* April, pp. 387–430.

Bergstrand, J. H., & Egger, P. (2007). A knowledge-and-physical-capital model of international trade flows, foreign direct investment, and multinational enterprises. *Journal of International Economics, 73*(2), 278–308.

Bevan, A., & Estrin, S. (2000). *The determinants of foreign direct investment in transition economies* (CEPR Discussion Paper No. 2638). London: Center for Economic Policy Research.

Bevan, A. A., & Estrin, S. (2004). The determinants of foreign direct investment into European transition economies. *Journal of comparative economics, 32*(4), 775–787.

Bevan, A., Estrin, S., & Grabbe, H. (2001). *The impact of EU accession prospects on FDI inflows to central and eastern Europe.* Sussex European Institute Policy Paper No. 06/01, UK: University of Sussex.

Bhavan, T., Xu, C., & Zhong, C. (2011). Determinants and growth effect of FDI in South Asian economies: Evidence from a panel data analysis. *International Business Research, 4*(1), 43–50

Billington, N. (1999). The location of foreign direct investment: An empirical analysis. *Applied Economics, 31*, 65–76.

Bitzenis, A. (2003). Universal model of theories determining FDI. Is there any dominant theory? Are the FDI inflows in the CEE countries and especially in Bulgaria a myth? *European Business Review, 15*(2), 94–104.

Blomström, M., & Kokko, A. (2002). *The economics of international investment incentives. International Investment Incentives, 165–183.* Research paper presented at the ECLAC/World Bank Seminar on Globalization, Santiago de Chile, 6–8 March, 2002.

Blomström, M., Kokko, A., & Mucchielli, J. L. (2003). *The economics of foreign direct investment incentives,* in Herrmann, H., & Lipsey, R. E. (2003). Foreign direct investment in the real and financial sector of industrial countries. (pp. 37–60). Berlin: Springer.

Blomström, M., Kokko, A., & Zejan, M. (2000). *Foreign direct investment. Firm and host country strategies.* London: Macmillan.

Blonigen, B. A. (1997). Firm specific assets and the link between exchange rate and foreign direct investment. *American Economic Review, 87*(3), 447–465.

Blonigen, B. A. (2005). A review of the empirical literature on FDI determinants. *Atlantic Economic Journal, 33*, 383–403.

Blonigen, B. A., & Davies, R. B. (2004). The effects of bilateral tax treaties on US FDI activity. *International Tax and Public Finance, 11*(5), 601–622.

Blonigen, B. A., Ellis, C. J., & Fausten, D. (2005). Industrial groupings and foreign direct investment. *Journal of International Economics, 65*(1), 75–91.

Blonigen, B. A., & Feenstra R. C. (1996). *Effects of U.S. Trade Protection and Promotion Policies* (NBER Working Paper No. 5285).

Blonigen, B. A., Tomlin, K., & Wilson, W. W. (2004). Tariff-jumping FDI and domestic firms' profits. *Canadian Journal of Economics/Revue canadienne d'économique, 37*(3), 656–677.

Botrić, V., & Škuflić, L. (2006). Main determinants of foreign direct investment in the southeast European countries. *Transition Studies Review, 13*(2), 359–377.

Braconier, H., & Ekholm, K. (2002). Competition for multinational activity in Europe: The role played by wages and market size. National Institute of Economic Research (Sweden), mimeo.

Brainard, S. L. (1997). An empirical assessment of the proximity-concentration trade-off between multinational sales and trade. *American Economic Review, 87*(4), 520–544.

Brenton, P., Di Mauro, F., & Luecke, M. (1999). Economic integration and FDI: An empirical analysis of foreign investment in the EU and in Central and Eastern Europe. *Empirica, 26,* 95–121.

Breuss, F., & Egger, P. (1999). How reliable are estimations of east-west trade potentials based on cross section gravity analysis? *Empirica, 26*(2), 81–94.

Bruno, L. R., & Campos, N. F. (2014). Foreign direct investment and economic performance: A systematic review of the evidence uncovers a new paradox. Unpublished mimeo.

Buch, C. M., & Lipponer, A. (2007). FDI versus exports: Evidence from German banks. *Journal of Banking & Finance, 31,* 805–826.

Buiter, W. H., Lago, R., & Rey, H. (1998, December). *Financing transition: Investing in enterprises during macroeconomic transition* (EBRD Working paper, No 35).

Campa, J. M. (1993). Entry by foreign firms in the U.S. under exchange rate uncertainty. *Review of Economics and Statistics, 75*(4), 614–622.

Campos, N. F., & Kinoshita Y. (2003). *Why does FDI go where it goes? New evidence from the transition economies* (IMF Working Paper 03/228). Washington, DC: International Monetary Fund.

Campos, J. E., Lien, D., & Pradhan, S. (1999). The impact of corruption on investment: Predictability matters. *World Development, 27*(6), 1059–1067.

Carstensen, K., & Toubal, F. (2004). Foreign direct investment in Central and Eastern European countries: A dynamic panel analysis. *Journal of Comparative Economics, 32*(1), 3–22.

Chakrabarti, A. (2001). The determinants of foreign direct investment: Sensitivity analysis of cross-country regressions. *Kyklos, 54,* 89–114.

Chang, S. J., & Xu, D. (2008). Spillovers and competition among foreign and local firms in China. *Strategic Management Journal, 29*(5), 495–518.

Choong, C. K., & Lim, K. P. (2007). Foreign direct investment in Malaysia: An economic analysis. *The IUP Journal of Applied Economics, 6*(1), 74–85.

Christie, E. (2002). Potential trade in South-East Europe: A gravity model approach. *SEER-South-East Europe Review for Labour and Social Affairs,* (04), 81–101.

Christie, E. (2003). *Foreign direct investment in Southeast Europe* (Working Paper No. 24). Vienna Institute for International Economic Studies.

Chuang, Y.-C., & Lin, C.-M. (1999). FDI, R&D and spillover efficiency: Evidence from Taiwan's manufacturing firms. *Journal of Development Studies, 35*(4), 117–137.

Claessens, S., Oks, D., & Polastri, R. (1998). *Capital flows to Central and Eastern Europe and the Former Soviet Union* (World Bank Policy Research Working Paper No. 1976). Washington, DC: World Bank.

Clausing, K. A., & Dorobantu, C. L. (2005). Re-entering Europe: Does European Union candidacy boost foreign direct investment? *Economics of Transition, 13*(1), 77–103.

Coughlin, C. C., Terza, J. V., & Arromdee, V. (1991). State characteristics and location of foreign direct investment within the United States. *Review of Economics and Statistics, 73*(4), 675–683.

Cuervo-Cazurra, A. (2006). Who cares about corruption? *Journal of International Business Studies, 37*(6), 807–822.

Culem, C. G. (1988). The locational determinants of direct investments among industrialized countries. *European Economic Review, 32*, 885–904.

Cushman, D. O. (1985). Real exchange rate risk, expectations, and the level of direct investment. *Review of Economics and Statistics, 67*(2), 297–308.

Damijan, J. P., Knell, M., Majcen, B., & Rojec, M. (2003). The role of FDI, R&D accumulation and trade in transferring technology to transition countries: Evidence from firm panel data for eight transition countries. *Economic Systems, 27*, 189–204.

Dehejia, V. H., & Weichenrieder, A. J. (2001). Tariff jumping foreign investment and capital taxation. *Journal of International Economics, 53*(1), 223–230.

Demekas, D. G., Balász, H., Ribakova, E., & Wu, Y. (2007). Foreign direct investment in European transition economies—The role of policies. *Journal of Comparative Economics, 35*(2), 369–386.

Demekas, D. G., Horváth, B., Ribakova, E., & Wu, Y. (2005). *Foreign direct investment in Southeastern Europe: How (and how much) can policies help?* (IMF Working Paper, WP/05/110).

Dencik, J., & Spee, R. (2012). *Global location trends-2013 annual report*. New York: IBM Institute.

Derado, D. (2013). Determinants of FDI in transition countries and estimation of the potential level of Croatian FDI. *Financial Theory and Practice, 37*(3), 227–258.

Desai, M. A., Foley, C. F., & Forbes, K. J. (2008). Financial constraints and growth: Multinational and local firm responses to currency crises. *Review of Financial Studies, 21*(6), 2857–2888.

Desai, M. A., Foley, F. C., & Hines, J. R., Jr. (2004). Foreign direct investment in a world of multiple taxes. *Journal of Public Economics, 88*(12), 2727–2744.

Devereux, M. P. (2006). *The impact of taxation on the location of capital, firms and profit: A survey of empirical evidence* (Working Paper from Oxford University Centre for Business Taxation No. 702).

Devereux, M. P., & Griffith, R. (1998). Taxes and the location of production: Evidence from a panel of US multinationals. *Journal of Public Economics, 68*(3), 335–367.

Devereux, M. P., & Griffith, R. (1999). *The taxation of discrete investment choices* (IFS Working Paper No. W98/16).

Di Mauro, F. (2000). *The impact of economic integration on FDI and exports: A gravity approach*. Brussels: Centre for European Policy Studies.

Dixit, A. (2009). Governance, institutions and economic activity. *American Economic Review, 99* (1), 5–24.

Driffield, N., & Taylor, K. (2000). FDI and the labour market: A review of the evidence and policy implications. *Oxford Review of Economic Policy, 16*(3), 90–103.

Dunning, J. H. (1993). *Multinational enterprises and the global economy*. Reading, MA: Addison-Wesley.

Dunning, J. H. (1999). *Globalization and the theory of MNE activity* (Discussion Papers in International Investment and Management 264). University of Reading.

Dunning, J. H. (2004). *Institutional reform, FDI and European transition economies* (Economics and Management Discussion Papers No. 2004-14). Reading: Henley Business School.

Dupasquier, C., & Osajwe, P. N. (2006). Foreign direct investment in Africa: Performance, challenges, and responsibilities. *Journal of Asian Economics, 17*(2), 241–260.

Easson, A. (2001). Tax incentives for foreign direct investment part 1: Recent trends and countertrends. *Bulletin for International Fiscal Documentation, 55*, 266–274.

Eicher, S. E. (2002). *Determinants of international capital flows: The saving-retention phenomenon and factors prompting foreign direct investment*. PhD dissertation, Kansas State University, Manhattan.

Ekholm, K., Forslid, R., & Markusen, J. R. (2007). Export-platform foreign direct investment. *Journal of the European Economic Association, 5*(4), 776–795.

Estrin, S., Hughes, K., & Todd, S. (1997). *Foreign direct investment in Central and Eastern Europe*. London: Cassel.

Estrin, S., & Uvalic, M. (2013). *Foreign direct investment into transition economies: Are the Balkans different?* (LEQS Paper, 64).

Estrin, S., & Uvalic, M. (2014). FDI into transition economies. *Economics of Transition, 22*, 281–312.

Feenstra, R. C., & Hanson, G. H. (1997). Foreign direct investment and relative wages: Evidence from Mexico's maquiladoras. *Journal of International Economics, 42*, 371–393.

Feenstra, R. C., Markusen, J. R., & Rose, A. K. (2001). Using the gravity equation to differentiate among alternative theories of trade. *Canadian Journal of Economics, 34*(2), 430–447.

Feld, L. P., & Heckemeyer, J. H. (2011). FDI and taxation: A meta-study. *Journal of Economic Surveys, 25*(2), 233–272.

Froot, K. A., & Stein, J. C. (1991). Exchange rates and foreign direct investment. An imperfect capital markets approach. *Quarterly Journal of Economics, 106*(4), 1191–1217.

Gastanaga, V., Nugent, J., & Pashamiova, B. (1998). Host country reforms and FDI inflows: How much difference do they make? *World Development, 26*(7), 1299–1314.

Glass, A. J., & Saggi, K. (2002). Multinational firms and technology transfer. *Scandinavian Journal of Economics, 104*(4), 495–513.

Goldberg, I. (2008). Globalization and technology absorption in Europe and Central Asia: The role of trade, FDI, and cross-border knowledge flows (No. 150). World Bank.

Goldberg, L. S., & Kolstad, C. D. (1995). Foreign direct investment, exchange rate variability and demand uncertainty. *International Economic Review, 36*(4), 855–873.

Goodspeed, T., Martinez-Vazquez, J., & Zhang, L. (2009). Public policies and FDI location: differences between developing and developed countries. International Studies Program Working Paper Series, GSU paper 0910, Andrew Young School of Policy Studies, Georgia State University.

Gordon, R. H., & Hines, J. R. (2002). International taxation. *Handbook of Public Economics, 4*, 1935–1995.

Gramlich, E. M. (1994). Infrastructure investment: A review essay. *Journal of Economic Literature, 32*(3), 1176–1196.

Grubert, H., & Mutti, J. (1991). Taxes, tariffs and transfer pricing in multinational corporate decision making. *Review of Economics and Statistics, 73*(2), 285–293.

Hailu, Z. A. (2010). Impact of foreign direct investment on trade of African countries. *International Journal of Economics and Finance, 2*, 122–133.

Hallward-Dreimeier, M. (2003). *Do bilateral investment treaties attract foreign direct investment? Only a bit ... and they could bite* (World Bank Working Paper, No. 3121).

Hanson, G., Mataloni, R., & Slaughter, M. (2001). *Expansion strategies of the U.S. multinational firms* (NBER Working Paper No. 8433). Cambridge, MA: National Bureau of Economic Research.

Hartman, D. G. (1984). Tax policy and foreign direct investment in the United States. *National Tax Journal, 37*(4), 475–487.

Haskel, J. E., Pereira, S. C., & Slaughter, M. J. (2002). *Does inward foreign direct investment boost the productivity of domestic firms?* (NBER Working Paper 8724). Cambridge, MA: National Bureau of Economic Research.

Hassett, K. A., & Hubbard, R. G. (1997). Tax policy and investment. In A. Shah (Ed.), *Fiscal policy: Lessons from economic research*. Cambridge, MA: MIT Press.

Helpman, E. (1984). A simple theory of international trade with multinational corporations. *Journal of Political Economy, 92*(3), 451–471.

Henisz, W. J. (2000). The institutional environment for multinational investment. *Journal of Law, Economics and Organization, 16*, 334–364.

Herrmann, H., & Lipsey, R. E. (2003). *Foreign direct investment in the real and financial sector of industrial countries*. Berlin: Springer.

Hines, J. R., Jr. (1995a). Altered states: Taxes and the location of foreign direct investment in America. *American Economic Review, 86*(5), 1076–1094.

Hines, J. R., Jr. (1995b). *Forbidden payment: Foreign bribery and American business after 1977* (NBER Working Paper No. 5266).

Hines, J. R., Jr. (1996). Altered states: Taxes and the location of foreign direct investment in America. *American Economic Review, 86*, 1076–1094.

Hines, J. R., Jr. (1999). Lessons from behavioral responses to international taxation. *National Tax Journal, 52*, 305–322.

Holland, D., & Pain, N. (1998). *The diffusion of innovations in Central and Eastern Europe: A study of the determinants and impact of foreign direct investment* (NIESR Discussion Paper No. 137). London: National Institute of Social and Economic Research.

Hwang, H., & Mai, C. C. (2002). The tariff-jumping argument and location theory. *Review of International Economics, 10*(2), 361–368.

Inglehart, R. F., Borinskaya, S., Cotter, A., Harro, J., Inglehart, R. C., Ponarin, E., & Welzel, C. (2014). Genetic factors, cultural predispositions, happiness and gender equality. *Journal of Research in Gender Studies, 4*, 32–100.

Ismail, R., & Yussof, I. (2003). Labour market competitiveness and foreign direct investment: The case of Malaysia. Thailand and the Philippines. *Papers in Regional Science, 82*, 389–402.

Jackson, S., & Markowski, S. (1995). The attractiveness of foreign direct investment-implications for the Asia-Pacific region. *Journal of World Trade, 29*(5), 159–180.

Jadhav, P. (2012). Determinants of foreign direct investment in BRICS economies: Analysis of economic, institutional and political factor. *Procedia-Social and Behavioral Sciences, 37*, 5–14.

Jaffe, A. B., Trajtenberg, M., & Henderson, R. (1993). Geographic localization of knowledge spillovers as evidenced by patent citations. *Quarterly Journal of Economics, 108*(3), 577–598.

Janicki, H. P., & Wunnava, P. V. (2004). Determinants of foreign direct investment: Empirical evidence from EU accession candidates. *Applied Economics, 36*(5), 505–509.

Jimborean, R., & Kelber, A. (2014). *Foreign direct investment drivers and growth in Central and Eastern Europe in the aftermath of the 2007 global financial crisis* (Working Paper 488). Paris: Banque de France.

Jun, K. W., & Singh, H. (1996). The determinants of foreign direct investment in developing countries. *Transnational Corporations, 5*(2), 67–105.

Kathuria, V. (2000). Productivity spillovers from technology transfer to indian manufacturing firms. *Journal of International Development, 12*(3), 343–369.

Keller, W. (2002). Geographic localization of international technology diffusion. *American Economic Review, 92*(1), 120–142.

King, M. A., & Fullerton, D. (1984). *The taxation of income from capital.* Chicago: University of Chicago Press.

Kinoshita, Y., & Mody, A. (1999). *Private and public information for foreign investment decisions* (CERGE-EI Working Paper Series (150)).

Klein, M. W., & Rosengren, E. S. (1994). The real exchange rate and foreign direct investment in the United States: Relative wealth vs. relative wage effects. *Journal of International Economics, 36*(3–4), 373–389.

Kogut, B., & Chang, S. J. (1996). Platform investments and volatile exchange rates: Direct investment in the U.S. by Japanese electronic companies. *Review of Economics and Statistics, 78*(2), 221–231.

Kokko, A. (1994). Technology, market characteristics, and spillovers. *Journal of Development Economics, 43*(2), 279–293.

Kokko, A. (1996). Productivity spillovers from competition between local firms and foreign affiliates. *Journal of International Development, 8*(4), 517–530.

Kornecki, L., & Raghavan, V. (2011). Inward FDI stock and growth in Central and Eastern Europe. *Review of Economics & Finance, 1*, 19–30.

Kravis, I. B., & Lipsey, R. E. (1982). The location of overseas production and production for export by U.S. multinational firms. *Journal of International Economics, 12*, 201–223.

Lankes, H. P., & Venables, A. J. (1996). Foreign direct investment in economic transition: The changing pattern of investments. *Economics of Transition, 4*(2), 331–347.

Leibrecht, M., & Riedl, A. (2010). *Taxes and infrastructure as determinants of foreign direct investment in Central and Eastern European countries revisited: New evidence from a spatially augmented gravity model* (Discussion papers SFB international tax coordination, 42). Vienna: WU Vienna University of Economics and Business.

Leitão, N. C. (2010). Foreign direct investment: The Canadian experience. *International Journal of Economics and Finance, 2*(4), 82.

Leitão, N. C., & Faustino, H. C. (2010). Determinants of foreign direct investment in Portugal. *Journal of Applied Business and Economics, 11*(3), 19–26.

Li, Q. (2008). Foreign direct investment and interstate military conflict. *Journal of International Affairs, 62*(1), 53–66.

Liebscher, K., Christl, J., Mooslechner, P., & Ritzberger-Grünwald, D. (2005). *European economic integration and South-East Europe: Challenges and prospects*. Cheltenham, UK: Edward Elgar.

Lim, E. G. (2001). *Determinants of, and the relation between, foreign direct investment and growth: A summary of the recent literature* (IMF Working Paper 01/175). Washington, DC: International Monetary Fund.

Lipsey, R. E. (2004). Home and host-country effects of foreign direct investment. In R. E. Baldwin & L. A. Winters (Eds.), *Challenges to globalization*. Chicago: University of Chicago Press.

Lipsey, R. E., & Sjoholm, F. (2005). The impact of inward FDI on host countries: Why such different answers. In T. H. Moran, E. M. Graham, & M. Blomström (Eds.), *Does foreign direct investment promote development*. Washington, DC: Institute for International Economics.

Lucas, R. (1993). On the determinants of direct investment: Evidence from East and South Asia. *World Development, 21*, 391–406.

Lunn, J. (1980). Determinants of U.S. direct investment in the E.E.C: Further evidence. *European Economic Review, 13*, 93–101.

Madiès, T., & Dethier, J. J. (2010). *Fiscal competition in developing countries: A survey of the theoretical and empirical literature*. World Bank Policy Research Working Paper Series.

Markusen, R. M., & Maskus, K. E. (1999). *Discriminating among alternative theories of the multinational enterprise* (NBER Working Paper No. 7164). Cambridge, MA: National Bureau of Economic Research.

Markusen, J. R., & Maskus, K. E. (2002). Discriminating among alternative theories of the multinational enterprise. *Review of International Economics, 10*(4), 694–707.

Markusen, J. R., & Venables, A. J. (1998). Multinational firms and the new trade theory. *Journal of International Economics, 46*(2), 183–203.

McLure, C. E. (1999). Tax holidays and investment incentives; A comparative analysis. *Bulletin for International Fiscal Documentation, 53*, 326–339.

Mohamed, S. E., & Sidiropoulos, M. G. (2010). Another look at the determinants of foreign direct investment in MENA countries: An empirical investigation. *Journal of Economic Development, 35*(2), 75–95.

Moosa, I. A. (2002). *FDI: Theory, evidence and practice*. New York: Palgrave.

Morgan, R. E., & Katsikeas, C. S. (1997). Theories of international trade, foreign direct investment and firm internationalization: A critique. *Management Decision, 35*(1), 68–78.

Navaretti, G. B., & Venables, A. J. (2004). *Multinational firms in the world economy*. Princeton, NJ: Princeton University Press.

Neven, D., & Siotis, G. (1993). Foreign direct investment in the European community: Some policy issues. *Oxford Review of Economic Policy, 20*, 72–93.

Nica, E. (2014). The development of transformational leadership. *Journal of Self-Governance and Management Economics, 2*, 26–31.

Noorbakhsh, F., Paloni, A., & Youssef, A. (2001). Human capital and FDI inflows to developing countries: New empirical evidence. *World Development, 29*(9), 1593–1610.

Nunnenkamp, P. (2002). *Determinants of FDI in developing countries: Has globalization changed the rules of the game?* (No. 1122). Kieler Arbeitspapiere.

OECD. (2003). *International investment perspectives*. Paris: Organization for Economic Cooperation and Development (OECD).

Oman, C. (2000). *Policy competition for foreign direct investment: A study of competition among governments to attract FDI*. Paris: OECD.

Peri, G. (2004). *Catching-up to foreign technology? Evidence on the "Veblen-Gerschenkron" effect of foreign investments* (No. w10893). National Bureau of Economic Research.

Popescu, G. H. (2014). FDI and economic growth in Central and Eastern Europe. *Sustainability, 6* (11), 8149–8163.

Razin, A., Yuen, C. W., & Sadka, E. (1998). *Capital flows with debt-and equity-financed investment-equilibrium structure and efficiency implications* (No. 98-159). International Monetary Fund.

Resmini, L. (2000). The determinants of foreign direct investment in the CEECs: New evidence from sectoral patterns. *Economics of Transition, 8*(3), 665–689.

Ricupero, R. (2000). *Tax incentives and foreign direct investment*. In United Nations Conference on Trade and Development, Geneva Advisory Studies (No. 16).

Sánchez-Martín, M. E., de Arce, R., & Escribano, G. (2014). Do changes in the rules of the game affect FDI flows in Latin America? A look at the macroeconomic, institutional and regional integration determinants of FDI. *European Journal of Political Economy, 34*, 279–299.

Schneider, F., & Frey, B. (1985). Economic and political determinants of foreign direct investment. *World Development, 13*, 161–175.

Schneider, K.H., & Matei, I. (2010). Business climate, political risk and FDI in developing countries: Evidence from panel data. *International Journal of Economics and Finance, 2*(5).

Shamsuddin, A. F. (1994). Economic determinants of foreign direct investment in less developed countries. *The Pakistan Development Review, 33*, 41–51.

Shatz, H. J., & Venables, A. (2000). *The geography of international investment* (Vol. 2338). Washington, DC: World Bank.

Singh, H., & Jun, K. (1996). The determinants of foreign direct investment in developing countries. *Transnational Corporations, 5*(2), 67–105.

Sjoholm, F. (1999). Technology gap, competition and spillovers from direct foreign investment: Evidence from establishment data. *Journal of Development Studies, 36*(1), 53–73.

Smarzynska, B. K., & Wei, S.-J. (2002). *Corruption and cross-border investment: Firm-level evidence* (William Davidson Institute Working Paper No. 494), pp. 1–29.

Suder, K. J., & Sohn, C. H. (2010). FDI in Central and Eastern European countries: Impact to neighbors and regional agglomeration effect. [Online] available at http://www.apeaweb.org/confer/bus11/papers/Sohn-Suder.pdf. Accessed 1 Feb 2013.

Swenson, D. L. (1994). The impact of U.S. tax reform on foreign direct investment in the United States. *Journal of Public Economics, 54*(2), 243–266.

Swenson, D. L. (1998). The effect of US state tax and investment promotion policy on the distribution of inward direct investment. In R. E. Baldwin, R. E. Lipsey, & D. Richardson (Eds.), *Geography and ownership as bases for economic accounting* (pp. 285–314). Chicago: University of Chicago Press.

Takii, S. (2001). *Productivity spillovers and characteristics of foreign multinational plants in Indonesian manufacturing 1990-1995* (INSEAD Working Paper 2001-14). Kitakyushu, Japan: ICSEAD.

Tashevska, B., & Trpkova, M. (2011). Determinants of economic growth in South-East Europe: A panel data approach. *Perspectives of Innovations, Economics and Business, PIEB, 1*(7), 12–15.

Taylor, C. T. (2000). The impact of host country government policy on US multinational investment decisions. *World Economy, 23*, 635–648.

Te Velde, D. W., & Bezemer, D. (2006). Regional integration and foreign direct investment in developing countries. *Transnational Corporations, 15*, 41–70.

Tintin, C. (2013). The determinants of foreign direct investment inflows in the Central and Eastern European countries: The importance of institutions. *Communist and Post-Communist Studies, 46*(2), 287–298.

Todo, Y., & Miyamoto, K. (2002). *Knowledge diffusion from multinational enterprises: The Role of domestic and foreign knowledge-enhancing activities* (OECD Technical Paper 196). Paris: OECD Development Centre.

Todorova, G., & Durisin, B. (2007). Absorptive capacity: Valuing a reconceptualization. *Academy of Management Review, 32*(3), 774–786.

Trevino, L. J., Daniels, J. D., & Arbelaez, H. (2002). Market reform and FDI in Latin America: An empirical investigation. *Transnational Corporations, 11*(1), 29–48.

Tsai, P. L. (1994). Determinants of foreign direct investment and its impact on economic growth. *Journal of Economic Development, 19*(1), 137–163.

Tytell, I., & Yudaeva, K. (2006). *The role of FDI in Eastern Europe and new independent states: New channels for the spillover effect* (Development Studies Working Paper No. 217). Centro Studi Luca d'Agliano.

UNCTAD. (1996a). *World investment report 1996*. New York: United Nations.

UNCTAD. (1996b). *Incentives and foreign direct investment. Current studies, series A, no. 30.* New York: United Nations.

Vernon, R. (1966). International investment and international trade in the product cycle. *Quarterly Journal of Economics, 80*, 190–207.

Vijayakumar, N., Perumal, S., & Rao, K. C. (2010). Determinants of FDI in BRICS countries: A panel analysis. *International Journal of Business Science and Applied Management, 5*(3), 1–13.

Walsh, J. P., & Yu, J. (2010). *Determinants of foreign direct investment: A sectoral and institutional approach* (IMF Working Papers). pp 1–27.

Wang, J.-Y., & Blomström, M. (1992). Foreign investment and technology transfer: A simple model. *European Economic Review, 36*(1), 137–155.

Wei, S. J. (2000). How taxing is corruption on international investors? *Review of Economics and Statistics, 82*(1), 1–11.

Wheeler, D., & Mody, A. (1992). International investment location decisions. *Journal of International Economics, 33*, 57–76.

Wilhelms, S. K. S., & Witter, M. S. D. (1998). Foreign direct investment and its determinants in emerging economies. United States Agency for International Development, Bureau for Africa, Office of Sustainable Development.

Yeaple, S. R. (2003). The role of skill endowments in the structure of U.S. outward foreign direct investment. *The Review of Economics and Statistics, 85*(3), 726–734.

Chapter 7
A Multidimensional Codifying of FDI Technological and Productivity Spillover Absorption Capacity and Threshold Effects

7.1 Brief Literature Review

The earliest discussions of spillovers in the literature on foreign direct investment date back to the 1960s (Blomström et al. 2003). The first author to systematically include spillovers (or external effects) among the possible consequences of FDI was MacDougall (1960), who analyzed the general welfare effects of foreign investment. Other early contributions were provided by Corden (1967), who looked at the effects of FDI on optimum tariff policy, and Caves (1971), who examined the industrial pattern and welfare effects of FDI.

7.2 The Importance, Benefits, and Advantages of Technological and Productivity Spillover

Understanding the channels and moderating factors of firms' adoption of foreign technology has important policy implications, as a clearer understanding of the exact mechanisms of learning via foreign investment will allow policymakers to better target appropriate forms of FDI. Multinational media corporations investing in foreign developing countries are believed to possess advantages enabling them to compete with better informed domestic firms. These advantages include intangible productive assets, such as technology know-how, management skills, reputation, etc.

© Springer International Publishing Switzerland 2016
Z. Vukanović, *Foreign Direct Investment Inflows Into the South East European Media Market*, Media Business and Innovation, DOI 10.1007/978-3-319-30512-7_7

7.3   The Analysis of Positive and Negative Impacts of Technological and Productivity Spillover

Spillovers from Foreign Direct Investment Multinational corporations (MNCs) produce, control, and own most of the world's technology, and they are responsible for almost 80 % of all private R&D expenditures worldwide (Dunning 1992). By encouraging MNCs to invest, developing countries hope to generate technology spillovers because FDI transfers intangible assets to the affiliate, which may then diffuse to local firms (Blomström and Kokko 1996). Kogut and Zander (1993) suggest that the more tacit or complex the technology, the more likely it is to be transferred to a wholly owned subsidiary. Studies employing cross-section data at the industry or firm level often discover positive spillovers to domestic firms, e.g., Caves (1974), Globerman (1979), Blomström and Persson (1983), Blomström and Wolf (1994), Kokko (1994), and Chuang and Lin (1999). Most studies employing firm-level panel data find no or negative evidence of spillovers to domestic firms, e.g., Haddad and Harrison (1993) and Aitken and Harrison (1999). The different results in the literature concerning the existence and the direction of spillovers from FDI are due to using aggregate versus firm-level data, to cross-section versus panel data analysis, and to different measures of spillovers at the industry level (Görg and Strobl 2001).

On the other hand, absorptive capacity of domestic firms plays a crucial role in reaping the benefits of FDI. In a dynamic industry environment characterized with rapid technology changes, higher FDI absorptive capacity is believed to lead to better adaptation to changing technology environment and exploitation of the opportunities (Zahra and George 2002; Todorova and Durisin 2007). Increased competition can push domestic firms to improve efficiency and increase their total factor productivity (TFP). This effect can also be considered a spillover.

In addition, a study by Kokko (1994, 1996) suggests that the economy and firm-level capacity to absorb technology is an important determinant of the spillover effect. This result is confirmed by Takii (2005) and Todo and Miyamoto (2002), who show that positive FDI spillovers are more pronounced in the case of firms that conduct their own R&D. In addition, Blalock and Gertler (2002) show that companies with more educated workforce derive greater benefits from foreign presence. In the case of developed countries, which are supposed to have enough absorptive capacity, Urban and Peri (2004) find evidence of the Veblen–Gerschenkron effect, according to which spillovers depend on the technological gap between foreign and domestic firms.

Moreover, the very presence of foreign-owned firms in an economy increases competition in the domestic market. The competitive pressure may spur local firms to operate more efficiently and introduce new technologies earlier than would otherwise have been the case. Because foreign firms are not able to extract the full value of these gains, this effect is commonly referred to as the spillover effect (Kokko 1994). The spillover effect has been identified as an important benefit accruing to domestic firms. It is also considered an important mechanism through which FDI promotes growth in a host country.

In this context, Wang and Blomström (1992) and Glass and Saggi (2002) argue that the entrance of foreign firms increases competition with host country and forces inefficient indigenous firms to use existing technology more efficiently or to look for new technology for survival. By upgrading intangible assets or investing in new machinery and equipment, domestic firms also increase their absorptive capacity. Wang and Blomström (1992) argue that competition reduces the technology gap between domestic and foreign firms, forcing foreign firms to transfer more technology to the host country.

Several recent studies point out that positive productivity spillovers are more likely to happen between vertically linked industries, rather than within the same industry sector. This is because multinational firms have an incentive to prevent knowledge leakage to competitors, but may transfer technology to local suppliers to get higher quality inputs at lower prices (Javorcik 2004; Blalock and Gertler 2002). Correspondingly, local firms could also improve efficiency for the same reasons when dealing with multinational suppliers. Javorcik (2004) finds positive spillovers from foreign-invested joint ventures to domestic firms in Lithuania in upstream industries, but not in horizontal or downstream industries. Foreign direct investment in the downstream sectors produces negative effects on the productivity for the whole sample and for domestic sectors, contrary to previous research that has found positive spillovers from foreign customers. Javorcik (2004) suggests that joint ventures are more likely than wholly owned foreign subsidiaries to source locally and thus transfer technology to local suppliers. Moreover, geographic distance does not have a significant effect on learning from multinationals. Zukowska-Gagelmann (2000) argues that as far as spillovers from foreign-owned to domestic firms are concerned, the direction of such spillovers depends on the size of domestic firms. Small firms, with less than 200 employees, are negatively affected by the entry of foreign firms. Total factor productivity of such domestic firms goes down with an increase in the share of foreign-owned firms in the total production of the industry. In contrast, foreign direct investments seem to have positive influence on domestic firms with 200–1000 employees.

Importantly, both knowledge spillovers and productivity spillover effects occur predominantly in the more educated and the low corrupted regions. As a result, FDI oriented firms are usually more productive than domestic firms. This prediction is supported by virtually all empirical studies conducted for both developing and developed countries (Lipsey 2004; Lipsey and Sjöholm 2005). Empirical studies also show that multinational companies usually pay higher wages than domestic ones (Aizenman and Spiegel 2002). FDI Technological and Productivity Spillover Absorption capacity/effects increase with the incremental and exponential technological development.

Moreover, it has recently been argued in the literature (see Moran 2005) that export-oriented foreign firms are better equipped to generate stronger positive spillovers for domestic firms than those attracted to protected domestic markets. The reason is that to be competitive in the international market, export-oriented foreign companies have to use advance/cutting-edge production technologies, while those aiming to supply protected domestic markets tend to use knocked-down and second-rate production processes.

Moreover, as more foreign capital flows in, foreign firms may become more inclined to introduce more advanced technologies (Tytell and Yudaeva 2006). This may happen for a number of reasons. Foreign firms may become more familiar with local conditions and, therefore, more confident in bringing in more advanced technologies. Competition among foreign firms themselves may create additional incentives to use the most recent technologies. They may also become more familiar with local producers and trust them with production of more sophisticated components. If this is the case, one would expect to see more positive spillovers in these countries.

Although some FDI promotion efforts are probably motivated by temporary macroeconomic problems such as low growth rates and rising unemployment, there are also more fundamental explanations for the increasing emphasis on investment promotion in recent years. Trade liberalization be it globally, through GATT and WTO, or regionally in the form of EU, NAFTA, AFTA, and other regional agreements has led to increasing market integration and reduced the importance of market size as a determinant of investment location (Blomström et al. 2003).

At the same time, national decision-makers have lost many of the instruments traditionally used to promote local competitiveness, employment, and welfare (Kokko 2003). The scope for active trade policy has diminished as a result of successful trade liberalization, and the internationalization of capital markets has limited the possibilities to use exchange rate policy as a tool to influence relative competitiveness (Blomström et al. 2003).

Kokko (1994), for example, argues that spillovers should not be expected in all kinds of industries. In particular, foreign MNCs may sometimes operate in enclaves, where neither products nor technologies have much in common with those of local firms. In such circumstances, there may be little scope for learning, and spillovers may not materialize. Conversely, when foreign affiliates and local firms are in more direct competition with each other, spillovers are more likely (Blomström et al. 2003; Sjöholm 1999).

Alongside, the results of Blomström et al.'s (1994) comprehensive cross-country study of 101 economies suggest that spillovers are concentrated in middle-income developing countries, while there was no evidence of such effects for the poorest developing countries. Thus, FDI is a "rich country good" and only the most advanced developing countries are able to benefit from FDI (Balasubramanyam 1998).

It seems clear from these studies that host country and host industry character-istics determine the impact of FDI and that systematic differences between coun-tries and industries should therefore be expected. There is strong evidence pointing to the potential for significant spillover benefits from FDI, but also ample evidence indicating that spillovers do not occur automatically (Blomström et al. 2003). The strongest substantial arguments in favor of public support to FDI alongside with the globalization are the increase of local employment, growth rates in cyclical down-turns, and knowledge spillovers.

A reasonable conclusion from the mixed findings of earlier studies is that the ability and motivation of local firms to engage in investment and learning to absorb foreign knowledge and skills is an important determinant of whether or not the potential spillovers will be realized.

Additionally, productivity of domestic firms tends to grow where firms with FDI are more productive (Liebscher et al. 2007). Accordingly, the author argues that effects of foreign presence may change as foreign capital accumulates. Namely, foreign firms may initially focus on labor-intensive activities in order to benefit from low labor costs in the host countries, but shift to more advanced technologies as their weight and experience in the area grows (Liebscher et al. 2007). In turn, they may also be unwilling initially to outsource high-technology jobs to local producers, but as they invest more in their relationship with domestic firms, they may trust the locals with production of more sophisticated components (Tytell and Yudaeva 2006). Importantly, it takes not only large foreign presence but also a longer period to see any positive spillover effect. Most transition economies of the South East Europe are middle-income countries known for their high level of education. Therefore, one can imagine that they have a sufficiently good capacity to absorb knowledge spillovers. However, they lack the practical and advanced technological skills as compared to developed countries.

In this context, FDI technological and productivity spillover and threshold effects primarily depend on

1. The way FDI production functions stimulate domestic companies' technological upgrade
2. The superiority of companies' FDI technologies.

Based on Chap. 8's major empirical evidence, finding, and analysis of the multiple-case studies of 16 SEECs media markets, the author confirms that in the more developed countries with better institutions and larger FDI inflows (Malta, Slovenia), foreign presence is associated with higher capital intensity and lower labor intensity of domestic firms. Even though foreign entry causes capital–labor ratios to decline initially, further accumulation of foreign capital tends to stimulate production function change by domestic firms toward more capital-intensive functions. This threshold effect may reflect better technologies brought in by foreign firms once they become established in the host country, as well as their increased willingness to outsource more sophisticated parts to local producers.

In this context, absorptive capacity of domestic firms is also important: the evidence of the production function change toward more capital-intensive technologies is strongest in areas where the labor force is more educated. In contrast, in the countries with worse institutions and correspondingly smaller FDI inflows (Albania, Moldova), foreign presence is associated with lower capital intensity and higher labor intensity of domestic firms. Importantly, in highly corrupt regions, foreign firms do not exhibit any productivity advantage over domestic firms, possibly as a result of the attitude of local authorities, which in turn is lobbied for by domestic producers.

To summarize, the author finds strong evidence showing that productivity and capital intensity of domestic firms are higher where foreign firms are more productive, holding their density constant in regions with more educated populations. Thus, the absorptive capacity, as proxied by education, is clearly important for reaping benefits from FDI.

References

Aitken, B. J., & Harrison, A. E. (1999). Do domestic firms benefit from direct foreign investment? Evidence from Venezuela. *American Economic Review, 89*, 605–618.

Aizenman, J., & Spiegel, M. M. (2002). *Institutional efficiency, monitoring costs and the investment share of FDI* (NBER Working paper No. 9324).

Balasubramanyam, V. N. (1998). *The MAI and foreign direct investment in developing countries* (Discussion Paper EC10/98). Lancaster University.

Blalock, G., & Gertler, P. (2002). *Technology diffusion from foreign direct investment through supply chain* (Working paper). Haas School of Business, UC Berkeley.

Blomström, M., & Kokko, A. (1996). Multinational corporations and spillovers. *Journal of Economic Surveys, 12*(2), 1–31.

Blomström, M., Kokko, A., & Mucchielli, J. L. (2003). *The economics of foreign direct investment incentives* (pp. 37–60). Berlin: Springer.

Blomström, M., Kokko, A., & Zejan, M. (1994). Host country competition and technology transfer by multinationals. *Weltwirtschaftliches Archiv, 130*, 521–533.

Blomström, M., & Persson, H. (1983). Foreign investment and spillover efficiency in an underdeveloped economy: Evidence from the Mexican manufacturing industry. *World Development, 11*(6), 493–501.

Blomström, M., & Wolf, E. (1994). Multinational corporations and productivity convergence in Mexico. In W. Baumol, R. Nelson, & E. Wolf (Eds.), *Convergence of productivity: Cross-national studies and historical evidence* (pp. 263–284). Oxford: Oxford University Press.

Caves, R. E. (1971). International corporations: The industrial economics of foreign investment. *Economica, 38*, 1–27.

Caves, R. E. (1974). Multinational firms, competition and productivity in host country markets. *Economica, 41*(162), 176–193.

Chuang, Y. C., & Lin, C. M. (1999). Foreign direct investment, R&D and spillover efficiency: Evidence from Taiwan's manufacturing firms. *The Journal of Development Studies, 35*(4), 117–137.

Corden, W. M. (1967). Protection and foreign investment. *Economic Record, 43*, 209–232.

Dunning, J. (1992). *Multinational enterprises and the global economy.* Harlow: Addison-Wesley.

Glass, A. J., & Saggi, K. (2002). Licensing versus direct investment: Implications for economic growth. *Journal of International Economics, 56*(1), 131–153.

Globerman, S. (1979). Foreign direct investment and "spillover" efficiency benefits in Canadian manufacturing industries. *Canadian Journal of Economics, 12*(1), 42–56.

Görg, H., & Strobl, E. (2001). Multinational companies and productivity spillovers: A meta-analysis. *Economic Journal, 111*(475), 723–739.

Haddad, M., & Harrison, A. (1993). Are there positive spillovers from direct foreign investment?: Evidence from panel data for Morocco. *Journal of Development Economics, 42*(1), 51–74.

Javorcik, B. S. (2004). Does foreign direct investment increase the productivity of domestic firms? In search of spillovers through backward linkages. *American Economic Review, 94*(3), 605–627.

Kogut, B., & Zander, U. (1993). Knowledge of the firm and the evolutionary theory of multinational corporation. *Journal of International Business Studies, 24*(3), 625–646.

Kokko, A. (1994). Technology, market characteristics, and spillovers. *Journal of Development Economics, 43*(2), 279–293.

Kokko, A. (1996). Productivity spillovers from competition between local firms and foreign affiliates. *Journal of International Development, 8*(4), 517–30.

Kokko, A. (2003). *Globalization and FDI policies. The development dimension of FDI: Policy and rule-making perspectives* (pp. 29–40). New York: UNCTAD.

Liang, F. H. (2009). Does foreign direct investment improve the productivity of domestic firms? Technology spillovers, industry linkages, and firm capabilities. Technology Spillovers, Industry Linkages, and Firm Capabilities.

Liebscher, K., Christl, J., Mooslechner, P., & Ritzberger-Grunwald, D. (2007). *Foreign direct investment in Europe: A changing landscape*. Cheltenham, UK: Edward Elgar.

Lipsey, R. E. (2004). Home-and host-country effects of foreign direct investment. In R. E. Baldwin & W. Alan (Eds.), *Challenges to globalization: Analyzing the economics* (pp. 333–382). Chicago: University of Chicago Press.

Lipsey, R. E., & Sjöholm, F. (2005). *The impact of inward FDI on host countries: Why such different answers. Does foreign direct investment promote development* (Working Paper No 192). pp 23–43.

MacDougall, G. D. A. (1960). The benefits and costs of private investment from abroad: A theoretical approach. *Economic Record, 36*, 13–35.

Moran, T. H. (2005). How does FDI affect host country development? Using industry case studies to make reliable generalizations. In T. H. Moran, E. M. Graham, & M. Blomström (Eds.), *Does foreign direct investment promote development*. Washington, DC: Institute for International Economics.

Sjöholm, F. (1999). Technology gap, competition and spillovers from direct foreign investment: Evidence from establishment data. *Journal of Development Studies, 36*(1), 53–73.

Takii, S. (2005). Productivity spillovers and characteristics of foreign multinational plants in Indonesian manufacturing 1990–1995. *Journal of Development Economics, 76*(2), 521–542.

Todo, Y., & Miyamoto, K. (2002). *Knowledge diffusion from multinational enterprises: The role of domestic and foreign knowledge-enhancing activities* (Technical Papers No. 196). OECD Development Centre.

Todorova, G., & Durisin, B. (2007). Absorptive capacity: Valuing a reconceptualization. *Academy of Management Review, 32*(3), 774–786.

Tytell, I., & Yudaeva, K. (2006). *The role of FDI in Eastern Europe and new independent states: New channels for the spillover effect*. Washington, DC: International Monetary Fund.

Urban, D. M., & Peri, G. (2004). *Catching-up to foreign technology? Evidence on the "Veblen-Gerschenkron" effect of foreign investments* (NBER Working Paper, w10893).

Wang, J. Y., & Blomström, M. (1992). Foreign investment and technology transfer: A simple model. *European Economic Review, 36*(1), 137–155.

Zahra, S. A., & George, G. (2002). Absorptive capacity: A review, reconceptualization, and extension. *Academy of Management Review, 27*(2), 185–203.

Zukowska-Gagelmann, K. (2000). Productivity spillovers from foreign direct investment in Poland. *Economics Systems, 24*(3), 232–256.

Chapter 8
Economic Profiles and Perspectives of FDI Inflows to SEECs Media Markets: Multiple-Case Study Research

8.1 Recent Global Trends in FDI

Reasons for the rapid expansion in FDI are attributed to several factors: increased levels and changes in technology, greater liberalization of trade and investment, and deregulation and privatization of markets in many countries. In fact, world FDI flows in the past three decades show exponential growth in the intensity of global exchanges and an ever more pronounced role of multinational corporations (MNCs) in creating a global economy. While in 1970, annual world FDI flows were a mere $12 million, in 1990 this figure was up to $200 billion, and by 2013 FDI had increased dramatically to $1.46 trillion (UNCTAD 2014). UNCTAD forecasts that FDI flows will rise gradually in 2014 and 2015, to US$1.6 trillion and US$1.8 trillion, respectively, as global economic growth gains momentum prompting investors to turn potentially their cash holdings into new investments.

8.2 Major Benefits of FDI Business Models

Benefits of effectively applied FDI business models are numerous and include specifically:

(a) Cost reduction
(b) Strategic flexibility
(c) Focus and specialization
(d) Rapid exploitation of new market product/service opportunities
(e) Shared and reduced risk of capital investment.

© Springer International Publishing Switzerland 2016
Z. Vukanović, *Foreign Direct Investment Inflows Into the South East European Media Market*, Media Business and Innovation, DOI 10.1007/978-3-319-30512-7_8

8.3   New Perspectives on Contextual Framing of FDI Business Model in SEECs Media Markets

Today, FDI business model is about much more than traditional investing into current and future markets. It is about reinventing disruptive business models and creating entirely new domestic and international markets to meet untapped customer, sellsumer, produser, and prosumer needs. In order to be successful, the business model in media industry has to be dynamic, adaptable, and transformative providing added value network to the corporation.

Despite a marked lack of high level of technological readiness, business efficiency, productivity, state of cluster development, and innovative capacity, the region of South-East Europe presents relatively promising economic market looking from a global point of view. The monograph offers a strong empirical and conceptual grounding as well as very thorough, exhaustive, and profound incorporation of the relevant literature. In this chapter, the author extrapolates key questions relating to the changing role of media globalization and FDI inflows.

8.4   International Business Research Design

The research design of international business is free from any single core paradigm pursuing no single dominant central research question, and not abiding by generally accepted and simplifying assumptions driving the choice of research methods and tightly bounding areas of research relevance. In other words, international business research design is multidisciplinary and eclectic in its approach, benefiting from the complementary insights provided by various theories (such as transaction cost economics, institutional theory). Despite its multidisciplinary, structural and methodological approach, qualitative research in international business has been rare, the main research streams of the field relying more on quantitative methods.

Although many notable topics in the IB field require a qualitative research approach (Buckley and Chapman 1996; Buckley 2002), qualitative studies remain an exception in the better IB journal until today. Werner (2002) reports that over the last 5 years only 8.5 % of the empirical international management research published in 20 top journals applied a qualitative research strategy. Comparably, Pauwels and Matthyssens (2004) conclude that approximately 10 % of all published international business research over the period 1991–2002 used a qualitative approach, with a notable last position taken by the Journal of International Business Studies with only 3 % qualitative studies over the same period. In order to avoid dogged empiricism of the quantitative research streams, the author utilizes the qualitative, longitudinal, and multiple-case study research data methodologies.

8.4.1 Research Design Methodology Aims and Approaches

To gain in-depth, refined, and empirical knowledge on the phenomenon and dynamics of the hybrid FDI business model in media industry/market, a multiple-case study approach was chosen. Although, the author acknowledges the richness of adopting a single-case study, studying multiple cases typically provides a stronger and more accurate, grounded, generalizable, and substantial base for developing a systematic theory (Yin 1994; Dyer and Wilkins 1991; Eisenhardt and Graebner 2007).

Thus, the research has been executed as a longitudinal, embedded multiple-case study. A longitudinal case study provides a single setting with multiple observations over an extended period of time (Yin 2003; Eisenhardt 1989). This allows researchers to study and explain managerial actions and involvement in depth, on a retrospective, processual, and real-time basis (Petigrew 1992). Moreover, case studies represent an appropriate and preferred methodology, research strategy, and tool (1) in the critical, early phases of creating a new management theory, when key variables and their relationships are explored (Gibbert and Ruigrok 2010; Eisenhardt 1989; Yin 2008); (2) when researchers are interested in learning how, when, or why some phenomenon occurs; (3) when the research focuses on contemporary events within some real-life context; and (4) when the investigator has little or no controls of behavioral events.

In line with the exploratory nature of the study, the current research on business models and hybrid FDI BM in media industry relied on comparative, longitudinal, and multiple-case study research to critically assess the hybrid nature, attributes, dynamics and complexion of FDI business model in media industry.

8.4.2 The Foundational Principles of Multiple-Case Study Research Design

The author conducts a multiple-case study as opposed to a holistic case study with embedded units, because (1) the multiple case study examines several cases to understand the similarities and differences between the cases; and (2) a holistic case study with embedded units only allows the researcher to understand one unique/extreme/critical case. Correspondingly, as a study contains more than a single case, than a multiple-case study is required. Moreover, as the context is different for each of the cases, a multiple-case study will allow the researcher to analyze within each setting and across settings.

Concurrently, multiple-case studies can be used to either (a) predict and replicate similar results or (b) predict contrasting results but for predictable reasons (Yin 2003). The advantage of this type of design includes robustness and reliability of aggregated, nomothetic, inferential, and hypothetical results, but it can also be extremely time-consuming and expensive to conduct. Among three terms describing case studies: intrinsic, instrumental, and collective, the author utilizes an instrumental and collective case study, because more than one case is being examined while there is the intent to gain insight and understanding of a particular situation or phenomenon. Moreover, the instrumental case study facilitates contextually a detailed insight into an issue of ordinary activity or helps the researcher pursue, provide or refine a theory (Stake 1995).

A multiple-case study enables the researcher to explore differences within and between cases. The goal is to replicate findings across cases. Because comparisons will be drawn, it is imperative that the cases are chosen carefully so that the researcher can predict similar results across cases or predict contrasting results based on a theory (Yin 2003).

The multiple-case design can be adopted with real-life events that show numerous sources of evidence through replication rather than sampling logic. By replicating the case through pattern matching, a technique linking several pieces of information from the same case to some theoretical proposition (Campbell 1975), multiple-case design enhances and supports the previous results. This helps raise the level of confidence in the robustness of the method. Thus, multiple-case studies strengthen research findings in the way that multiple experiments strengthen experimental research findings (Benbasat et al. 1987; Yin 1994). For a multi-case study, the case records are presented intact, accompanying a cross-case analysis with some emphasis on the binding concept or idea (Stake 2006). A multi-case study approach is needed to overcome the shortcomings of much of the previous research reported in the literature, which has concentrated on a single organization. As discussed above, the multi-case study approach allows a more direct comparison between the similarities and differences of the implementation practices in the different contexts considered (Silverman 2000). It also enables more generic conclusions to be reached (Eisenhardt and Graebner 2007).

In multiple-case studies, research data can be treated cumulatively. Accordingly, multiple cases should be considered as multiple experiments or multiple surveys (i.e., follow a replication logic), instead of as multiple respondents in a survey (Yin 1994). The multiple-case study has one significant benefit over a traditional case study approach; the number of investigated hypothesis is greater in number and scope. Thus, a causal covariational relationship increases validity, breadth, case comparability, representativeness, and the consequential likelihood of a conjectural, inferential, and presumptive magnitude of a scalar outcome.

Importantly, the multiple-case study research has to shed light on both causal mechanisms and/as well as its true causal effect. As a result, multiple-case studies are often useful in conjunction with a cross-sectional unit study for the purpose of investigating and elucidating causal mechanisms (i.e., process tracing and pattern matching). Consequently, its characteristic style of evidence—gathering-over-time and within-unit variation—is likely to provide clues into what connects a purported X to a particular Y.

Multiple-case study research design was chosen given the need to gather in-depth, rich data on the phenomenon of FDI inflows in media industry. When a researcher is examining correlative relationships or proximate causal relationships, the multiple-case study format seems less problematic and is often highly informative. The author uses the synthesis of heuristic, instrumental, disciplined configurative, and building block multiple-case studies. Disciplined configurative case studies use established theories to explain a case. Heuristic case studies identify new causal paths. Outlier cases may be especially valuable here. Building block studies of particular phenomenological types or subtypes identify common patterns or serve a particular kind of heuristic purpose. Multiple-case study is a research design best defined as an intensive study of a single unit (a relatively bounded phenomenon) where the scholar's aim is to elucidate features of a larger class of similar phenomenon (Gerring 2004).

A research design is an action plan that guides research from the questions to the conclusions and includes steps for collecting, analyzing, and interpreting evidence according to preestablished propositions, units of analyses, a logic for linking the data to the propositions, and application of set criteria for interpreting the findings (Yin 2003).

The term methodology, like case study, has little definitional clarity and is commonly used interchangeably with the term method. For example, Sjoberg, Williams, Vaughn, and Sjoberg (1991) defined methodology as "the analysis of the intersection (and interaction) between theory and research methods and data." However, in this scenario, case study is not a methodology because it does not provide a parsimonious theory of how research should proceed with conceptually coherent methods and accompanying data collection procedures that map onto the theory. Accordingly, case study is the unit of analysis, rather than an independent method, research design, and/or methodology.

8.4.3 Pragmatical Guidelines for Evaluating Multiple-Case Study Research

Guidelines for evaluating case study research include seven parameters: (1) definition of a priori research question (i.e., provides better grounding of construct measures); (2) selecting specific cases (i.e., constrains extraneous variation and sharpens external validity); (3) crafting instruments and protocols (i.e., strengthens multiple qualitative and quantitative data research methodology by triangulation of evidence fostering synergistic and divergent view of evidence); (4) entering the field (i.e., speeds overlap data collection and analysis, revealing helpful adjustments to data collection and allowing investigators to take advantage of emergent themes and unique case features); (5) analyzing data (i.e., within-case analysis, gaining familiarity with preliminary data; and cross-case pattern search using divergent techniques, forcing investigators to look beyond initial impressions and see evidence through multiple lenses); (6) shaping hypothesis (i.e., iterative tabulation of evidence for each construct; sharpening, and confirming construct definition, validity, and measurability); and (7) enfolding literature (i.e., comparison with conflicting and with similar literature—building, sharpening, and raising internal validity of construct definitions) (Eisenhardt 1989).

8.4.4 Multiple-Case Study Research in International Business

Within the current "niche" of qualitative IB research, multiple-case study methodology remains the most important research method by far (Werner 2002). Hartley (1994) defines a case study as "a detailed investigation, often with data collected over a period of time, of one or more organizations, or groups within organizations, with a view to providing an analysis of the context and processes involved in the phenomenon under study." The ultimate aim of multiple-case study research is the construction of explanatory middle range theory (Frederickson 1983). In middle range theory building, the researcher disaggregates complex contexts and situations into more discrete, carefully defined chunks and then reintegrates these bits with an explicit analysis of their context (Bourgeois 1979; Peterson 1998).

8.5   The Economic Potential and Importance for SEECs Markets to Attract Prospective FDI

Despite a marked lack of high level of technological readiness, business efficiency, productivity, state of cluster development, and innovative capacity, the region of SEECs presents relatively promising economic market looking from a global point of view. The main reason for such an observation is based on the fact that the region's annual GDP generates $1.68 trillion equaling that of Texas' annual GDP. With the population of approximately 155 million, this region covers the area of almost 1.7 million square kilometers. The foreign direct investment (FDI) in 2014 reached $34.3 billion representing 2.03 % of the region's annual GDP. Only four countries in the region (i.e., Cyprus, Malta, Montenegro, and Slovenia) received more than $500 per capita in FDI. Accordingly, the region of SEECs media markets provides a substantial potential and ample opportunities for prospective FDI. Moreover, SEECs feature a versatile type of media industries and companies including 804 daily newspapers, 1737 TV stations, and 4144 radio stations.

The case for FDI is particularly compelling in transition economies as developing economies are often in need of stable sources of foreign financing in order to leverage their growth potential (Wolf 2005). As the economic growth in the SEECs depends on net private capital inflows, the FDI inflow in the SEECs has been a key component augmenting economic development in the first transformative phase of the privatization process throughout the transition period (Popescu 2014). FDI into SEECs economies is dominantly horizontal (Popescu 2014). Furthermore, FDI has an essential function in SEECs transition economies, being an outstanding sign of the globalization process in the region as well as a notable addition to domestic savings.

The need for extensive enterprise restructuring and modernization in view of SEECs limited domestic resources creates an environment where the potential benefits of FDI are especially valuable. Also, transition economies are well placed to benefit from the technology and knowledge transfer associated with FDI: they are relatively developed and possess a highly educated labor force. Borensztein et al. (1998) find that the net positive impact of FDI on growth is larger when the host country labor force is highly educated. Finally, the balance of payments crises of the 1980s and 1990s have highlighted the importance of non-debt-creating capital flows for external sustainability during the transition process (which is underscored by the evidence presented in Frankel and Rose 1996). As a result, attracting FDI has become a prominent item on the policy agenda, especially in transition economies, and research on the determinants of FDI has been expanding rapidly. Specifically, SEECs should raise their FDI for the purpose of intensifying alterations and decreasing unemployment to compete for EU membership. On the other hand, the loss of FDI has made it more difficult for the SEECs to finance their present account deficits (Labaye et al. 2013).

As FDI has become the most ordinary sort of capital flow during the transition period in the SEECs, the governments of the SEECs economies (De Beaufort and Summers 2014) have been advancing formal FDI promotion strategies and policies supplying relevant stimulants for foreign corporations. In this region, the need for FDI to substitute for limited domestic savings is great, but the low levels of income suggest that the region may have limited absorptive capacity (Cohen and Levinthal 1990; Zahra and George 2002) and therefore find it hard to exploit potential spillovers from FDI. However, SEECs have a notable capacity for economic growth because of (a) relatively low level of exports; (b) unsaturated markets, and (c) a relevant level of FDI desirability due to the geopolitical significance of the region (Popescu 2014). Moreover, the nations that guarantee the most significant returns and minimum expenditures will attract the most FDI (Popescu 2014).

The last decade has seen a remarkable growth of European but also US outward direct investments in SEECs. This growth is often regarded as being driven by the process of integration of SEECs into the European Union and the associated elimination of the barriers to FDI and acceleration of the transition process of those economies.

Correspondingly, the South East European Countries (SEECs) have attracted a considerable amount of FDI so far: the average annual growth of inward FDI in the SEECs reached 26 % over the 2001–2008 period (Bellak et al. 2010a, Bellak et al. 2010b). Nevertheless, capital is still a scarce production factor in SEECs and hence there is room and the need for additional FDI (e.g., FIPA 2008). Accordingly, the SEECs are far from homogeneous and both the level and growth of FDI differ across these countries. While the countries such as Malta, Croatia, Hungary, Cyprus, and Slovenia have attracted a good amount of foreign capital, countries including Bosnia and Herzegovina, Kosovo, Moldova, Romania, Bulgaria, Macedonia FYR, and Greece lag considerably behind (Carstensen and Toubal 2004).

The SEECs are defined here to include Albania, Bosnia and Herzegovina, Bulgaria, Croatia, Cyprus, Greece, Hungary, Kosovo, Macedonia FYR, Malta, Moldova, Montenegro, Romania, Serbia, Slovenia, and Turkey. Also the SEECs have developed various strategies actively attracting (promoting) FDI to their countries rather than relying solely on market size, low taxes, and low wage costs as location factors. Indeed, the attraction of FDI has become an important policy goal for regional development of SEECs. Therefore, especially corporate income taxes play a dominant role in the policy mix used by SEECs' governments to attract FDI. As a very general remark, corporate income taxes (henceforth TAX) have been lowered (e.g., Bellak and Liebensteiner 2011) and the institutional environment toward FDI (henceforth INST) has been considerably revised in the SEECs (e.g., EBRD 2010).

The author's findings suggest that the potential for SEECs to attract FDI upon changes in these policy areas varies substantially within the group of SEECs. Yet, as a general picture, most SEECs have to improve substantially their institutional environment as well as their infrastructure endowment to attract FDI. The tax instrument, in contrast, is largely exhausted as a means to attract FDI. Every reduction of the effective tax rate in the SEECs by one percentage point increases inward FDI ceteris paribus by 4.3 %, which clearly is a non-negligible amount. One should keep in mind that there are strong magnitude variations in the results depending on the time frame, method applied, tax measure used, FDI indicator employed, the quality of data in general, etc (DeMooij and Ederveen 2008). This result is also in line with the findings of Overesch and Wamser (2010) based on firm-level data. Furthermore, the relevance of corporate income taxes as location factor is also shown by the meta-study of Feld and Heckemeyer (2011). Thus, there is a broad agreement in the literature that corporate income taxes matter for FDI. In addition, the paper by Bellak et al. (2009) also includes evidence that FDI in SEECs is attracted by increases in the infrastructure endowment. These findings are consistent with Wheeler and Mody (1992) who study the importance of infrastructure for the location decision of US MNEs. They find that infrastructure, measured via a comprehensive index capturing various dimensions, is an important location factor, especially in less developed countries.

Bevan and Estrin (2004) find in their empirical work that FDI between developed Western and transition countries is determined by unit labor costs, host and source country size, and proximity. FDI flows to the transition countries are not affected remarkably by market assessments of country-specific risk (Bevan and Estrin 2004). Cheng and Kwan (2000) find support for the fact that a favorable transport infrastructure is a relevant determinant of FDI into Chinese regions. Goodspeed et al. (2006) explain FDI in a broad range of countries and include the consumption of electric power, the number of mainline telephone connections, and a composite infrastructure index in their regressions. For the latter two proxies, they find a significant positive impact upon FDI. In a related paper, Goodspeed et al. (2009) find that a favorable infrastructure endowment attracts FDI to developed as well as to less developed countries. Thus, the impact is larger in the latter country group. They use a composite infrastructure index comprising transport, telecommunication, energy, and environmental infrastructures. Similarly, Mollick et al. (2006) analyze the role of telecommunications and transport infrastructure for FDI in Mexico and find a positive impact of both types of infrastructure. Bénassy-Quéré et al. (2007b) use data on the net stock of public capital as proxy for the quantity and quality of production-related infrastructure. They analyze FDI from the US to 18 EU countries and find a significant positive impact of the net stock of public capital on FDI. Thus, the available empirical evidence suggests that production-related material infrastructure is an economically and statistically significant determinant of FDI, especially in developing and in transition economies.

An "investor-friendly" institutional environment of an economy, that is, the formal and informal norms shaping the behavior of economic agents, secure property rights, low barrier entry to a particular market, is frequently seen as a necessary condition for a country to receive FDI. Conversely, a poor institutional infrastructure (e. g. legal structure, economic policy enforcement, etc.) leads to potentially higher costs of investments, increasing the probability of expropriation of firms' assets which, in turn, make investment activity less likely in the host country (e.g., Blonigen 2005; Bénassy-Quéré et al. 2007a). Thus, reducing FDI activity. Blonigen 2005; Bénassy-Quéré et al. 2007a). Nevertheless, Dhakal et al.'s (2007) study shows that stronger government regulations have a statistically negative impact on FDI inflows.

Although, this empirical analysis implies that most SEECs are already competitive in terms of the taxation of proceeds from FDI, a tax regime instrument used to attract more FDI in the short run is almost exhausted. This is especially the case if the SEECs consider joining the EU in the near future as the EU prohibits many tax base-related measures through its state aid regulations. Yet, as shown by Bellak et al. (2009) low corporate income taxes compensate to some extent MNEs for a lack in the infrastructure endowment. Thus, for the SEECs it was essential to reduce TAX to compensate for the lack in infrastructure.

In a medium- to long-run perspective, SEECs need to improve their infrastructure endowment to make FDI sustainable and to climb up the value chain of MNEs. Despite low taxes attracting FDI even in the case of an inferior infrastructure endowment, its policy will only enable the SEECs to attract FDI where productivity of the private capital does not primarily depend on complementary public material infrastructure. Relatedly, improved ICT infrastructure is critical if the region wants to attract higher value-added production (Bellak et al. 2010a).

Specifically, if the SEECs want to attract higher stages of the various value chains of production of public material infrastructure, ICT infrastructure will become increasingly fundamental factor spurring this transformation (see e.g., FIAS 2007). It has to be stressed that to climb up the value chain via the attraction of more sophisticated FDI also creates the need to focus and prioritize more strongly on complementary investments in intangible infrastructure (education, skill development, etc.) and infrastructure investments into production-related material infrastructure. Furthermore, improving the infrastructure endowment should also receive high political priority, as the low-wage advantage of SEECs may vanish over time, as the recent experiences in Hungary and in Poland have shown (e.g., Austrian Central Bank 2010). Thus, any compensatory effects low wages (or low taxes) have with respect to the lack of infrastructure may quickly be eroded during the catching-up process.

Among the world's top 20 ranking destination countries measured by the number of jobs created by FDI in 2014, two countries are from the region of South East Europe (i.e., Romania and Hungary) (Dencik and Spee 2012). Measured by the number of jobs relative to the size of the population, Macedonia is positioned as the top destination country in the world, while Hungary is eight. In addition, Serbia, Bulgaria, Romania and Bosnia and Herzegovina are ranked among top 20 destination countries by estimated jobs—per million inhabitants (Dencik and Spee 2012). Similarly, Turkey is now ranked among the world's top 20 sources of investment, highlighting how Turkish companies are expanding their global footprints in response to new opportunities (i.e., overall levels of greenfield FDI). Thus, the number of estimated jobs as a result of the FDI in Turkey increased by 379 % between 2012 and 2013, while for example in the United States it increased by 16 %, India 11 %, and Australia 8 %.

SEECs had experienced an export boom as well as a surge in capital inflows up to the outbreak of the economic and financial crisis. Thus, FDI stocks nearly doubled in CESEE countries between 2004 and 2009 (Fidrmuc and Martin 2011). Correspondingly, most of the countries in Central, Eastern, and Southeastern Europe (CESEE) are seen as good examples of the growth-enhancing effect of downhill capital flows, i.e., capital flows from relatively capital-rich to relatively capital-poor countries. In addition, they are good examples for an export-led growth strategy. Especially in more recent papers on growth in the region, it is, however, often emphasized that in the years before the recent economic and financial crisis, growth had been overly consumption driven (EBRD 2010). These two facets of the CESEE region's recent growth experience—substantial capital inflows and a very strong export performance—are closely interrelated. Besides, they need to be seen in the context of the region's gradual EU integration, which, in 2004 and 2007, culminated in the accession of ten CESEE countries to the EU. First, a large share of the capital flows into the region originated from the EU. These inflows, in particular inward FDI, arguably helped build up the capital stock in the CESEE countries, which was expected to facilitate export growth. Second, EU integration provided a major boost for the CESEE exporting industries by opening up a large market at the region's doorstep (Fidrmuc and Martin 2011).

To sum up, this analysis shows that SEECs which aim to increase FDI inflows should first reduce legal barriers toward FDI. Second, SEECs should keep corporate income taxes low at least in the short and the medium run. Third, SEECs need to free financial means to improve their infrastructure endowment in the medium to long run. Of course, securing financial means to improve infrastructure endowment in the case of low corporate income taxes implies that other revenue sources have to be used. For instance, SEECs with a low public debt level could consider increasing public borrowing. Moreover, measures to reduce tax fraud and to reduce the importance of the informal sector may be implemented. Financial means should also come from European institutions as the catching up of the SEECs should be in the economic interest of the EU as the experience with the CEECs has proven. Fourth, once the institutional environment and the infrastructure endowment have improved, SEECs might even consider to increase corporate income taxes again as accruing "infrastructure rents" can be taxed without losing FDI (see Bellak et al. 2009).

8.6   A Systematic, Meta-synthetic, and Preliminary Scholarly Literature Review on SEECs Media Industry and Markets

European media scholars and researchers have dominantly analyzed media through two mirrors: the reflection of political and social forces reinforcing, fostering and reordering the media sector, and the reflection and display of "a wider entertainment and 'information' network beyond national constraints" (Rooke 2009). At the same time, the sector of media economics has been largely neglected until the beginning of 1990s. The rise of neoliberal and global capitalism and the collapse of Soviet-style communism in the Central, Eastern, and Southeastern Europe started to dictate more dynamic capitalist rules. Moreover, the increase in market competition followed by the rollout of new-digital technologies prompted media companies to pay more attention at economic, business, and market values in the media industry as well as consumers' demand.

Historically, media researchers have neglected the topic of foreign direct investment (FDI) inflow to SEEC media markets. Nevertheless, in terms of the holistic academic depth, accuracy, and relevancy, only a few pertinent works have been published in the field of SEEC media business, market, and entrepreneurship studies [e. g. Tsourvakas (2010), Sanchez-Tabernero and Carvajal (2002), Medina (2004), Gulyás (2003), Leandros (2010), van der Wurff (2002), Fardigh (2010), Schalt (2008), Splichal (1994, 2004), Jakubowicz (2007), Jakubowicz and Sükösd (2008), Perusko and Popovic (2008), Downey and Mihelj (2012), Dobek-Ostrowska et al. (2010), Jakubowicz and Sükösd (2008), and Gross (2004)].

There are at least two valid reasons for apparent absence of profoundly systematized and holistic longitudinal, empirical, comparative, and analytical conceptual or case study analysis: (1) The tradition of capitalist, liberal, and free market has been very scarce as 12 out of 16 countries were former communist countries—until 1991; (2) The SEECs with the exception of Turkey and Romania are (a) relatively small in territorial and demographic size and are (b) ethnically and culturally very diverse. In fact, it is the ethnic, linguistic, and cultural fragmentation making their prospective economic and technological cooperation more challenging to maintain. From a cultural viewpoint, four countries are mainly Catholic (Croatia, Hungary, Malta, and Slovenia), another four countries are dominantly Muslim (Albania, Kosovo, Turkey, and Bosnia and Herzegovina), and the rest of them are mainly Orthodox (Bulgaria, Serbia, Montenegro, Romania, Cyprus, Greece, FYR Macedonia, and Moldova). Accordingly, it is advisable to point that high ethnic diversity is particularly present in Bosnia and Herzegovina, Bulgaria, Montenegro, Serbia, FYR Macedonia, and Moldova, while only five countries in the entire region (Malta, Slovenia, Hungary, Greece, and Cyprus) maintain low ethnic diversity.

Thus, the ethnic, cultural, and linguistic fragmentation of the European media channeled scholars' attention more toward the social, cultural, political, and regulatory issue of media rather than to economic, market, business, and entrepreneurial aspect of media science. This notion is apparently evident in the number of published books (160) and articles (940) covering the issue of European media from 1990 to 2011.

Therefore, the predominant concentration of scholarly literature on the European media was based on the analysis of digital switchover in Europe (Iosifidis 2006a, Iosifidis 2006b; Rooke 2009); media rights (Craufurd Smith 2004); European media policy (Papathanassopoulos and Negrine 2011; Downey and Mihelj 2012; Harcourt 2005); media ownership (Craufurd Smith 2004, Williams 2003); media regulation (Harcourt 2005; Venturelli 1999; Rooke 2009; Holoubek et al. 2006); media self-regulation (Baydar et al. 2011); media systems (Färdigh 2010; Downey and Mihelj 2012; Kristovic 2008); media pluralism (Iosifides 1997); media content (Rohman 2011); media and European integration (Meyer 2010; Christensen and Nezih 2009; Trenza 2008; Chaban and Holland 2008; Michalis 2007; Papathanassopoulos and Negrine 2011; Rooke 2009); the European public broadcasting service (Jusić and Amer 2008; Nissen 2006; Venturelli 1999; Collins 1998; Iosifidis 2006a, b); media discourse analysis (Van De Steeg 2005; Koopmans and Statham 2010; Eastern European); media transition (Gross 2004; Jakubowicz and Sükösd 2008; Downey and Mihelj 2012; Mertelsmann 2011); media politics (Voltmer 2005; Papathanas-sopoulos and Negrine 2011; Downey and Mihelj 2012; Beumers et al. 2011; Venturelli 1999; Lange and Ward 2004; Triandafyllidou et al. 2009; Papathanas-sopoulos 2005; Blain and O'Donnell 2003; Koch-Baumgarten and Voltmer 2010); media culture (Downey and Mihelj 2012; Bondebjerg and Madsen 2009; Bondebjerg and Golding 2004; Rooke 2009); media consumption (Downey and Mihelj 2012; Färdigh 2010); media and gender (in)equality (Downey and Mihelj 2012); European media law (Castendyk et al. 2008; Keller 2011; Baldi and Hasebrink 2007); media ethics and freedom of expression (Baydar et al. 2011); media and religion (Morán 2008; Doe 2004); media representation of immigrants and ethnic minorities (Christensen and Nezih 2009; Frachon and Vargaftig 2000); media rhetoric (Deirdre 2003); media and identity (Crain and Hughes-Freeland 1998); media and European public sphere (Harrison and Wessels 2009; Meyer 2010); media democracy (Bondebjerg and Madsen 2009); media and nationalism (Jakubowicz and Sukosd 2011); media and European identities (Jakubowicz and Sukosd 2011; Papathanassopoulos and Negrine 2011); media concentration policy (Iosifides 1997); and media diversity (Rooke 2009).

8.7 Historical Background and Brief Overview of the Literature on FDI in SEECs

Over the past 15 years, there has been a flourishing literature on FDI in Southeastern Europe. This is not surprising, since foreign capital has played an important role in most countries during the 20-year transition to market economy. A number of studies have looked into the key features of FDI in Eastern Europe—its volume, forms, origins, destination by economic activity, and case studies (see, for example, Lankes and Venables 1996; Meyer 1998; Estrin et al. 2000; Bartlett 2009; Kalotay 2010; Hunya 2011, 2012), as well as the determinants of FDI based on econometric research (for example, Bevan and Estrin 2004; Bevan et al. 2004; Janicki and Wunnava 2004; Dikova and van Witteloostuijn 2007).

8.8 Introduction to the Critical Research of FDI Business Models in Media Industry and Business

As no consensus or attempt exists to prioritize or establish critical research questions, frameworks as well as streams regarding the definition and practical implementation FDI business models in the field of media industry and market by researchers, the purpose of this study is to propose an integrative, synthetic, polycentric, composite, multi-variant, holistic, complementary, multidimensional, interrelated, sustainable and interdependent framework for characterizing the hybrid FDI business model in media business and industry.

The closest research available in the MNCs' FDI business models in the media industry relates to the basic variants/modifications of the microeconomic model of trade liberalization elaborated and published independently by several different set (s) of authors studying trade in films and television programs in the late 1980s and early 1990s (Hoskins & Mirus, 1988; Waterman, 1988; Wildman & Siwek, 1987; Wildman & Siwek, 1988; Frank, 1992; Owen & Wildman, 1992; Wildman & Siwek, 1993; Wildman 1995).

One of the main reasons for the late development and adoption of FDI business models in the media business deals with the unique ubiquitous, pervasive and intangible nature of media industries, enterprises, institutions, and personnel to society. Lavine and Wackman (1988) identified five characteristics differentiating media industries from other types of businesses. These include (a) the perishable commodity of the media product, (b) the highly creative employees, (c) the organizational structure, (d) the societal role of the media (e.g., awareness, influence), (e) the blurring of lines separating traditional media, and (f) short product and service business cycles. Similarly, Caves (2000) offers a distinction between media firms and other businesses through the theory of contracts and the differences involved in dealing with creative individuals and demand uncertainty.

8.9   Common Characteristics of SEEC Media Markets

In this context, the major characteristics of SEECs media include: low levels of newspaper circulation (Hallin and Mancini 2004); a tradition of advocacy reporting (Hallin and Mancini 2004); instrumentalization of privately-owned media (Papathanassopoulos 2000); politicization of public broadcasting and broadcast regulation (Papathanassopoulos 2000); limited development of journalism as an autonomous profession; the legacy of the Communist system – "post-Communist countries"; the lack of the political consensus and media self-regulation; unclear and incomplete legislative framework (Zlatev 2011); underdeveloped, repressive, partly free industrialist capitalist market development and a political instability; high market concentration, as there has been a transition from state concentration to commercial media market deregulation and liberalization (Tsourvakas 2010); late democratization and transition to democracy (Terzis 2008) characterizing incomplete, or (in some cases) underdeveloped and weak civil society, well-organized and cohesive pressure groups and rational-legal authority combined in many cases with a dirigiste State (Statham 1996; Marletti and Roncaloro 2000; Papatheodorou, Machin 2003; Mancini 2000; Hallin, Papathanassopoulos 2002) (e.e. "State paternalism", "political clientelism", and panpoliticismo—a situation when political elites pervade and influence many state's social, economic and judical systems as well as media sector (Terzis 2008). Unsurprisingly, liberal institutions were only consolidated in Greece from about 1975–1985, while Turkey has witnessed three military coups (1960, 1971, 1980) (Terzis 2008).

Another common social and economic features of SEECs include absence of a strong civil society, underdevelopment of capitalism, a weak civil society and well-organized and cohesive pressure groups, lack of the political consensus and media self-regulation, and unclear and incomplete legislative framework (Zlatev 2011). All these features have made the state an autonomous and dominant factor, yet the capacity of the state to intervene effectively is often limited by lack of resources and clientelist relationships which diminish the capacity of the state for unified action (Hallin and Mancini 2004). The final feature of the media markets in Southeast European countries is that they are highly concentrated, as there has been a transition from state concentration to market concentration (Tsourvakas 2010).

8.10   The Dynamic Development of FDI Thematic Research Field and the Lack of FDI Business Models Scholarly Research

In recent years, economists have successfully explained several varieties of foreign direct investment (FDI): greenfield (Nocke and Yeaple 2007), mergers (Horn and Persson 2001; Portes and Rey 2005), acquisitions (Davies and Kristjánsdóttir 2010; Head and Ries 2008), foreign affiliate sales (Bergstrand and Egger 2007; Kleinert and Toubal 2010), and partial ownership (Fatica 2010; Van Assche and Schwartz 2013). These models have spurred the development of empirical studies highlighting the rich variety of FDI inflow types (Hijzen et al. 2008; Hyun and Kim 2010; Qiu and Wang 2011).

While extant literature provides a firm theoretical footing upon which to base empirical research on some FDI types, there is a limited substantial and systematic research with respect to determinants of FDI inflow business models in SEECs media industry. Moreover, the literature on FDI inflow business models in media industry is predominantly marginal compared to FDI inflows into other industries. Despite the policy and economic interest and the importance of FDI, scholars apparently fail to examine in full the underlying mechanisms, key insights, and conceptual frameworks of FDI inflows business models into media industry. Thus FDI and media industry/economics studies fail to provide holistic, comprehensive, and profound empirical findings as well as ground economic and business model to explain FDI inflows business models into media industry.

Therefore, the coverage of media FDI inflows into SEECs is scant, patchy, inconsistent, and largely absent from the existing literature. With the exception of Vukanovic's (2011), systematic research paper "Exploring and Crossing Communication and Media Industry Frontiers: Creating a Strategy to Expand Foreign Direct Investment (FDI) Inflow in SEEC," published in the Romanian journal—Eurolimes, there has been almost no profoundly systematic, integrative, comprehensive, holistic, meta-synthetic analysis of this theme in academic scholarship and journal literature. Despite continuous increase in recent scholarship on FDI inflows into SEECs, only a dozen papers were cited more than 20 times (i.e., Christie 2002; Bijsterbosch and Kolasa 2010; Demekas et al. 2005; Stoian and Filippaios 2008; Bitzenis 2003, 2006; Slaveski and Nedanovski 2002; Arbatli 2011; Johnson 2006; Gardo and Martin 2010; Botrić and Škuflić 2006; Artige and Nicolini 2006). This further implies that scholarship on the issue of FDI inflows into SEECs is still fragmented and in need of a further holistic, synthetic, and systematic integration, overview, and analysis. Linguistic and cultural differences existing between the SEECs may also pose problems in the case of covering of the topic of FDI inflows into SEECs.

8.11   The Need and Importance for a Hybrid Media FDI Business Model

The main rationale, principle, and aim of this subchapter is to provide an input as to which KPIs-key performance indicators, main empirical drivers, variables, indices, coefficients, scores, metrics, and parameters should be included in a hybrid media FDI business model. Moreover, once the systematically structural and applicative paradigm of the hybrid media FDI business model is established, researchers and managers will more effectively understand casual relations between media industry, market and business as well as prospective potential for current and future FDI inflows into media markets.

Importantly, the emerging digital media technologies demand a rapid expansion of knowledge base and intensive collaboration across various organizational, technological, business, entrepreneurial, industrial, and market sectors. Global media corporations are seeing their raisons d'tre swiftly eroded by the rising technological tide. With the transformation and rebirth of business models at dizzying speeds, the larger social impact is profound. Consequently, the new global and technological change in media business models and media FDI inflows is fast outstripping our critical frames of reference. Hence, it is necessary to establish a diverse set of business models' methods and perspectives for studying this critical moment in media business and industry.

At the same time, little is known to date about the extent to which FDI business models are implemented in the media business and industry. The media industry response to FDI inflows into media markets has been uneven and at times hesitant. Moreover, published empirical studies on FDI spillover effects on growth and value-added activities of SEECs media market are almost nonexistent. Therefore, this study is an important contribution to the international media business literature because SEECs media market potential is still under-researched.

The dynamic and fast-growing media, ICT, and telecommunications industries now account for 10 % of global GDP representing only 27.77 % of the global ICT business potential. Its unique and complex of innovative, commercial, experiential, creative, and technical resources (i. e. content, distribution, competition, and audience analysis) have attracted much research attention from various media business and industry disciplines (Gershon 2015; Friedrichsen and Mühl-Benninghaus 2013; Ferrell Lowe and Brown 2015; Lugmayr and Dal Zotto 2015a, Lugmayr and Dal Zotto 2015b; Feldmann, 2005; Georgiades 2015; Razmerita et al. 2016; Van Kranenburg and Dal Zotto 2009). Nevertheless, working with corporate media businessmen, entrepreneurs, and emerging ventures, the author saw a firsthand an evident lack of deeper, more profound, and sophisticated development of a practical, pertinent, relevant and applicative media FDI business model. Moreover, media corporations did not develop right/targeted FDI market opportunities, despite pursuing, following, and leading the innovative technology or regulatory politics. Consequently, the most pressing need is building the right set of capabilities around the media FDI business models' core strategy.

Thus, the author proposes implementing of a specific and multidisciplinary hybrid FDI media business model, as generic FDI business models provide impractical and unfeasable value. As a matter of fact, these generic business models generally fail to account for the differences between industrial sectors, market conditions, and business cycles. Specifically, the hybrid FDI business model is important for two reasons. First, it closes the gap between the media corporations' FDI strategy and its competitive landscape. Second, it focuses on sharing best practices associated with launching, expanding, and sustaining digital platform businesses.

Moreover, the hybrid FDI business model analyzes, explains, and estimates the prospective opportunities for FDI into regional and global media markets by aggregating seven composite and dynamic factors. At the same time, it makes new commercial initiatives via effective, efficient, and scalable capturing of prospective media markets. Relatedly, the hybrid FDI business model provides innovative substitution patterns according to its basic assumptions and model foundations. The importance of the hybrid FDI business model is further reinforced, fostered, and articulated via a current absence of consensus or even emerging widespread/universal agreement on any alternative to the application of this specific and multidisciplinary business model. Accordingly, the hybrid FDI business model may serve as role model to other media corporations planning to invest their capital, assets, and human resources into regional and global markets.

8.11.1 The Common Denominator, Basic Principles, and Dynamics of the Hybrid FDI Business Model

The hybrid FDI business specifically draws on the provision of so-called experiential digital/new media services and applications. Hybrid business model research streams draw primarily on two theoretical models: the resource-based view (RBV) and transaction cost economics (TCE). The former gives primacy in decision-making to the relationship between what resources a firm possesses and what resources it seeks to acquire (Sullivan and Jiang 2010). The latter gives primacy to the transaction costs associated with acquiring the resources under different ownership arrangements (Sullivan and Jiang 2010). Most scholars have found that both of these frameworks are useful and that which takes priority depends on the situation. Shao (2010) argues that where the goal is to acquire new products or capabilities, RBV is likely to better predict which form investment will (should) take, and when the goal is to acquire new markets or customers, TCE is the preferred framework.

Moreover, the hybrid FDI business model provides more adaptable and sustainable digital and network media services than traditional, static, and old media business models. As a result of today's symbiotic market linkages, it takes into consideration a widespread network architecture connectivity speeding up the service/product life cycle as well as the speed of business model disruptive innovation. The hybrid FDI business model and many of these proposed variables require further development and analysis. In this process, economic feasibility and market acceptance need to be balanced sensitively.

8.12 Multiple-Case Studies of SEECs Media Markets

8.12.1 Albanian Media Market Outlook

The Albanian media market characterizes high market competition of daily newspapers. Unsurprisingly, in print media, only a small number of boulevard newspapers are profitable, such as the weekly Paloma, which sells 30,000–35,000 copies, while the largest daily newspapers in the country, such as Panorama, Shqip, Shekulli, and Gazeta Shqiptare, incur losses.

The case study analysis of the Albanian media market shows that among 56 radio stations only two hold a national license. Moreover, among 71 television stations holding a local license, only two of them hold a national license. The main TV stations in Albania are Top Channel TV, TV Klan, Vizion Plus TV, TV News 24, ABC News, ORA News TV, A1 Report, and Albanian Screen. The main radio stations are Top Albania Radio and +2 Radio.

Given the lack of publicly available audience and readership research as well as accurate data on advertising, it is difficult to reach a safe conclusion on this aspect. Annual advertising revenue in media sector ranges from 48 to 55 million euros. The value of the Albanian TV advertising market in 2011 is estimated at 34 million euros.

The spending on Internet advertising has increased from 0.5 % in 2007 to 0.9 % in 2011, while the advertising expenditure on Television decreased from 86.3 % in 2004 to 66.8 % in 2011. The main advertisers in the Albanian media are telecom operators, banks, and big companies (food and beverages, such as Coca-Cola). In 2011, the telecommunications sector accounted for 69 % of the TV advertising market, followed by coffee trading companies, which accounted for 14 %. This trend has been more or less stable.

Some editors claim that their newspapers have a significantly larger readership online, rather than on newsstands. This can be explained by the fact that content is still free online and also accessed by the large number of Albanians living abroad. Indeed, according to the IREX, Media Sustainability Index 2010, "the internet website of a daily newspaper that sells about 5000 copies has about 16,000 visitors per day, most of whom are emigrants abroad."

Apart from traditional media on the web, new players have joined the media scene, represented by the so-called news aggregators or news agencies. Among them the most important are the public Albanian Telegraphic Agency (ATA), BalkanWeb, NOA, Gazeta Start, and Lajmi Fundit. ATA and the commercial agency NOA publish news from Albania, Kosovo, and Macedonia. Their websites offer an array of information and topics, similar to the main daily newspapers.

In addition, they have some interactive content, such as commenting, forums, and the possibility of RSS feeds. At the moment, 26 daily newspapers are published in Albania. While their circulation and number of sold copies are not made public, the total combined circulation is believed not to exceed 70,000 copies, with the biggest-selling newspaper having a circulation below 25,000 copies (Goga 2009). These papers include three party newspapers—Zëri i Popullit, of the leftwing Socialist Party, Rilindja Demokratike, of the rightwing Democratic Party, and Integrimi, of the leftwing Socialist Movement for Integration (Lëvizja Socialiste për Integrim)—and some sports newspapers.

Competition from television and new media, combined with the lack of improvement of quality in reporting, has led to a steady fall in the popularity of newspapers, especially among young people. In the Open Society Foundation for Albania survey "Use of Facebook, Twitter, YouTube, and Blogging" (2010) of more than 2000 people aged 15–39, almost 72 % said that they did not read newspapers at all.

Of all existing national analog television stations, the public broadcaster Radio Televizioni Shqiptar (RTSH) enjoys the greatest coverage: 80.5 % of the territory, followed by TV Klan with 70.2 %, and Top Channel with 62.1 %. If estimates of the advertising market are taken into account, TV Klan, Top Channel, Ora News, News 24, KohaTelevizion, TVSH, Vizion Plus, and Alsat TV (Albanian Screen TV) account for 81 % of the advertising market.

According to global website traffic ranking, the most popular online media are Top Channel, BalkanWeb, Telegrafi, and Shekulli. Given the sizable number of Albanians who live abroad, the Internet is becoming increasingly more popular source of information especially among younger youth.

The most significant foreign ownership presence today is Germany's WAZ–Mediengruppe, which bought from Albanian-owned company Media Vizion the majority shares of Vizion Plus, an important television station in Tirana, which also has a national satellite-broadcasting license and a digital terrestrial and satellite multiplex. One of the most important media groups is Top Media, comprising Top Albania Radio, the first private radio station to receive a national license; Top Channel; DigitAlb, the first digital terrestrial and satellite multiplex; the daily newspaper Shqip; and Top Gold Radio. Shekulli Media Group owns the daily newspapers Shekulli, considered by journalists to be one of the dailies with the highest circulation, and SportiShqiptar. It also owns the publishing house Botimet Max, A1 Televizion, and the national radio station +2 Radio, as well as Abbisnet, one of the large Internet service providers in the country. Other important groups are Media Vizion (owner of the Tring Digital multiplex) and the Panorama group, which owns Panorama, reputedly the daily paper with the highest circulation, Panorama Sport, and Psikologjia magazine. Finally, the Klan group owns the national station TV Klan and the daily newspaper Koha Jone.

Another group that certainly deserves a mention is Edisud Group, which owns the daily newspaper Gazeta Shqiptare and the online news agency BalkanWeb. This company also owns Edisud Radio TV, including Radio Rash and News 24. Recently, this group sold its outlets to Focus Group, owned by two businessmen, Artan Santo, involved in banking, and Irfan Hysenbelliu, who owns other media outlets, including the Panorama group.

What these groups have in common is the cross-ownership of several media outlets, their location in the capital, and, with a few exceptions, their owners' involvement in other sectors apart from the media. Subscriptions remain extremely low, whereby a paper with the highest circulation of 23,000 copies per day counts only 400 subscriptions.

8.12.2   Bosnian and Herzegovinian Media Market Outlook

The media market in Bosnia and Herzegovina characterizes high advertising market share of TV, low advertising market share of print media, high ethnic diversity and potential to broadcast multicultural programs, low market competition of TV stations, and low market competition of daily newspapers.

Importantly, the media market remains poor and fragmented, with a large number of small broadcasters. The level of professionalism and the quality of journalism remain weak, with widespread self-censorship, low reporting quality, lack of investigative journalism, and disrespect for basic standards as defined in the Press Code.

The newspaper market in Bosnia and Herzegovina is highly concentrated as the first four newspapers receive more than 50 % of the total advertising revenues in the market (Tsourvakas 2010). The rapid commercialization of reading women's magazines from Croatia and Bosnia is steadily increasing—Azra (Reading rate 14.7 %) and Gloria (12.5 %) have taken lead, in front of serious political magazines, such as Dani (9.4 %) and Slobodna Bosna (7.2 %) (Tsourvakas 2010). Major daily newspapers in Bosnia and Herzegovina in terms of annual advertising revenues are Dnevni Avaz, Dnevni list, Oslobodjenje, and Nezavisne novine.

In addition, there are 144 radio stations active in the market of which 65 are public and 79 are privately financed. There are 45 registered TV stations of which 30 are private and 15 are public. Four most dominant private TV stations are Al Jazeera, NTV Hayat, Pink BH, and OBN.

8.12.3   Bulgarian Media Market Outlook

Seven important international media corporations are present in Bulgarian media market: German newspaper group WAZ (Westdeutsche Algemeine Zeitung), the Swedish Modern Times Group, Central European Media Enterprises (CEME), the Irish Communicorp Group, SBS Broadcasting Group (Scandinavian Broadcasting System became in 2007 a part of ProSiebenSat.1 Media AG), US Emmis Communications, and News Corporation Group (owned by Rupert Murdoch).

The Bulgarian media market characterizes the high ethnic diversity and potential to broadcast multicultural programs and high market competition of daily newspapers. Moreover, reading rates of women's and lifestyle magazines are steadily decreasing.

Importantly, the aging of the Bulgarian media audience and readership is becoming increasingly visible as the share of demographic group of those over 65 years old is 19.3 % in 2014. Bulgaria is experiencing demographic crisis as its population is now shrinking at an alarming rate, losing 627,000 citizens in 10 years. By 2005, approximately 1.2 million people, mostly younger adults, left the country permanently, and the fertility rate is well below the replacement rate. 1/3 of households have just one member, and 76 % of families do not have children under 16. Bulgaria has one of the lowest birth rates in the world. By 2060, the UN projects that Bulgaria will have a population of just over 5.384 million, a huge drop from 1988's 8.981 million. Its median age increased from 30 in 1960 to 42 in 2012, the third-highest median age in the EU, surpassed only by Germany and Italy. Between 1950 and 1990, Bulgaria's population grew from 7.3 to 8.8 million before falling back. The population of northern Bulgaria is decreasing seven times faster compared to the population in the southern parts of the country. Bulgaria has one of the highest median age levels in Europe, 42 years and 8 months, with 19 % of the population being senior citizens aged 65+. In 2012, a total of 24 settlements were erased from Bulgaria's map, and 172 were on the verge of extinction because they had been completely depopulated. According to statistics, Bulgaria's population declines at a rate of 62,700 people a year topping the global ranking by rate of population extinction. Thus, the media market niche for middle-aged and retired population is growing and printed publications capturing these largely untapped media market niches would be increasingly profitable.

Currently, there are four television networks with nationwide coverage. BNT is the public service broadcaster with four regional and one satellite television networks. bTV is the commercial television network with the highest ratings. It is owned by US-based Central European Media Enterprises (CME) after its purchase from the Balkan News Corporation in April 2010. The second largest commercial network by audience is Nova, owned by Sweden's Modern Times Group (MTG). In August 2009, the Swedish Modern Times Group transferred and merged its assets in the Balkan Media Group (previously owned with Apace Media) into its subsidiary Nova Televizia. This includes the channel Nova TV (and also the Diema channels and MM channels), which in 2009 had a market share of 20.6 % (an increase from 17.1 % in 2008). The fourth network, bTV Action, is also owned by CME. In the years after 2000, when bTV was launched, the three nationwide television networks gathered a total combined market share of 70 %, a figure that in 2010 was down to 62.5 %.

The cable network has been developing quickly and most recent data (from the second half of 2009) show that over 70 % of households in the country are cable-operator subscribers. About 22 % of homes had satellite services (15 % pay satellite) at the end of 2009. Moreover, Bulgaria now has three satellite platforms: Bulsatcom, Total TV (formerly ITV Partner and rebranded in 2010 by Mid Europa Partners), and Vivacom (launched in September 2010).

The share of households with DTH platforms increased from 13 % in 2008 to 21 % in 2010. This growth was at the expense of cable television, whose share in the total number of television households dropped between 2008 and 2010. Linear Internet television access is still negligible, although the major channels do make content available on demand via the Internet.

Between 2001 and 2006, the average daily time spent in front of a television set rose from 285.6 to 307 minutes. In 2010, it rose further to 341 minutes. The most loyal viewers are over 55 years old and spend more than 6 h every day watching television.

The major dailies are Trud, Telegraph, and 24 Chasa. Dailies Trud and 24 Chasa, published by the German newspaper group WAZ (Westdeutsche Algemeine Zeitung), are the most typical examples of "hybrid" newspapers identifying themselves as "serious and quality" ones. The traditionally strong lifestyle and women's magazines, such as Eva, Cosmopolitan, and Grazia, are losing advertisers. In 2011, some 181 newspaper titles were printed in Sofia, which is equal to the number in all other regions of Bulgaria combined. According to Capital weekly compiled data report in June 2011, the Telegraph is the most popular title with a circulation of 115,000 copies. It belongs to the largest print media group in the country, the New Bulgarian Media Group. Next in the rankings are Trud and 24 Chasa, with circulations of 60,000 and 50,000, respectively. Their previous owner was the German media group Westdeutsche Allgemeine Zeitung (WAZ), but since 2011 they have been owned by a Bulgarian company, Media Group Bulgaria. In December 2012, Media Group Bulgaria transferred its ownership to Investbank. The fourth largest daily newspaper by circulation, Standart, is stated to have a circulation of 40,000. It is owned by Todor Batkov, an influential lawyer and local businessman. Moreover, the shareholders in Standart include Georgi Georgiev, who also controls other newspapers with a total circulation of approximately 250,000 copies.

Of the weekly newspapers, Weekend is the biggest with a circulation of 263,000. It is closely followed by Treta vazrast with roughly the same circulation. Weekend is part of the New Bulgarian Media Group, the same publishing house that owns Telegraph and a significant number of other newspapers. It also has a major influence on the newspaper distribution market.

In recent years radio market in Bulgaria has consolidated. Four foreign radio companies shape the image of the radio sector—the Irish Communicorp Group, SBS Broadcasting Group (Scandinavian Broadcasting System became in 2007 a part of ProSiebenSat.1 Media AG), US Emmis Communications, and News Corporation Group (owned by Rupert Murdoch). The foreign investors own almost 20 radio stations, most of them in Sofia (Tsourvakas 2010).

The public service broadcaster BNR has retained a large audience despite numerous competitors who rely primarily on music content. Despite the decrease in advertising revenue, radio stations still accounted for 7 % of the total advertising spend in 2012. The top 20 radio stations by reach are controlled by seven entities. According to a report by Market Links, commissioned by BNR, Horizont, which is BNR's main channel, has the biggest monthly reach of any radio station in Bulgaria, with 23.0 % (Market Links Report 2012). In second place is Veselina commercial radio station, which forms part of a company that also owns Vitosha, Magic FM, and a radio and television station called The Voice. Since 2011, its proprietor has been a company related (according to media reports) to a shareholder in Standart newspaper, who is also an owner of the newspapers Show and Doctor, and the news website Blitz.bg. Third by monthly reach is Darik, a polythematic commercial network, followed by NJOY, owned by bTV Media Group. It also owns Z Rock, Melody, Classic FM, and Jazz FM. Fourth by reach is Radio 1, owned by the Irish company Communicorp, which also controls Radio 1 Rock, BG Radio, Energy, City, Veronica, and Nova (not to be confused with the television broadcaster of the same name). Communicorp's stations are all in the top 10 by reach, with the exception of Nova. Apart from its dominance of the Bulgarian Radio market, Communicorp owns stations in Ireland, Czech Republic, Estonia, Finland, Hungary, Jordan, Latvia, and Ukraine.

Another significant player is the owner of Radio Fresh, FM+, and Star FM. Prior to 2012, these were part of US-based company Emmis. The buyer is Reflex media, a Bulgarian company, with no previous presence in the media market. The seventh major company owns Focus, a radio news station. In recent years, K2, a Sofia radio station, is often quoted by other media due to its consistent (albeit one-sided) low-cost coverage of politics. A particular case of cross-promotion is evident in radio stations owned by bTV Media Group, which are heavily promoted by the most popular television station, bTV. Overall, the departure of foreign investors from the local radio market caused a stalled growth.

The average daily time spent listening to the radio has decreased slightly in recent years. Between 2009 and 2011, this indicator fell from 215 to 195 min. Bulgarians spend 11.7 h a week listening to radio compared with 16 h surfing online, according to a study by the local branch of the IAB. An estimated 57 % of Internet users listen to radio online every month, while 17 % listen to radio online daily. According to 2010 research, people aged 30–50 listen to radio most often while driving and at work. The younger and more educated prefer the radio not only for music but also for short news bulletins. Most often they listen to radio online or via mobile devices.

In addition, there was a tenfold increase in the number of Internet users in Bulgaria between 2002 and 2011, according to data from the International Tele-communication Union (ITU). More specifically, the Internet penetration increased from 17 % of total number of households in 2006 to 50.9 % in 2012. Concurrently, there are significant regional inequalities in Internet penetration. Southwest Bulgaria has the highest share of Internet access (57.3 %), which is explained by the fact that this region is supplied with relatively good optic-fiber infrastructure, the largest number of Internet service providers (ISPs), and the strongest consumer demand. Thus, the first decade of the twenty-first century in Bulgaria was marked by the rise of the Internet and the corresponding decline in sales of print media. According to the NSI, the number of newspaper titles fell from 545 in 2000 to 369 in 2011, while at the same time, the annual combined circulation of all newspapers in the country fell by 15 %. Nevertheless, the percentage of people who read daily newspapers has stayed stable: roughly 36 %.

Moreover, the four most popular Bulgarian-owned online media services measured by the daily unique browsers and monthly reach (i.e., Abv.bg, Vbox7.com HP, Netinfo, and Gbg.bg) are owned by Netinfo digital media company (Glowacki 2011).

8.12.4 Croatian Media Market Outlook

The main features of the Croatian media market include: high Internet usage, low free newspaper distribution, high TV viewing time per viewer, high audience share of Public TV, low market competition of daily newspapers, low advertising market share of print media, and high advertising market share of TV. In addition, the share of advertisement revenues at the state-owned HRT (Hrvatska Radio-Televizija or Croatian Radio-Television) increased for television to 77 % or nearly 700 million euros in 2009, matching an increasing entertaining but also news reporting content of the four national broadcasters. The audience leadership belongs to the public television, but private televisions are narrowing the gap to it.

The government controls approximately 40 % of radio stations. There are six licensed national Radio stations. Two private music-only stations are leaders among radio audience. Although, there is a steady decline in production of newspaper, the increasing number of Internet users proves to be a fertile ground for a growing number of Internet portals. Importantly, all major newspapers online websites (Jutarnji list, Vecernji list, and Slobodna Dalmacija) are featured among the top 20 Croatian sites.

The magazine market is led by women's magazines Gloria and Story with 8 and 5 %, of average readership respectively. The sales of daily newspapers have declined steadily since 2007.

8.12.5 Cypriot Media Market Outlook

The Cyprus media market characterizes a small market size, high Internet usage, low TV viewing time per viewer, high audience share of commercial TV, low audience share of Public TV, and high market competition of radio stations.

In addition, the top six channels account for around 75 % of daily audiences (+1.5 % compared to 2008). Cyprus media market is very promising for prospective FDI in the daily newspapers industry as well as TV industry. TV media market is the most sustainable for FDI inflows, closely followed by daily newspapers. The radio market is the least profitable for prospective FDI inflows.

8.12.6 Greek Media Market Outlook

The Greek media market characterizes: high free newspaper distribution, high TV viewing time per viewer, high audience share of commercial TV, low audience share of Public TV, high market competition of daily newspapers, high market competition of radio stations, low advertising market share of print media, and low advertising market share of TV.

Free sheets have the highest percentages of readership (City press Free Daily 271.000 and Metro Free Daily 250.000) as well as the largest advertising revenues. Demand in Greece for foreign publications is very high due to the number of tourists visiting the country. Correspondingly, there are 33 periodicals in English, 1 in French, 7 in German, 6 in Italian, and many more in Spanish, Chinese, Russian, Albanian, Turkish, Bulgarian, Armenian, Polish, Dutch, and Arab. Moreover, 2 %

of Greek newspapers and magazines are exported to Cyprus, the United States, Germany, and Great Britain. There are 600 newsagents and 500 subagencies in the Greek provinces for the distribution of printed media. Within Greece, there are 12,000 places where the print media is sold. The number of agents, agencies, and distribution centers exceeds the demand and the general population's needs in comparison to the other nations in the European Union. Newspaper industry continually experiences a high percentage of unsold newspapers (30–35 %), thus, increasing its production costs. The print media ownership is highly concentrated as most of the leading newspapers belong to few media organizations such as Lambrakis Press S.A., Pegasus Publishing and Printing S.A (Bobolas Publishing Group), Tegopoulos Publishing S.A (Tegopoulos Publishing Group), Kathimerini Publications S.A. (Alafouzos Publishing Group), and Acropolis, (Apogevmatini Publishing Group) (Tsourvakas 2010).

The use of online news portals is constantly increasing, but is still relatively low in comparison with other European countries. Most radio stations broadcast news and music. In terms of audience, Skai Radio (owned by Alafouzos Publishing Company) takes the lead (10.8 %) over Rythmos (8.4 %), which has a music format. In recent years, there has been an increase in sport radio programs with Nova Sport FM in the lead with 7.1 % of the market. Multicultural radio is also on a development track due to the cultural diversity of the Greek society. In terms of viewership, Mega Channel (20.8 %) and Antenna (18.1 %) control the market, followed by Alpha TV (13.5 %) and Star (11.4 %). On the other hand, public channels enjoy less market share in comparison to the private channels (NET - 10.09 %, ERT 1 - 10.5 %, and ERT 2 - 8.4 %).

8.12.7 Hungarian Media Market Outlook

The Hungarian media market is one of the most sophisticated in South East Europe featuring high Internet usage, high TV viewing time per viewer, high audience share of commercial TV, low market competition of daily newspapers, TV and Radio stations, low advertising market share of print media, high newspaper readership, and high advertising market share of TV. However, the VAT tax on newspapers and magazines is 15 %, making it one of the highest in Europe.

The two terrestrial commercial channels, RTL Klub which is owned by a consortium of CLT, Bertelsmann, Pearson, and the telecom company T-com and TV2 whose majority owner is Scandinavian Broadcasting System (SBS) dominate the television scene since their launching in 1997. The Swedish Modern Times Group manages the Budapest edition of Metro while Ringier-owned Népszabadság and Blikk share the highest circulation among the Hungarian daily newspapers. The private broadcasters with the highest viewing rates are RTL Klub and TV 2, established in 1997. Online news sites are growing in importance and picking up the slack as the print media's readership declines. Currently the news portals Index and Origo have the most visitors.

8.12.8   Kosovar Media Market Outlook

The Kosovar media market characterizes the high Internet usage, high audience share of Public TV, and low market competition of TV stations.

Specifically, out of 21 TV stations, three major broadcasters have Kosovo-wide coverage, covering 75 % of Kosovo's population: the public broadcaster Radio and Television of Kosovo (RTK) and the privately owned broadcasters—Radio and Television 21 (RTV21) and Kohavision (KTV). Their broadcasting ratings are as follows: RTK 52 %, RTV21 49 %, and KTV 28 %. There are additional 18 local TV stations.

There are between 25,000 and 35,000 copies sold every day in Kosovo. Koha ditore and Kosova Sot have the highest circulation. The weak distribution and sales system are the main reasons and indicators for the low circulation of newspapers.

Local radios have significantly larger share of the audience in comparison with national radios—60.76 % compared to 33.54 % for national radio emitters (5.68 % are for foreign and/or other radio stations). There are four nationwide radio stations, two public (Radio Kosova and Radio Blue Sky) and two private (Radio 21 and Radio Dukagjini). The country has also 90 local radio stations.

In a territory with a high percentage of young people, it is particularly profitable that public and commercial broadcasters appeal to the young audience and opinion formers.

8.12.9   FYR Macedonian Media Market Outlook

The main features of the Macedonia media market include high ethnic diversity and a strong potential to broadcast multicultural programs, high free newspaper distribution, high TV viewing time per viewer, high audience share of commercial TV, low audience share of Public TV, and high market competition of TV stations.

Apart from three terrestrial MRT broadcast channels (MTV1, MTV2, and Parliamentary Channel) as well as MKTV-SAT, a satellite channel for the Diaspora, there are four national broadcasters in Macedonia: Kanal 5 TV, Sitel TV, Telma TV, and ALSAT-M-TV.

Among 77 TV broadcasting licenses issued in FYR Macedonia, there are four national terrestrial, 16 national satellite, 10 regional, and 47 local TV channels. Additionally, there are three radio stations with national coverage (Antenna 5, Kanal 77, and Metropolis).

Leading Macedonian-language newspapers are Dnevnik, Vest, Utrinski Vesnik, Vecer, and Nova Makedonija. Leading Albanian-language newspapers are Lajm, Zhurnal plus, Koha, and Fakti. During the last decade, the combined circulation of all newspapers shrank from 150,000 to 60,000.

8.12.10   Maltese Media Market Outlook

Main characteristics of the Maltese media market are a small market size, high Internet usage, high market competition of radio stations, high advertising market share of print media, and low advertising market share of TV.

Times of Malta is Malta's top media house and the oldest daily newspaper still in circulation in Malta. Founded in 1935, by the Strickland Foundation - and independent media organization it is the oldest daily newspaper still in circulation in Malta. It has the widest circulation of 37,000 copies a day and is seen as the daily newspaper of "reference" of the Maltese press. The newspaper and its popular website timesofmalta.com are known to be the most influential media sources in Malta. Locally, Timesofmalta.com is by far the most accessed website in Malta overall. Other popular online news media include Malta Today—Weekly Maltese newspaper, Independent.com.mt, Dailymail.co.uk, BBC.com, and tvm.com.mt.

The media advertising market in Malta is estimated at 30 million euro. Fifty percent of the total national advertising budget is spent on the print media, while 39 % is spent on the broadcast media (Borg 2009).

About 15 % of viewers watch the Mediaset stations and 7 % watch the RAI stations.

Accessing RAI stations either terrestrially or through cable was introduced in 1992. Around 80 % of Maltese households are now subscribed via Cable TV.

8.12.11   Moldovan Media Market Outlook

The Moldovan media market characterizes a low circulation of dailies (varying from 3000 to 9000 copies), a weak distribution system of the newspapers in the rural areas, low newspaper concentration, high audience share of Public TV, and high ethnic diversity and potential to broadcast multicultural programs.

There are four TV channels and six radio stations with nationwide coverage. The most popular TV stations are "Prime" TV (3.1 % rating and 23.8 % market share), "Pro TV" (1.2 % rating and 9 % market share), "NIT" (1.1 % rating and 8.1 % market share), and "Moldova 1" (0.9 % rating and 6.6 % market share) (The Eastern Partnership Civil Society Forum 2011). The most viewed international broadcast media (with local programs) are "Perviy Kanal," Russia, "CTC," Russia, "NTV," Russia, and "Pro TV," Romania. Romanian and Russian programming has a heavy presence on Moldovan television. "Jurnal TV" was launched by Jurnal Trust Media in March 2010 with investments from Reinstein Media Management (German Company) (The Eastern Partnership Civil Society Forum 2011). In 2010, the TV advertising market accounted for about 16 million euros a year.

The Internet usage increased from 13.1 % in 2005 to 48.8 % in 2014. This increase corresponds with the take-up of IPTV. The number of households watching IPTV increased from 108,000 to 226,000 between 2005 and 2009.

The most popular online media, judging by the number of unique visitors, are "Unimedia" (about 16,000 daily visitors), Jurnal.md (about 5600 visitors), and Publika.md (4600 visitors). StireaZilei.md has about 2400 daily unique visitors, OMG.md—2100, Azi. md—1200, and Hotnews.md—1100 (The Eastern Partnership Civil Society Forum 2011). Among the newspapers with Internet platforms, the most popular include Timpul (Timpul.md) and Jurnal (Jurnal.md) with approximately 100,000 unique visitors per month.

8.12.12 Montenegrin Media Market Outlook

Main characteristics of the Montenegrin media are high ethnic diversity and potential to broadcast multicultural programs, small market size, and high market competition of TV and Radio stations.

The size of the advertising market in 2014 was about 9 million euros, of which 5.5 million euros went to advertising in broadcast media. The record annual advertising market in Montenegro in the past decade was around 13,000,000 euros. In addition, more than 80 % of advertising is taken by dominant advertising agencies, and the remaining 20 % is the result of direct negotiations between advertisers and media companies. In order to gain a minimal profitability, an average television station in Montenegro has to raise 160,000 euros per month.

8.12.13 Romanian Media Market Outlook

Main characteristics of the Romanian media include large market size, low Internet usage: 58 %, high free newspaper distribution, high TV viewing time per viewer, high audience share of Public TV, high market competition of TV stations, low advertising market share of print media, and high advertising market share of TV.

Television takes the lion share of the advertising pie (about two-thirds) amounting to a total of US $177 million in 2014. Revenue in the social media advertising segment amounts to US $15.6 million in 2016. Revenue is expected to show an annual growth rate (CAGR 2016–2020) of 6.97 % resulting in a market value of US $20.4 million in 2020.

According to the Media Factbook 2009, the most popular TV shows among Romanians are football games, Romanian soap operas, prime-time news, entertainment shows, and international contests such as the Eurovision or big sporting events. Reception via analogue cable is at 66.8 %. Pro TV (owned by CME—Central European Media Enterprises) and Antena 1 (owned by Intact Media Group) are the most popular TV channels in Romania. Companies owned by the MediaPro group are Publimedia, MediaPro Studios, MediaPro Pictures, MediaPro Distribution, ProVideo, Mediafax, MediaPro Interactiv, Indoor Media, Coprint, and the Pro Foundation. In addition, MediaPro owns film studios in Romania.

As far as the publications distributed across the nation are concerned, the past few years have seen a decline in circulation of quality newspapers, whereas the two national sports dailies have done relatively well, and the tabloids even better. Nevertheless, according to information provided by the National Study of Audience (Studiul National de Audienta—SNA Focus), a study by the Bureau of Circulations and Audit for the Romanian press (BRAT—Biroul Roman de Audit al Tirajelor), the newspaper market declined severely over the past 5 years for 65 %. More specifically, the quality newspapers' sales market share has declined dramatically in the last 5 years in Romania. Accordingly, out of newspapers sold, quality newspapers fell from a market share of 32.6 % in 2009 to 16.1 % market share in the first 9 months of 2014. Importantly, unlike papers in Bucharest, local newspapers usually have not received any attention from big investors.

Lifestyle magazines covering the issues of automobiles, computers, cooking, house and gardening, and other niche products are popular in Romania. One of the most popular is *Practic in Bucatarie*, a cooking magazine owned by Burda Romania, selling more than 250,000 copies a month. Femeia de azi, a women's weekly published by Sanoma Hearst, also sells more than 100,000 copies per issue. National TV guides are doing well, too; TV Mania (Ringier) and ProTV Magazin (MediaPro), for example, each sell around 75,000 copies a week.

Tabloids continue to be Romania's most-read newspapers, although their audience is in a slight decline, as is the case for most printed publications. Click! remains the most-read newspaper in Romania, with 554,000 readers per edition, according to BRAT's SNA for 4 June 2012—4 May 2014. Libertatea, a tabloid published by Ringier, ranks second highest with audiences, with 436,000 readers per edition on average. For the analyzed period, the sports newspapers are the next most read, with Gazeta Sporturilor having a medium readership per edition of 324,000. This is followed by ProSport, with 339,000 readers. Among quality publications, Jurnalul National keeps hold of its leadership with 169,000 readers per edition, followed by Evenimentul Zilei with 154,000 readers and Adevarul with 141,000 readers. The most-read newspapers also posted the highest decreases in readership: Click! lost 33,000, Libertatea lost 32,000, and Jurnalul National lost 18,000.

According to the regulatory body ANCOM, the number of subscribers to television broadcasting services reached 6.4 million at the end of 2013. Most of them (4.1 million) prefer cable services (of whom 1.5 million have access to digital services), 2.2 million were subscribers to satellite networks, and 56,000 received those programs through IP technology.

In January 2014, German ProSiebenSat.1 sold all media it owned in Romania. The Greek Antenna Group bought Kiss TV, Kiss FM, Magic FM, One FM, and Rock FM.

The participation of Western publishers in the Romanian press market (i.e., the local press and magazine market) is low compared with other Eastern European countries. Accordingly, the FDI inflows into press market are dominantly untapped.

Most successful private radio stations belong to strong networks: Europa FM (owned by French group Lagardere) and Info Pro (CME).

After the cable subscriptions, satellite subscriptions are on the second place and are mainly popular in rural areas, where cable television and optical fiber networks are not widely available. IP Television is popular in business, rather than consumer sector. It is dominantly provided by Telekom Romania (formerly Romtelecom) and INES (an Internet, IPTV, and Internet provider). Due to old network architecture affecting the IP Television's program quality, this media service is way behind cable and satellite television.

8.12.14   Serbian Media Market Outlook

The Serbian media market characterizes low newspaper concentration, high audience share of Public service TV, low free newspaper distribution, high TV viewing time per viewer, high ethnic diversity and potential to broadcast multicultural programs, high audience share of Public TV, low concentration of daily newspapers, high market concentration of TV stations, and high market concentration of radio stations. Revenue in the social media advertising segment amount to US $5.7 million in 2016. Revenue is expected to show an annual growth rate (CAGR 2016–2020) of 12.99 % resulting in a market volume of US $9.2 million in 2020.

The FDI to the Serbian media market is most dominant in the printed media. In 2014, the value of media advertising market in Serbia is 155 million euros. In 2015, most people read Kurir (122,000 copies), Vecernje Novosti (119,000), Blic (103,968), Alo! (89,511), and Politika (55,970). Swiss company Ringier is well positioned in the media market owning three dailies in Serbia (Blic, Alo!, and free paper 24 sata) and three weeklies (NIN, Puls, Blic zena, and monthly Blic zena kuhinja). Their dailies are the third (Blic) and fourth (Alo!) on the readership list. NIN is the first among political and economic magazines; in March 2009 Ringier bought 70 % stocks of the old Serbian newsweekly NIN, and in April 2010 the company purchased an additional 13.2 %. The company claims a 25 % increase in circulation, now 16,200, since it has become the majority owner. Blic zena is second among women's magazines and Puls fourth among celebrity magazines. In March 2010, Ringier and German publishing concern Axel Springer formed a joint venture that unites their business activities in the east and southeast of Europe, including Serbia. In spring 2010, the company reported five million euros profit for their Serbian businesses in 2009, 150 % more than in 2008.

Moreover, The Westdeutsche Allgemeine Zeitung(WAZ) Media Group has been represented in the Serbian media market since October 2001 by a joint venture with newspaper publisher Politika AD, based in Belgrade. The WAZ Group holds 50 % of the shares in the company. In Serbia, WAZ publishes national daily Politika, regional daily Dnevnik, and licensed car magazine Auto Bild. Other foreign media companies publish lifestyle, fashion, and various specialized weeklies and monthlies. They include but are not limited to Adria Media (Story, Cosmopolitan, Men's Health, Lisa, Elle, Gala, National Geographic, Kuhinjske tajne, Moj stan, Basta, Zivot sa cvecem, and Sensa), Europapress (Gloria and OK!), and Attica Media Serbia (Grazia, Maxim, Playboy, and Sale & Pepe).

The leading magazine publisher in Serbia is CPG—Color Press Group. In terms of circulation, among 20 top weekly, biweekly, and monthly magazines in Serbia, 16 belong to the Color Press Group. The first three magazines are women's magazines (Pošalji recept—175,768 copies; Blic žena—125,889; Torte i kolači—120,485) closely followed by celebrity magazines (Scandal—68,933 copies; Svet—51,061; Star—44,116).

TV Broadcast ratings of top four TV stations are as follows: RTS1—Public Media Service, 18.5 %; TV Pink—15.8 %; TV Prva—10.7 %; TV B92—6.9 %.

8.12.15   Slovenian Media Market Outlook

Main characteristics of the Slovenian media market include high Internet usage: 73 %, high free newspaper distribution, low TV viewing time per viewer, high audience share of Public TV, low concentration of daily newspapers, small market size, high newspaper readership, high advertising market share of print media—30 %, high advertising market share of TV-55 %, and high market concentration of TV and radio stations.

After 2000 important foreign media actors on Slovenian market are Bonnier AG (Sweden), Styria Verlag, Leykam (Austria), and Burda (Germany).

The two public radio broadcasters Val 202 and Ra SLO1 are still the most popular in the country.

Apart from the national and regional public stations, private television broadcasters—POP TV (a member media group Pro Plus d.o.o. owned by Dutch CME Media Enterprises B.V.) and Kanal A—have a large number of viewers.

The gross value (without discounts) of the advertising pie in Slovenian media in 2008 was 522.5 million euro, 15 % higher than in 2007. More than half of the advertising income goes to television (55 %) and print media share of advertising pie is 30.2 %, while outdoor media (7.1 %), radio stations (4.4 %), and online media (3.5 %) together get approximately 15 % of the pie. Importantly, in 2016 social media advertising reached US \$4.9 million. Revenue is expected to show an annual growth rate (CAGR 2016-2020) of 11.50 % resulting in a market volume of US \$7.6 million in 2020.

Unlike in the print and radio market, foreign owners play an important role in the Slovenian commercial television market. Three of the largest commercial channels are all owned by foreign companies: Pop TV (audience share: 27 %) and Kanal A (9 %) are owned by the same company, American-owned Central European Media Enterprises (CME), while TV3 (2 %) is owned by the Swedish company Modern Times Group—MTG AB. In Slovenia, the television market is dominated by the channels of the Central European Media Enterprises (CME) Group (Pop TV, Kanal A, and the Pro Plus family of channels). Pop TV has an average rating share (7 pm–11 pm)—32.1 %; TV Slovenija 1—14.2 %; Kanal A—12.6 %; TV Slovenija 2—5.0 %;

Planet TV—3.7 %; Planet TV—3.7 %; TV3 Medias—2.2 %; POP Non-Stop—1.1 %; TV Slovenija 3—0.7 %. In February 2012, another significant player TV3 (part of the Modern Times Group—MTG) ceased operating and left the Slovenian market claiming an unfair domination of the CME Group in the advertising market. This case is still pending with the competition authorities. Cable served more than 30 % of homes at the end of 2012. The main operator is Telemach (formerly Mid Europa Partners who sold its investment in Telemach to UnitedGlobalCom), with approximately 200,000 subscribers. Telemach has gradually been taking over smaller operators including Elektro Turnsek and Kabel TV in the summer of 2013.

More than 26 % of Slovenian homes use IPTV services and three different services are available. SiOL (Telekom Slovenije) had approximately 126,636 subscribers in March 2013 (56 % of the market). Further data from 2012 (Post and Electronic Communications Agency of the Republic of Slovenia—AKOS) show that T2 had 32 % of the market. The only satellite package, Total TV (Mid Europa Partners), launched in 2007, has approximately 25,000 customers.

The main multiplex of RTV Slovenija has eight national and four regional channels. Six more local channels are provided on local multiplexes. Norkring (Multiplex B) left in February 2012 claiming that the public service broadcaster violated competition regulations by hosting commercial channels. Norkring dismantled the second Multiplex in Slovenia. A tender was launched for a third Multiplex (C) in October 2012, and this Multiplex was also granted to RTV Slovenija. In June 2012, the Media Act was amended providing free transmission of TV channels of special importance on the DTT multiplex operated by RTV Slovenija. Also in June 2012, the Digital Broadcasting Act was amended to forbid the hosting of commercial TV channels on the public multiplex when other DTT multiplexes are available.

As a result of stable economic and political situation, advanced ICT infrastructural development, and lacking strategic as well as competitive private ownership, Slovenian media market is relatively profitable for FDI inflows.

8.12.16   Turkish Media Market Outlook

Main characteristics of the Turkish media market include large market size, increasing readership of daily newspapers, high advertising market share of TV, high advertising market share of print media, high internet access spending, low market competition of radio stations, low market competition of TV stations, low audience share of Public TV, high audience share of commercial TV, high TV viewing time per viewer, and low free newspaper distribution.

In Turkey, all the major commercial channels and newspapers belong to following media groups and conglomerates including Doğan, Turkuvaz, Ciner, Çukurova, Doğuş Merkez, İhlas, and Feza. They use their media outlets to protect and expand their interests and activities in other sectors of the economy (tourism, finance, car industry, construction, and banking). Moreover, the distribution of the print media is in the hands of Doğan Group's Yay-Sat and Turkuvaz Group's Turkuvaz Dağıtım Pazarlama.

Newspapers in Turkey are growing in popularity despite increasing Internet use. For the first time in Turkish history, newspaper circulation at the weekend achieved a distribution of six million copies, according to data from two distribution companies. Overall, circulation has grown by 59 % since 2001, and there has also been a rapid increase in advertising revenues. Istanbul represents 45 % of the total newspaper sales in Turkey.

The market for imported press represents only 3 % of the total press market in Turkey as foreign population living in Turkey represents over 460,000 expatriates. The top ten foreign newspapers in Turkey are Bild, The Sun, International Herald Tribune, De Telegraaf, Het Laatste Nieuws, Financial Times, Daily Mail, Daily Mirror, Daily Star, and The Wall Street Journal Europe. The top ten foreign magazines/weeklies are Bild am Sonntag, The Economist, Newsweek, Ok Weekly, Time, Bild der Frau, Der Spiegel, Nur TV, and Sternand TV Direkt. 95 % of the foreign publications are imported by air, the main hub being Istanbul. In summer, Antalya is used as a second hub.

The Turkish TV market is one of the largest in Europe with almost 18 million television households. Kanal D (Doğan Group) had the largest daily audience market share in 2009 with 14.1 %, ahead of Show TV (Çukurova group, with 10.7 %), ATV (Çalık Group, 8.9 %), Fox Türk (News Corp group, 8 %), and Star (Doğan Group, 8 %). The public channels of the broadcaster TRT are a long way behind their private competitors, with the first public channel TRT 1 only recording a 3.1 % daily audience market share in 2009. The most important reception platforms are terrestrial and satellite, with almost 50 % of homes using satellite TV services (of these 15 % were pay services) at the end of 2009.

8.12.16.1 The Competitive Importance of Turkish Media Markets

Turkey's printed media industry provides ample opportunities for TNC's FDI inflows as the country (along with Croatia and Serbia) has relatively low level of newspaper readership, unlike some other countries in the region, most notably Greece, Romania, Slovenia, and FYR Macedonia. Furthermore, together with Romania, Turkey provides foreign media corporations with the largest untapped market size in the SEE region. Also, very low audience share of Public Service broadcasting implies that entry barriers in the Turkish television market are considerably lower as opposed to other SEECs markets. The main competitive advantage of Turkey in printed and TV media business as compared to the rest of the SEECs is its dominant market size, a high TV viewing time per viewer, as well as high advertising market share of television market (57 %) and high advertising share of printed media (31 %). Moreover, Internet access is the biggest segment in Turkish media by a wide margin, with revenue of US $3.5 bn in 2013 - well ahead of TV second TV advertising of US $1.3 bn in 2015, up from US $1 bn in 2011. In addition, Internet advertising will be Turkey's second - fastest growing segment during the five-year forecast period, rising at a CAGR of 12.5 % to reach US $1.3 bn in 2018. The growth in Internet advertising will strongly outpace TV advertising, Turkey's second-biggest segment, which will rise at a CAGR of 7.8% to US $2.3 bn in 2018. Revenue in the social media advertising segment amounts to US $100.8 million in 2018. Revenue is expected to show an annual growth rate (CAGR 2016–2020) of 10.71 % resulting in a market volume of US $151.4 million in 2010. TV subscriptions and licence fees revenue in 2013 reached US $1.5 bn. Another fast-growing segment of media advertising in Turkey over the next five years will be radio, expanding at a CAGR of 8.8 % to reach US $280 mn in 2018.

Additionally, the Turkish media market is particularly beneficial for the prospective media investors due to its FDI inflows and GDP growth. In 2014, Turkey had the world's 17th largest GDP-PPP. In parallel, Turkey has more than tripled its GDP reaching US$800 billion in 2014, up from US$231 billion in 2002. Concurrently, the export industry sector in Turkey increased by 350 % between 2004 and 2014. Accordingly, Turkey's nominal GDP is expected to grow to $4.45 trillion by 2050 becoming the twelfth largest in the world. Moreover, recent HSBC estimates that in 2020 Turkey's GDP will overtake Canada's and then South Korea's (2031), Spain's (2035), and Italy's (2042). In addition, the latest IMF forecasts project that Average Annual GDP Growth in Turkey for the period between 2009 and 2050 will be 4.33 % (the fourth largest after India, Indonesia, and China—among 19 largest global producers). During the period 2010–2011, Turkey achieved the largest annual increase in real GDP growth rate in Europe—8.2 %. In much the same way, Net FDI inflows in Turkey increased from US$783 million in 1999 to US$22.047 billion in 2007.

At the same time, Turkey's population is growing rapidly as well as the level of education, economic and infrastructural development, technological readiness, and investment in innovative technology. Moreover, Turkey's unique position linking three continents, being at the same time a European, Asian, Caucasian, Middle Eastern, Mediterranean, and Black Sea country, enables foreign companies wanting to use the crossroads between Europe and Asia as a production base for exports to the EU. Nevertheless, FDI to Turkey has dropped sharply since the financial crisis: UN data show it at $12.7 bn in 2014 as opposed to $28.9 bn in 2007. Consequently the share of greenfield in the total last year was a healthy 92 %, in 2007 just 49 % of Turkey's FDI was greenfield. Nevertheless, Turkey's economy grew at an average rate of 7.5 % between 2002 and 2006, faster than any other OECD country. Over the past 20 years, Turkey has made significant improvements in economic freedom expanding monetary and fiscal freedom as well as freedom from corruption. However, these advancements have, nevertheless, been undermined by Turkey's deteriorating property rights.

8.13   The Key Drivers and Propositions of the Hybrid Media FDI Business Model

In order to meet a complex and highly competitive media business demands, the author identifies and proposes an application as well as implementation of new business model—the FDI hybrid media business model consisting of seven synthetic, underlying, unique, and multidisciplinary factors/indicators/propositions/dimensions/variables/indices/key drivers and building blocks: (1) Media market concentration (Number of daily newspapers, radio stations, and TV stations per million); (2) ICT Competitiveness—The WEF Networked Readiness Index; (3) WIPO, Cornell University, and INSEAD Global Innovation Index; (4) The WEF Global Competitiveness Index; (5) SEECs forecasted GDP per capita (PPP) Index (2010–2019); (6) SEECs forecasted population prospects via the UN Medium variant (%), 2015–2100; and (7) Average annual HDI growth (%), 2000–2013. Additionally, these seven indicators instrumentally influence and shape the potential for strategically intensive and sustainable FDI into increasingly competitive SEECs media markets. Importantly, the hybrid FDI business media model is applicable to any global media corporation. In Tables 8.1, 8.2, 8.3, 8.4, 8.5, 8.6, 8.7, 8.8, 8.9, 8.10, and 8.11, the author examines specific parameters, indicators, indices, indexes, variables, and factors of SEECs media markets' hybrid FDI business models.

Table 8.1 Quantitative analysis of printed and broadcast media markets in SEECs

Country (or territory)	Number of daily newspapers	Number of TV stations	Number of radio stations	Number of daily newspapers per million Rank (out of 16) Lower number means less competition	Number of TV stations per million Rank (out of 16) Lower number means less competition	Number of radio stations per million Rank (out of 16) Lower number means less competition
Albania	23	73	58	7.2	22.85	18.15
Bosnia and Herzegovina	9	43	142	2.34	11.21	37
Bulgaria	62	103	83	8.75	14.53	11.71
Croatia	10	31	158	2.35	7.28	37.13
Cyprus	9	27	72	7.5	22.5	60
Greece	122	131	1058	10.96	11.77	95
Hungary	34	95	96	3.45	9.63	9.74
Kosovo	7	21	92	3.78	11.35	49.72
Macedonia, FYR	11	66	81	5.17	31.05	38.11
Malta	4	9	50	9.41	21.17	117.64
Moldova	38	69	56	10.7	19.44	15.77
Montenegro	4	23	52	6.62	38.07	86.09
Romania	159	606	614	8	30.48	30.88
Serbia	20	116	334	2.82	16.36	47.1
Slovenia	8	69	98	3.92	33.82	48.03
Turkey	280	255	1100	3.6	3.28	14.18
Total	804	1616	4010			

Table 8.2 SEECs the WEF Networked Readiness Index 2015

Country (or territory)	The WEF Networked Readiness Index 2015 Rank (out of 148)	Rank (out of 14) Coefficient ratio
Albania	92	14/14 = 1
Bosnia and Herzegovina	n/a	n/a
Bulgaria	73	12/14 = 0.857
Croatia	54	7/14 = 0.5
Cyprus	36	2/14 = 0.2
Greece	66	10/14 = 0.714
Hungary	53	6/14 = 0.428
Kosovo	n/a	n/a
Macedonia	47	4/14 = 0.285
Malta	29	1/14 = 0.071
Moldova	68	11/14 = 0.785
Montenegro	56	8/14 = 0.571
Romania	63	9/14 = 0.642
Serbia	77	13/14 = 0.928
Slovenia	37	4/14 = 0.214
Turkey	48	5/14 = 0.357

Table 8.3 SEECs WIPO, Cornell University, and INSEAD Global Innovation Index 2015

Country (or territory)	WIPO, Cornell University, and INSEAD Global Innovation Index 2015 Rank (out of 143)	Rank (out of 15) Coefficient ratio
Albania	94	15/15 = 1
Bosnia and Herzegovina	81	14/15 = 0.933
Bulgaria	44	7/15 = 0.466
Croatia	42	5/15 = 0.333
Cyprus	30	3/15 = 0.2
Greece	50	8/15 = 0.533
Hungary	35	4/15 = 0.266
Kosovo	n/a	n/a
Macedonia	60	12/15 = 0.8
Malta	25	1/15 = 0.066
Moldova	43	6/15 = 0.4
Montenegro	59	11/15 = 0.733
Romania	55	10/15 = 0.666
Serbia	67	13/15 = 0.866
Slovenia	28	2/15 = 0.133
Turkey	54	9/15 = 0.6

Table 8.4 The WEF Global Competitiveness Index 2015

Country (or territory)	The WEF Global Competitiveness Index 2015 Rank (out of 140)	Rank (out of 15) Coefficient ratio
Albania	93	13/15 = 0.866
Bosnia and Herzegovina	111	15/15 = 1
Bulgaria	54	4/15 = 0.266
Croatia	77	10/15 = 0.666
Cyprus	65	8/15 = 0.533
Greece	81	11/15 = 0.733
Hungary	63	7/15 = 0.466
Kosovo	n/a	n/a
Macedonia FYR	60	6/15 = 0.4
Malta	48	1/15 = 0.066
Moldova	84	12/15 = 0.8
Montenegro	70	9/15 = 0.6
Romania	53	3/15 = 0.2
Serbia	94	14/15 = 0.933
Slovenia	59	5/15 = 0.333
Turkey	51	2/15 = 0.133

Table 8.5 SEECs forecasted GDP per capita (PPP) Index (%), 2010–2019

Country (or territory)	SEECs forecasted GDP per capita (PPP) Index (%), 2010–2019	Rank (out of 16) Coefficient ratio
Albania	64	3/16 = 0.187
Bosnia and Herzegovina	50.22	6/16 = 0.375
Bulgaria	51.32	5/16 = 0.312
Croatia	23.38	14/16 = 0.875
Cyprus	3.66	16/16 = 1
Greece	18.98	15/16 = 0.937
Hungary	38.45	9/16 = 0.562
Kosovo	34.70	12/16 = 0.750
Macedonia	52.99	4/16 = 0.25
Malta	35.15	11/16 = 0.687
Moldova	68.24	1/16 = 0.062
Montenegro	45.36	8/16 = 0.5
Romania	65.94	2/16 = 0.125
Serbia	35.23	10/16 = 0.625
Slovenia	24.74	13/16 = 0.812
Turkey	50.03	7/16 = 0.437

Table 8.6   SEECs forecasted population prospects via the UN Medium variant (%), 2015–2100

Country (or territory)	SEECs forecasted population prospects via the UN Medium variant (%), 2015–2100	Rank (out of 16) Coefficient ratio
Albania	−45.05	11/16 = 0.687
Bosnia and Herzegovina	−49.96	14/16 = 0.875
Bulgaria	−51.92	15/16 = 0.937
Croatia	−38.54	10/16 = 0.625
Cyprus	15.5	1/16 = 0.0625
Greece	−33.56	8/16 = 0.5
Hungary	−33.98	9/16 = 0.562
Kosovo	−56.99	16/16 = 1
Macedonia	−30.02	7/16 = 0.435
Malta	−18.11	4/16 = 0.25
Moldova	−47.7	13/16 = 0.812
Montenegro	−27.64	6/16 = 0.375
Romania	−46.17	12/16 = 0.75
Serbia	−23.89	5/16 = 0.312
Slovenia	−15.51	3/16 = 0.187
Turkey	13.5	2/16 = 0.125

Table 8.7 SEECs average annual HDI growth (%), 2000–2013

Country (or territory)	SEECs average annual HDI growth (%), 2000–2013	Rank (out of 15) Coefficient ratio
Albania	0.69	5/15 = 0.333
Bosnia and Herzegovina	0.29	15/15 = 1
Bulgaria	0.66	7/15 = 0.466
Croatia	0.64	8/15 = 0.533
Cyprus	0.43	12–13/ 15 = 0.833
Greece	0.51	10/15 = 0.666
Hungary	0.43	12–13/15
Kosovo	n/a	n/a
Macedonia	(2005–2013) 0.67	6/15 = 0.4
Malta	0.57	9/15 = 0.6
Moldova	0.8	3/15 = 0.2
Montenegro	(2005–2013) 0.74	4/15 = 0.266
Romania	0.82	2/15 = 0.133
Serbia	0.34	14/15 = 0.933
Slovenia	0.48	11/15 = 0.733
Turkey	1.16	1/15 = 0.066

Table 8.8 The methodological dataset of the hybrid FDI business model for Albania, Bosnia and Herzegovina, Bulgaria, Croatia, and Cyprus

Country	Albania	Bosnia and Herzegovina	Bulgaria	Croatia	Cyprus
Number of daily newspapers per million	7.2	2.34	8.75	2.35	7.5
Rank (out of 16) Lower number means less competition Coefficient ratio	10/16 = 0.625	1/16 = 0.062	13/16 = 0.812	2/16 = 0.125	11/16 = 0.687
Number of TV stations per million	22.85	11.21	14.53	7.28	22.5
Rank (out of 16) Lower number means less competition Coefficient ratio	12/16 = 0.75	4/16 = 0.25	7/16 = 0.437	2/16 = 0.125	11/16 = 0.687
Number of radio stations per million	18.15	37	11.71	37.13	60
Rank (out of 16) Coefficient ratio Lower number means less competition	5/16 = 0.312	7/16 = 0.437	2/16 = 0.125	8/16 = 0.5	13/16 = 0.812
The WEF Networked Readiness Index 2015 Rank (out of 148)	92	n/a	73	54	36
Rank (out of 14) Coefficient ratio	14/14 = 1	n/a	12/14 = 0.857	7/14 = 0.5	2/14 = 0.142
WIPO, Cornell University, and INSEAD Global Innovation Index 2015 Rank (out of 143)	94	81	44	42	30
Rank (out of 16) Coefficient ratio	15/15 = 1	14/15 = 0.933	7/15 = 0.466	5/15 = 0.333	3/15 = 0.2
The WEF Global Competitiveness Index 2014–2015 Rank (out of 140)	97	n/a	54	77	58
Rank (out of 16) Coefficient ratio	14/14 = 1	n/a	3/14 = 0214	10/14 = 0.714	4/14 = 0.285
SEECs Average Annual HDI growth (%) 2000–2013	0.69	0.23	0.66	0.64	0.43
Coefficient ratio	(4/15 = 0.266)	(15/15 = 1)	(5/15 = 0.333)	(6/15 = 0.4)	(12–13/15 = 0.833)

(continued)

Table 8.8 (continued)

Country	Albania	Bosnia and Herzegovina	Bulgaria	Croatia	Cyprus
SEECs forecasted GDP per capita (PPP) Index 2010–2019 (%)	64	50.22	51.32	23.38	3.66
Rank (out of 16) Coefficient ratio	3/16 = 0.187	6/16 = 0.375	5/16 = 0.312	14/16 = 0.875	16/16 = 1
SEECs forecasted population prospects via the UN Medium variant (%), 2015–2100	−45.05	−49.96	−51.92	−38.54	15.5
Rank (out of 16) Coefficient ratio	11/16 = 0.687	14/16 = 0.875	15/16 = 0.937	10/16 = 0.625	1/16 = 0.062

Table 8.9 The methodological dataset of the hybrid FDI business model for Greece, Hungary, Kosovo, Macedonia FYR, and Malta

Country	Greece	Hungary	Kosovo	Macedonia FYR	Malta
Number of daily newspapers per million	10.96	3.45	3.78	5.17	9.41
Rank (out of 16) Lower number means less competition Coefficient ratio	$16/16 = 1$	$4/16 = 0.25$	$6/16 = 0.375$	$8/16 = 0.5$	$14/16 = 0.875$
Number of TV stations per million	11.77	9.63	11.35	31.05	21.17
Rank (out of 16) Lower number means less competition Coefficient ratio	$6/16 = 0.375$	$3/16 = 0.187$	$5/16 = 0.312$	$14/16 = 0.875$	$10/16 = 0.625$
Number of radio stations per million	95	9.74	49.72	38.11	117.64
Rank (out of 16) Lower number means less competition Coefficient ratio	$15/16 = 0.937$	$1/16 = 0.062$	$12/16 = 0.75$	$9/16 = 0.562$	$16/16 = 1$
The WEF Networked Readiness Index 2015 Rank (out of 148)	66	53	n/a	47	29
Rank (out of 14) Coefficient ratio	$10/14 = 0.714$	$6/14 = 0.428$	n/a	$4/14 = 0.285$	$1/14 = 0.071$
WIPO, Cornell University, and INSEAD Global Innovation Index 2014 Rank (out of 143)	50	35	n/a	60	25
Rank (out of 15) Coefficient ratio	$8/15 = 0.533$	$4/15 = 0.266$	n/a	$12/15 = 0.8$	$1/15 = 0.066$
The WEF Global Competitiveness Index 2015 Rank (out of 140)	81	66	n/a	60	48
Rank (out of 15) Coefficient ratio	$11/15 = 0.733$	$7/15 = 0.466$	n/a	$6/15 = 0.4$	$1/15 = 0.066$
SEECs Average Annual HDI growth (%), 2000–2013	0.51	0.43	n/a	0.67 (2005–2013)	0.57
Rank (out of 15) Coefficient ratio	$10/15 = 0.666$	$12–13/15 = 0.833$	n/a	$6/15 = 0.4$	$9/15 = 0.6$

(continued)

Table 8.9 (continued)

Country	Greece	Hungary	Kosovo	Macedonia FYR	Malta
SEECs forecasted GDP per capita (PPP) Index (%), 2010–2019	18.98	38.45	34.70	52.99	35.15
Rank (out of 16) Coefficient ratio	15/ 16 = 0.937	9/ 16 = 0.562	12/ 16 = 0.75	4/16 = 0.25	11/ 16 = 0.687
SEECs forecasted population prospects via the UN Medium variant (%), 2015–2100	−33.56	−33.98	−56.99	−30.02	−18.11
Rank (out of 16) Coefficient ratio	8/16 = 0.5	9/ 16 = 0.562	16/16 = 1	7/16 = 0.435	4/ 16 = 0.25

Table 8.10 The methodological dataset of the hybrid FDI business model for Moldova, Montenegro, Romania, Serbia, Slovenia, and Turkey

Country	Moldova	Montenegro	Romania	Serbia	Slovenia	Turkey
Number of daily newspapers per million	10.7	6.62	8	2.82	3.92	3.6
Rank (out of 16) Lower number means less competition Coefficient ratio	15/ 16 = 0.937	9/16 = 0.562	12/ 16 = 0.75	3/ 16 = 0.187	7/ 16 = 0.437	5/ 16 = 0.312
Number of TV stations per million	19.44	38.07	30.48	16.36	33.82	3.28
Rank (out of 16) Lower number means less competition Coefficient ratio	9/ 16 = 0.562	16/16 = 1	13/ 16 = 0.812	8/16 = 0.5	15/ 16 = 0.937	3/ 16 = 0.187
Number of radio stations per million	15.77	86.09	30.88	47.1	48.03	14.18
Rank (out of 16) Lower number means less competition Coefficient ratio	4/ 16 = 0.25	14/ 16 = 0.875	6/ 16 = 0.375	10/ 16 = 0.625	11/ 16 = 0.687	3/ 16 = 0.187
The WEF Networked Readiness Index 2015 Rank (out of 148)	68	56	63	77	37	48
Rank (out of 14) Coefficient ratio	11/ 14 = 0.785	8/14 = 0.571	9/ 14 = 0.642	13/ 14 = 0.928	3/ 14 = 0.214	5/ 14 = 0.37
WIPO, Cornell University, and INSEAD Global Innovation Index 2014 Rank (out of 143)	43	59	55	67	28	54
Rank (out of 15) Coefficient ratio	6/15 = 0.4	11/ 15 = 0.733	10/ 15 = 0.666	13/ 15 = 0.866	2/ 15 = 0.133	9/15 = 0.6
The WEF Global Competitiveness Index 2015 Rank (out of 140)	84	70	53	94	59	57
Rank (out of 15) Coefficient ratio	12/ 15 = 0.8	9/15 = 0.6	3/15 = 0.2	14/ 15 = 0.933	5/ 15 = 0.333	2/ 15 = 0.133
SEECs Average Annual HDI growth (%), 2000–2013	0.8	0.74 (2005–2013)	0.82	0.34	0.48	1.16

(continued)

Table 8.10 (continued)

Country	Moldova	Montenegro	Romania	Serbia	Slovenia	Turkey
Rank (out of 15) Coefficient ratio	3/15 = 0.2	4/15 = 0.266	2/ 15 = 0.133	14/ 15 = 0.933	11/ 15 = 0.733	1/ 15 = 0.066
SEECs forecasted GDP per capita (PPP) Index (%), 2010–2019	68.24	45.36	65.94	35.23	24.74	50.03
Rank (out of 16) Coefficient ratio	1/ 16 = 0.062	8/16 = 0.5	2/ 16 = 0.125	10/ 16 = 0.625	13/ 16 = 0.812	7/ 16 = 0.437
SEECs forecasted population prospects via the UN Medium variant (%), 2015–2100	−42.7	−27.64	−46.17	−23.89	−15.51	13.5
Rank (out of 16) Coefficient ratio	13/ 16 = 0.812	6/16 = 0.375	12/ 16 = 0.75	5/ 16 = 0.312	3/ 16 = 0.187	2/ 16 = 0.125

Table 8.11 Individual and cumulative average hybrid FDI inflows coefficient ratio for daily newspapers, TV stations, and Radio stations in SEECs media markets

Country	Daily newspapers' average hybrid FDI inflows coefficient ratio Rank (out of 16) Lower number means more profitable prospects for FDI	TV stations' average hybrid FDI inflows coefficient ratio Rank (out of 16) Lower number means more profitable prospects for FDI	Radio stations' average hybrid FDI inflows coefficient ratio Rank (out of 16) Lower number means more profitable prospects for FDI	Cumulative average hybrid FDI inflows coefficient ratio for daily newspapers, TV stations, and Radio stations in SEECs media markets Rank (out of 16) Lower number means more profitable prospects for FDI
Albania	0.68—13/16	0.698—15/16	0.636—12/16	0.671—12/16
Bosnia and Herzegovina	0.649—12/16	0.686—13/16	0.724—14/16	0.686—13/16
Bulgaria	0.561—9/16	0.508—7/16	0.463—5/16	0.51—7/16
Croatia	0.51—7/16	0.51—8/16	0.563—11/16	0.527—9/16
Cyprus	0.458—4/16	0.458—3/16	0.476—7/16	0.464—5/16
Greece	0.726—16/16	0.636—12/16	0.717—13/16	0.693—14/16
Hungary	0.57—11/16	0.561—10/16	0.543—9/16	0.558—11/16
Kosovo	0.708—15/16	0.687—14/16	0.833—16/16	0.742—16/16
Macedonia, FYR	0.438—3/16	0.492—6/16	0447—4/16	0.459—4/16
Malta	0.448—6/16	0.452—2/16	0.506—8/16	0.482—6/16
Moldova	0.569—10/16	0.507—9/16	0.472—6/16	0.519—8/16
Montenegro	0.515—8/16	0.577—11/16	0.56—10/16	0.55—10/16
Romania	0.466—5/16	0.475—4/16	0.413—2/16	0.451—3/16
Serbia	0.682—14/16	0.727—16/16	0.745—15/16	0.718—15/16
Slovenia	0.406—2/16	0.477—5/16	0.441—3/14	0.441—2/16
Turkey	0.29—1/16	0.271—1/16	0.271—1/16	0.277—1/16

8.14 Final Conclusions, Implications, and Summary of Main Findings: Benchmarking, Refocusing, and Repositioning the Future FDI Inflows Potential and Competitiveness of SEECs Media Markets

After a detailed meta-analysis of multiple-case studies of the SEECs media markets (including 804 daily newspapers, 1737 TV stations, and 4144 radio stations), the author argues that printed media markets are least concentrated as opposed to broadcasting media (TV and particularly radio media). The lowest market competition of daily newspapers is attributable to Bosnia and Herzegovina, Croatia,

Serbia, and Hungary. Conversely, the highest market competition is noticeable in Greece, Moldova, Malta, and Bulgaria. Concurrently, the highest media competition in TV industry is visible in Montenegro, Slovenia, FYR Macedonia, and Romania. In addition, the lowest competition of TV media market is present in Turkey, Croatia, Hungary, and Bosnia and Herzegovina. In parallel, countries featuring the highest radio market competition include Malta, Greece, Montenegro, and Cyprus. Conversely, countries outstripping its competition by having considerably lower concentration of radio markets are Hungary, Bulgaria, Turkey, and Moldova. Overall, most saturated and competitive media markets in SEECs are in Malta, Montenegro, Greece, and Cyprus. Conversely, countries with the lowest media competition market in South East Europe include Hungary, Turkey, Croatia, and Bosnia and Herzegovina.

Additionally, the most profitable SEECs markets for FDI inflows in daily newspapers industry include Turkey, Slovenia, FYR Macedonia, and Cyprus. The FDI inflows in TV media are highly recommended to Turkey, Malta, Cyprus, and Romania. FDI in radio industry is the least profitable business because of the low consumption of this media as well as high market competition in SEECs markets. Nevertheless, SEECs markets recommended for FDI inflows in radio industry include Turkey, Romania, Slovenia, and FYR Macedonia. In contrast, the least profitable SEECs markets in daily newspapers industry include Greece, Kosovo, Serbia, and Albania. FDI inflows in TV media are least recommended to Serbia, Albania, Kosovo, and Bosnia and Herzegovina. The least profitable SEECs markets for FDI in radio industry include Kosovo, Serbia, Bosnia and Herzegovina, and Greece. Overall, the most profitable SEECs media markets for FDI in daily newspapers, TV, and Radio industry include Turkey, Slovenia, Romania, and FYR Macedonia. In contrast, the least profitable SEECs media markets for FDI include Kosovo, Serbia, Greece, and Bosnia and Herzegovina.

Moreover, the main findings also show a clear relation between the high urban population and high level of newspaper readership. Consequently, the high level of rural population connotes a low level of newspaper readership. This is particularly the case in Malta, Hungary, Slovenia (dominantly urban population), and Moldova and Albania (dominantly rural population). Moreover, rural population increasingly favors watching television program as evidenced by high TV viewing time in FYR Macedonia and Turkey. Importantly, most dominant and specific features of SEECs media markets are given in Table 8.12.

Table 8.12 The dominant features of SEECs media markets

A specific feature of SEECs media markets	Country
The most profitable SEECs markets for FDI in daily newspapers industry	Turkey, Slovenia, FYR Macedonia, and Cyprus
The least profitable SEECs markets for FDI in daily newspapers industry	Greece, Kosovo, Serbia, and Albania
The most profitable SEECs markets for FDI in TV industry	Turkey, Malta, Cyprus, and Romania
The least profitable SEECs markets for FDI in TV industry	Serbia, Albania, Kosovo, and Bosnia and Herzegovina
The most profitable SEECs markets for FDI in Radio industry	Turkey, Romania, Slovenia, and FYR Macedonia
The least profitable SEECs markets for FDI in Radio industry	Kosovo, Serbia, Bosnia and Herzegovina, and Greece
The most profitable SEECs markets for FDI in daily newspapers, TV, and Radio industry	Turkey, Slovenia, Romania, and FYR Macedonia
The least profitable SEECs markets for FDI in daily newspapers, TV, and Radio industry	Kosovo, Serbia, Greece, and Bosnia and Herzegovina
Low Internet usage	Moldova—47.9 %, and Romania—58 %
High Internet usage	Cyprus—95 %, Kosovo—84.4 % , Hungary—76.1 %, Croatia—75 %, Malta—79.6 %, Slovenia—72.8 %
High free newspaper distribution	FYR Macedonia, Romania, Greece, Slovenia
Low free newspaper distribution	Turkey, Croatia, Serbia
High TV viewing time per viewer	Greece, Croatia, FYR Macedonia, Romania, Serbia, Hungary, Turkey
Low TV viewing time per viewer	Cyprus, Bulgaria, Slovenia
High audience share of commercial TV	Hungary, FYR Macedonia, Cyprus, Turkey, Greece
High audience share of Public TV	Croatia, Serbia, Kosovo, Slovenia, Moldova, Romania
Low audience share of Public TV	Greece, FYR Macedonia, Cyprus, Turkey
Low market competition of daily newspapers	Bosnia and Herzegovina, Croatia, Serbia, and Hungary
High market competition of daily newspapers	Greece, Moldova, Bulgaria, and Albania
Low market competition of TV stations	Turkey, Hungary, Bosnia and Herzegovina, and Kosovo
High market competition of TV stations	Montenegro, Slovenia, FYR Macedonia, and Romania
Low market competition of radio stations	Hungary, Bulgaria, Turkey, and Moldova
High market competition of radio stations	Malta, Greece, Montenegro, and Cyprus
High ethnic diversity and potential to broadcast multicultural programs	Bosnia and Herzegovina, Bulgaria, Moldova, FYR Macedonia, Serbia
High advertising market share of print media	Malta—50 %. Turkey (31 %) and Slovenia (30 %)

(continued)

Table 8.12 (continued)

A specific feature of SEECs media markets	Country
Low advertising market share of print media	Bosnia and Herzegovina (7 %), Romania (9 %), Hungary (10 %), Croatia (14 %), and Greece (16 %)
Low advertising market share of TV	Greece—31 %, Malta—39 %
High newspaper readership	Slovenia and Hungary
High advertising market share of TV	Bosnia and Herzegovina—90 %, Croatia—68 %, Romania and Hungary—64 %, Turkey—57 %, Slovenia—55 %

8.15   The Major Disadvantages in SEECs Media Markets

Notably, the major disadvantages for prospective foreign investors in the media market of South-East Europe are insufficient cluster development, low level of innovation, access to financing, inefficient government bureaucracy, restrictive labor regulations, corruption, policy instability, inadequately educated workforce, poor work ethic in national labor force, property rights, business and monetary freedom, relatively low credit rating outlook, low FDI per capita and current account in % of GDP, and low country brand index (only three countries—Greece, Croatia, and Malta—are positioned among 50 most successful global brand countries as measured by the Future Brand Country Index in 2015).

8.16   Further Research, Limitations, and Advances

The further development of the key challenges and dynamic behavior of FDI business model ontology, planning, application, system, modeling, and simulation methods will be dominantly influenced by the dynamics and technological transformation of global market, the length and quality of business lifecycles, added value networks/ecosystems and the multinationals' FDI spillover effects absorption capacity.

References

Arbatli, E. C. (2011). *Economic policies and FDI inflows to emerging market economies* (IMF Working Papers). pp. 1–25.

Artige, L., & Nicolini, R. (2006). Evidence on the determinants of foreign direct investment. The case of three European regions (No. 0607). Centre de Recherche en Economie Publique et de la

Population (CREPP) (Research Center on Public and Population Economics) HEC-Management School, University of Liège.

Austrian Central Bank. (2010). Recent economic developments in selected countries. In *Focus on European Economic Integration, Vienna*.

Baldi, P., & Hasebrink, U. (2007). *Broadcasters and citizens in Europe: Trends in media accountability and viewer participation*. Bristol: Intellect.

Bartlett, W. (2009). Economic development in the European super-periphery: Evidence from the Western Balkans. *Economic Annals, 54*(181), 21–44.

Baydar, Y., Hulin, A., Lani, R., Mollerup, J., Turtia, T. Vilović, G. & Zlatev, O. (2011). Journalism and self-regulation: New media, old dilemmas in South East Europe and Turkey, United Nations Educational, Scientific and Cultural Organization, Paris.

Bellak, C., Damijan, J., & Leibrecht, M. (2009). Infrastructure endowment and corporate income taxes as determinants of Foreign Direct Investment in Central- and Eastern European countries. *The World Economy, 32*(2), 267–290.

Bellak, C., Leibrecht, M., & Liebensteiner, M. (2010a). Attracting foreign direct investment: The public policy scope for South East European countries. *Eastern Journal of European Studies, 1* (2), 37–53.

Bellak, C., Leibrecht, M., & Stehrer, R. (2010b). The role of public policy in closing foreign direct investment gaps: An empirical analysis. *Empirica, 37*, 19–46. Special Issue on FDI Policies, Bellak, C. & Wolfmayr-Schnitzer, Y. (eds.).

Bellak, C., & Liebensteiner, M. (2011). Direct taxation of business in South East European countries. In D. Sternad & T. Döring (Eds.), *Handbook of doing business in South East Europe*. Basingstoke, UK: Palgrave Macmillan.

Bénassy-Quéré, A., Coupet, M., & Mayer, T. (2007a). Institutional determinants of foreign direct investment. *The World Economy, 30*(5), 764–782.

Bénassy-Quéré, A., Gobalraja, N., & Trannoy, A. (2007b). Tax and public input competition. *Economic Policy*, April, 387–430.

Benbasat, I., Goldstein, D. K., & Mead, M. (1987). The case research strategy in studies of information systems. *Management Information Systems Quarterly, 11*(3), 369–386.

Bergstrand, J. H., & Egger, P. (2007). A knowledge-and-physical-capital model of international trade flows, foreign direct investment, and multinational enterprises. *Journal of International Economics, 73*(2), 278–308.

Beumers, B., Hutchings, S., & Rulyova, N. (2011). *The post-Soviet Russian media: Conflicting signals*. London: Taylor & Francis.

Bevan, A. A., & Estrin, S. (2004). The determinants of foreign direct investment into European transition economies. *Journal of Comparative Economics, 32*(4), 775–787.

Bevan, A., Estrin, S., & Meyer, K. (2004). Foreign investment location and institutional development in transition economies. *International Business Review, 13*(1), 43–64.

Bijsterbosch, M., & Kolasa, M. (2010). FDI and productivity convergence in Central and Eastern Europe: An industry-level investigation. *Review of World Economics, 145*(4), 689–712.

Bitzenis, A. (2003). Universal Model of theories determining FDI: Is there any dominant theory? Are the FDI inflows in the CEE countries and especially in Bulgaria a myth? *European Business Review, 15*(2), 94–104.

Bitzenis, A. (2006). Decisive FDI barriers that affect multinationals' business in a transition country. *Global Business and Economics Review, 8*(1–2), 87–118.

Blain, N., & O'Donnell, H. (2003). *Media, monarchy and power: The postmodern culture in Europe*. Bristol: Intellect.

Blonigen, B. A. (2005). A review of the empirical literature on FDI determinants. *Atlantic Economic Journal, 33*, 383–403.

Bondebjerg, I., & Golding, P. (2004). *European culture and the media*. Bristol: Intellect Books.

Bondebjerg, I., & Madsen, P. (2009). *Media democracy and European culture*. Bristol: Intellect.

Borensztein, E., Gregorio, J., & Lee, J. W. (1995). *How does foreign direct investment affect economic growth*. (NBER Working Paper, 5057).

Borensztein, E., De Gregorio, J., & Lee, J. W. (1998). How does foreign direct investment affect economic growth? *Journal of International Economics, 45*(1), 115–135.

Borg, J. (2009). Malta's media landscape: An overview. In J. Borg, A. Hillman, & M. A. Lauri (Eds.), *Exploring the Maltese media landscape* (pp. 19–33). Malta: Allied.

Botrić, V., & Škuflić, L. (2006). Main determinants of foreign direct investment in the southeast European countries. *Transition Studies Review, 13*(2), 359–377.

Bourgeois, L. J. (1979). Toward a method of middle-range theorizing. *Academy of Management Review, 4*(3), 443–447.

Buckley, P. J. (2002). Is the international business research agenda running out of steam? *Journal of International Business Studies, 33*(2), 365–373.

Buckley, P. J., & Chapman, M. (1996). Theory and method in international business research. *International Business Review, 5*(3), 233–245.

Campbell, D. (1975). Degrees of freedom and the case study. *Comparative Political Studies, 8*, 178–185.

Carstensen, K., & Toubal, F. (2004). Foreign direct investment in Central and Eastern European countries: A dynamic panel analysis. *Journal of Comparative Economics, 32*(1), 3–22.

Castendyk, O., Dommering, E. J., & Scheuer, A. (2008). *European media law*. Alphen a/d Rijn: Kluwer.

Caves, R. E. (2000). *Creative industries. Contracts between art and commerce*. Cambridge, MA: Harvard University Press.

Chaban, N., & Holland, M. (2008). *The European Union and the Asia-Pacific: Media, public and elite perceptions of the EU*. London: Taylor & Francis.

Cheng, L. K., & Kwan, Y. K. (2000). What are the determinants of the location of foreign direct investment? The Chinese experience. *Journal of International Economics, 51*(2), 379–400.

Christensen, M., & Nezih, E. (2009). *Shifting landscapes: Film and media in European context*. Newcastle: Cambridge Scholars.

Christie, E. (2002). Potential trade in South-East Europe: A gravity model approach. *SEER-South-East Europe Review for Labour and Social Affairs*, (04), 81–101.

Cohen, W. M., & Levinthal, D. A. (1990). Absorptive capacity: A new perspective on learning and innovation. *Administrative Science Quarterly, 35*(1), 128–152.

Collins, R. (1998). *Satellite to single market: New communication technology and European public service television*. London: Taylor & Francis.

Crain, M. M., & Hughes-Freeland, F. (1998). *Recasting ritual: Performance, media, identity*. London: Taylor & Francis.

Craufurd Smith, R. (2004). Rethinking European Union competence in the field of media ownership: The internal market, fundamental rights and European citizenship. *European Law Review, 5*, 652–672.

Daude, C., & Stein, E. (2007). The quality of institutions and foreign direct investment. *Economics & Politics, 19*(3), 317–343.

Davies, R. B., & Kristjánsdóttir, H. (2010). Fixed costs, foreign direct investment, and gravity with zeros. *Review of International Economics, 18*(1), 47–62.

De Beaufort, V., & Summers, L. (2014). Women on boards: Sharing a rigorous vision of the functioning of boards, demanding a new model of corporate governance. *Journal of Research in Gender Studies, 1*, 101–140.

Deirdre, K. (2003). *Europe in the media: A comparison of reporting, representation, and rhetoric in national media systems in Europe*. London: Taylor & Francis.

Demekas, D. G., Horváth, B., Ribakova, E., & Wu, Y. (2005). *Foreign direct investment in Southeastern Europe: How (and how much) can policies help?* (IMF Working Paper, WP/05/110).

DeMooij, R., & Ederveen, S. (2008). Corporate tax elasticities: A reader's guide to empirical findings. *Oxford Review of Economic Policy, 24*(4), 680–697.

Dencik, J., & Spee, R. (2012). *Global location trends-2013 annual report*. New York: IBM Institute.

Dhakal, D., Mixon, F., Jr., & Upadhyaya, K. (2007). Foreign direct investment and transition economies: Empirical evidence from a panel data estimator. *Economics Bulletin, 6*(33), 1–9.

Dikova, D., & Van Witteloostuijn, A. (2007). Foreign direct investment mode choice: Entry and establishment modes in transition economies. *Journal of International Business Studies, 38*(6), 1013–1033.

Dobek-Ostrowska, B., Glowacki, M., Jakubowicz, K., & Sukosd, M. (2010). *Comparative media systems: European and global perspective*. Budapest: Central European University Press.

Doe, N. (2004). *The portrayal of religion in Europe: The media and the arts*. Leuven: Peeters.

Downey, J., & Mihelj, S. (2012). *Central and Eastern European media in comparative perspective*. Farnham: Ashgate.

Dyer, W. G., & Wilkins, A. L. (1991). Better stories, not better constructs, to generate better theory: A rejoinder to Eisenhardt. *Academy of Management Review, 16*(3), 613–619.

EBRD. (2010). Invigorating trade integration and export-led growth. Transition report 2010. Chapter 4, pp. 66–77.

Eisenhardt, K. M. (1989). Building theories from case study research. *Academy of Management Review, 14*, 532–550.

Eisenhardt, K. M., & Graebner, M. E. (2007). Theory building from cases: Opportunities and challenges. *Academy of Management Journal, 50*(1), 25–32.

Estrin, S., Richet, X., & Brada, J. C. (2000). *Foreign direct investment in Central Eastern Europe: Case studies of firms in transition*. London: ME Sharpe.

Färdigh, M. A. (2010). Comparing media systems in Europe: Identifying comparable country-level dimensions of media systems. QoG Working Paper Series, The Quality of Government Institute, Department of Political Science, University of Gothenburg.

Fatica, S. (2010). Investment liberalization and cross-border acquisitions: The effect of partial foreign ownership. *Review of International Economics, 18*(2), 320–333.

Feld, L. P., & Heckemeyer, J. H. (2011). FDI and taxation: A meta-study. *Journal of Economic Surveys, 25*(2), 233–272.

Feldmann, V. (2005). *Leveraging mobile media: Cross-media strategy and innovation policy for mobile media communication*. Berlin: Springer.

Ferrell Lowe, G., & Brown, C. (2015). *Managing media firms and industries: What's so special about media management?* Berlin: Springer.

FIAS. (2007). Attracting investment to South East Europe: Survey of FDI trends and investor perceptions. Washington, DC.

Fidrmuc, J., & Martin, R. (2011). FDI, trade and growth in CESEE countries. *Focus on European Economic Integration, Q1*, 70–113.

FIPA (Foreign Investment Promotion Agency of Bosnia-Herzegovina). (2008). Investment opportunities in Bosnia-Herzegovina. 5th edn.

Frachon, C., & Vargaftig, M. (2000). *European television: Immigrants and ethnic minorities*. London: Libbey.

Frank, B. (1992). A note on the international dominance of the U.S. in the trade in movies and television fiction. *Journal of Media Economics, 5*(1), 31–38.

Frankel, J. A., & Rose, A. K. (1996). Currency crashes in emerging markets: An empirical treatment. *Journal of International Economics, 41*(3), 351–366.

Frederickson, J. W. (1983). Strategic process research: Questions and recommendations. *Academy of Management Review, 8*(4), 565–575.

Friedrichsen, M., & Mühl-Benninghaus, W. (2013). *Handbook of social media management: Value chain and business models in changing media markets*. Heidelberg: Springer.

Gardo, S., & Martin, R. (2010). The impact of the global economic and financial crisis on central, eastern and south-eastern Europe: A stock-taking exercise. ECB occasional paper.

Georgiades, S. (2015). Communication process to achieve employee engagement. In *Employee engagement in media management* (pp. 39–59). Springer International Publishing.

Gerring, J. (2004). What is a case study and what is it good for? *American Political Science Review, 98*(02), 341–354.

Gershon, R. (2015). *Digital media and innovation: Management and design strategies in communication*. Thousand Oaks, CA: SAGE Publications, Inc.

Gibbert, M., & Ruigrok, W. (2010). The "what" and "how" of case study rigor: Three strategies based on published research. *Organizational Research Methods, 13*(4), 710–737.

Glowacki, M. (2011). 'A sleeping mechanism' for the time being? Media accountability online in Bulgaria. media ACT Working Paper series on 'media accountability practices on the internet.' Journalism Research and Development Centre, University of Tampere, Finland.

Goga, T. (2009). *Footprint of financial crisis in the media.* Open Society Institute.

Goodspeed, T., Martinez-Vazquez, J., & Zhang, L. (2006). Are other government policies more important than taxation in attracting FDI? Andrew Young School of Policy Studies Research Paper, (06-28).

Goodspeed, T., Martinez-Vazquez, J., & Zhang, L. (2009). Public policies and FDI location: Differences between developing and developed countries, International Studies Program Working Paper Series, GSU paper 0910, Andrew Young School of Policy Studies, Georgia State University.

Gross, P. (2004). Between reality and dream: Eastern European media transition. *Transformation, Consolidation, and Integration, East European Politics & Societies, 18,* 110–131.

Gulyás, A. (2003). Print media in post-Communist East Central Europe. *European Journal of Communication, 18*(1), 81–106.

Hallin, D. C., & Papathanassopoulos, S. (2002). Political clientelism and the media: Southern Europe and Latin America in comparative perspective. *Media, Culture and Society, 24*(2), 175–196.

Hallin, D. C., & Mancini, P. (2004). *Comparing media systems: Three models of media and politics.* Cambridge: Cambridge University Press.

Harcourt, A. (2005). *The European Union and the regulation of media markets.* Manchester: Manchester University Press.

Hartley, J. F. (1994). Case studies in organizational research. In C. Cassel & G. Symon (Eds.), *Qualitative methods in organizational research: A practical guide* (pp. 208–229). London: Sage.

Harrison, J., & Wessels, B. (2009). *Mediating Europe: New media, mass communications and the European public sphere.* New York: Berghahn Books.

Head, K., & Ries, J. (2008). FDI as an outcome of the market for corporate control: Theory and evidence. *Journal of International Economics, 74*(1), 2–20.

Hijzen, A., Görg, H., & Manchin, M. (2008). Cross-border mergers and acquisitions and the role of trade costs. *European Economic Review, 52*(5), 849–866.

Holoubek, M., Damjanovic, D., & Traimer, M. (2006). *Regulating content: The European regulatory framework for the media and related creative sectors.* Alphen a/d Rijn: Kluwer.

Horn, H., & Persson, L. (2001). The equilibrium ownership of an international oligopoly. *Journal of International Economics, 53*(2), 307–333.

Horowitz, M. J., Milbrath, C., Jordan, D. S., Stinson, C. H., Ewert, M., Redington, D. J., et al. (1994). Expressive and defensive behavior during discourse on unresolved topics: A single case study of pathological grief. *Journal of Personality, 62*(4), 527–563.

Hoskins, C., & Mirus, R. (1988). Reasons for U.S. dominance of the international trade in television programmes. *Media, Culture and Society, 10,* 499–515.

Hunya, G. (2011). Diverging patterns of FDI recovery (No. 2011-05). The Vienna Institute for International Economic Studies, wiiw.

Hunya, G. (2012). Short-lived recovery (No. 2012-05). The Vienna Institute for International Economic Studies, wiiw.

Hyun, H.-J., & Kim, H. H. (2010). The determinants of cross-border M&As: The role of institutions and financial development in the gravity model. *World Economy, 33*(2), 292–310.

Iosifides, P. (1997). Pluralism and media concentration policy in the European Union. *Javnost, 4* (1), 85–104.

Iosifidis, P. (2006a). *Public TV in small EU countries: The Greek case.* Conference presentation at the Research Institute of Applied Communications, Cyprus.

Iosifidis, P. (2006b). Digital switchover in Europe. *The International Communication Gazette, 68* (3), 249–268.

Jakubowicz, K. (2007). *Rude awakening: Social and media change in Central and Eastern Europe.* Cresskill, NJ: Hampton Press.

Jakubowicz, K., & Sükösd, M. (Eds.). (2008). *Finding the right place on the map: Central and Eastern European media change in a global perspective.* Intellect Books.

Jakubowicz, K., & Sukosd, M. (2011). *Media, nationalism and European identities.* Budapest: Central European University Press.

Janicki, P. H., & Wunnava, P. V. (2004). Determinants of foreign direct investment: Empirical evidence from EU accession candidates. *Applied Economics, 36*, 505–509.

Johnson, A. (2006). FDI inflows to the transition economies in Eastern Europe: Magnitude and determinants. The Royal Institute of Technology, CESIS (Centre for Excellence for Studies in Science in Innovation), Paper No, 59.

Jusić, T., & Amer, D. (2008). Bosnia and Herzegovina. In S. Bašić-Hrvatin, M. Thompson, & T. Jusić (Eds.), *Divided the fall: Public service broadcasting in multiethnic states (PDF).* Sarajevo: Mediacentar. Accessed 12 Jan 2011.

Kalotay, K. (2010). Patterns of inward FDI in economies in transition. *Eastern Journal of European Studies, 1*(2), 55–76.

Keller, P. (2011). *European and international media law: Liberal democracy, trade and the new media.* Oxford: Oxford University Press.

Kleinert, J., & Toubal, F. (2010). Gravity for FDI. *Review of International Economics, 18*(1), 1–13.

Koch-Baumgarten, S., & Voltmer, K. (2010). *Public policy and the mass media: The interplay of mass communication and political decision making.* London: Routledge.

Koopmans, R., & Statham, P. (2010). *The making of a European public sphere: Media discourse and political contention.* Cambridge: Cambridge University Press.

Kristovic, M. (2008). 2000 Political influence on the media system in Serbia: What was changed after? In *58th Political Studies Association annual conference, democracy, governance and conflict: Dilemmas of theory and practice.* Swansea University.

Labaye, E., Sjatil, P. E., Bogdan, W., Novak, J., Mischke, J., Fruk, M., & Ionutiu, O. (2013). *A new dawn: Reigniting growth in Central and Eastern Europe.* New York: McKinsey Global Institute.

Lange, B.-P., & Ward, D. (2004). *The media and elections: A handbook and comparative study.* London: Taylor & Francis.

Lankes, H. P., & Venables, A. J. (1996). Foreign direct investment in economic transition: The changing pattern of investments. *Economics of Transition, 4*(2), 331–347.

Lavine, J. M., & Wackman, D. B. (1988). *Managing media organizations.* New York: Longman.

Leandros, N. (2010). Media concentration and systemic failures in Greece. *International Journal of Communication, 4*, 886–905.

Lugmayr, A., & Dal Zotto, C. (2015a). *Media convergence handbook—Vol. 1: Journalism, broadcasting, and social media aspects of convergence.* Berlin: Springer.

Lugmayr, A., & Dal Zotto, C. (2015b). *Media convergence handbook—Vol. 2: Firms and user perspectives.* Berlin: Springer.

Mancini, P. (2000). Political complexity and alternative models of journalism: The Italian case. In J. Curran & M.-J. Park (Eds.), *De-westernizing media studies* (pp. 265–279). London: Routledge.

Market Links report commissioned by BNR. "Slideshare. Bulgarian radio stations' national audience—February 2012," Market Links, at http://www.slideshare.net/andriangeorgiev/nr-feb-2012. Accessed 31 Oct 2015.

Marletti, C., & Roncarolo, F. (2000). Media Influence in the Italian transition from a consensual to a majoritarian democracy. In R. Gunther & A. Mugham (Eds.), *Democracy and the media. A comparative perspective* (pp. 195–240). Cambridge: Cambridge University Press.

Medina, M. (2004). *European television production. Pluralism and concentration.* Media Management Department of the University of Navarra School of Communication.

Mertelsmann, O. (2011). *Central and Eastern European media under dictatorial rule and in the early Cold War.* Frankfurt: Peter Lang.

Meyer, K. (1998). *Direct investment in economies in transition.* Cheltenham, UK: Edward Elgar.

Meyer, J.-H. (2010). *The European public sphere: Media and transnational communication in European integration 1969-199.* Stuttgart: Franz Steiner.

Michalis, M. (2007). *Governing European communications: From unification to coordination.* Lanham, MD: Lexington Books.

Mollick, A. V., Ramos-Duran, R., & Silva-Ochoa, E. (2006). Infrastructure and FDI into Mexico: A panel data approach. *Global Economy Journal, 6,* 1–25.

Morán, G. M. (2008). Religion and media: Legal control & regulations: Comparative analysis in Europe and USA. Foro, *Nueva época,* núm. 8:13–39.

Nissen, C. S. (2006). *Making a difference: Public service broadcasting in the European media landscape.* Bloomington, IN: Indiana University Press.

Nocke, V., & Yeaple, S. R. (2007). Cross-border mergers and acquisitions vs. greenfield foreign direct investment: The role of firm heterogeneity. *Journal of International Economics, 72*(2), 336–365.

Open Society Foundation for Albania, "Përdorimi i Facebook, Twitter, YouTube dhe Blogjeve për ligjërim politik mes të rinjve dhe kandidatëve për bashki e komuna" (Use of Facebook, Twitter, YouTube, and Blogging for political deliberation between the youth and candidates for local office), 2010, available at http://www.soros.al/2010/article.php?id=274. Accessed 31 Oct 2015 (hereafter, Open Society Foundation for Albania, "Use of Facebook, Twitter, YouTube, and Blogging").

Overesch, M., & Wamser, G. (2010). The effects of company taxation in EU accession countries on German FDI. *Economics of Transition, 18,* 429–457.

Owen, B. M., & Wildman, S. S. (1992). *Video economics.* Cambridge, MA: Harvard University Press.

Papathanassopoulos, S. (2000). *Television and its audience.* Athens: Kastaniotis Editions [In Greek].

Papathanasopoulos, S. (2005). *Politics and media: The case of Southern Europe.* Athens: Kastaniotis.

Papathanassopoulos, S., & Negrine, R. M. (2011). *European media: Structures, politics and identity.* Polity: Cambridge.

Papatheodorou, F., & Machin, D. (2003). The umbilical cord that was never cut: The post-dictatorial intimacy between the political elite and the mass media in Greece and Spain. *European Journal of Communication, 18*(1), 31–54.

Pauwels, P., & Matthyssens, P. (2004). The architecture of multiple case study research in international business. In R. Piekkari & C. Welch (Eds.), *Handbook of qualitative research methods for international business* (pp. 125–143). Cheltenham, UK: Edward Elgar.

Peruško, Z., & Popović, H. (2008). Media concentration trends in Central and Eastern Europe. In K. Jakubowicz & M. Sükösd (Eds.), *Finding the right place on the map: Central and Eastern European media change in a global perspective* (pp. 165–189). Bristol: Intellect Books.

Peterson, M. F. (1998). Embedded organizational events: The units of process in organization science. *Organization Science, 9*(1), 16–33.

Pettigrew, A. M. (1992). The character and significance of strategy process research. *Strategic Management Journal, 13*(Special Issue, Winter), 5–16.

Popescu, G. H. (2014). FDI and economic growth in Central and Eastern Europe. *Sustainability, 6* (11), 8149–8163.

Portes, R., & Rey, H. (2005). The determinants of cross-border equity flows. *Journal of International Economics, 65*(2), 269–296.

Qiu, L. D., & Wang, S. (2011). FDI policy, greenfield investment and cross-border mergers. *Review of International Economics, 19*(5), 836–851.

Razmerita, L., Phillips-Wren, G., & Jain, L. C. (2016). Innovations in knowledge management: The impact of social media, semantic web and cloud computing (Intelligent Systems Reference Library).

Rohman, I. K. (2011). How important is the media and content sector in the European economy? In *26th European communications policy research conference (EuroCPR)*.

Rooke, R. (2009). *European media in the digital age: Analysis and approaches*. London: Pearson.

Sánchez-Tabernero, A., & Carvajal, M. (2002). *Media concentration in the European market. New trends and challenges*. Media Management Department of the University of Navarra School of Communication.

Schalt, C. (2008). Going East: How media companies successfully enter the Eastern European radio market: A case of Hungary. *Journal of Radio & Audio Media, 15*(2), 249–260.

Shao, G. (2010). Venturing through acquisitions or alliances? Examining U.S. media companies' digital strategy. *Journal of Business Media Studies, 7*(1), 21–39.

Silverman, D. (2000). Analyzing talk and text. In N. Denzin & Y. Lincoln (Eds.), *Handbook of qualitative research* (pp. 821–834). Thousand Oaks, CA: Sage.

Sjoberg, G., Williams, N., Vaughn, T. R., & Sjoberg, A. F. (1991). The case study approach in social research: Basic methodological issues. In J. R. Feagin & A. Orum (Eds.), *A case for the case study* (pp. 27–79). Chapel Hill, NC: University of North Carolina Press.

Slaveski, T., & Nedanovski, P. (2002). Foreign direct investment in the Balkans: The case of Albania, FYROM, and Bulgaria. *Eastern European Economics, 40*(4), 83–99.

Splichal, S. (1994). *Media beyond socialism: Theory and practice in East-Central Europe*. Boulder, CO: Westview Press.

Splichal, S. (2004). Privatization: The cost of media democratization in East and Central Europe? In P. N. Thoas & Z. Nain (Eds.), *Who owns the media. Global trends and local resistances*. Penang: Southbound.

Stake, R. E. (1995). *The art of case study research*. Thousand Oaks, CA: Sage.

Stake, R. E. (2006). *Multiple case study analysis*. New York: Guilford Press.

Statham, P. (1996). Television news and the public sphere in Italy. Conflicts at the media/politics interface. *European Journal of Communication, 11*(4), 511–556.

Stoian, C., & Filippaios, F. (2008). Dunning's eclectic paradigm: A holistic, yet context specific framework for analysing the determinants of outward FDI: Evidence from international Greek investments. *International Business Review, 17*(3), 349–367.

Sullivan, D., & Jiang, Y. (2010). Media convergence and the impact of the internet on the M&A activity of large media companies. *Journal of Media Business Studies, 7*(4), 21–40.

Terzis, G. (2008). *European media governance: National and regional dimensions*. Bristol: Intellect Books.

The Eastern Partnership Civil Society Forum. (2011).Media landscape of Eastern partnership Countries. Yerevan Press Club.

Trenza, H.-J. (2008). Understanding media impact on European integration: Enhancing or restricting the scope of legitimacy of the EU? *Journal of European Integration, 30*(2), 291–309.

Triandafyllidou, A., Wodak, R., & Krzyzanowski, M. (2009). *The European public sphere and the media: Europe in crisis*. Basingstoke: Palgrave Macmillan.

Tsourvakas, G. (2010). Economic opportunities and threats for Southeast European media companies. Media in Southeast Europe trends and challenges, 22/23 November, Bonn.

UNCTAD. (2014). *World investment report 2014*, Geneva Switzerland.

Van Assche, A., & Schwartz, G. A. (2013). Contracting institutions and ownership structure in international joint ventures. *Journal of Development Economics, 103*, 124–132.

Van De Steeg, M. (2005). The public sphere in the European Union: A media analysis of public discourse on EU enlargement and on the Haider case, ate: Series/Report no.: EUI PhD theses.

Van der Wurff, R. (2002). With two feet on firm ground and diverse heads up in the air. Conclusions of four expert meetings on media and open societies in East and West. In: Gazette: *The International Journal for Communication Studies, 64*(5), 407–423.

Van Kranenburg, H., & Dal Zotto, C. (2009). *Management and innovation in the media industry*. Cheltenham, UK: Edward Elgar.

Venturelli, S. (1999). *Liberalizing the European media: Politics, regulation, and the public sphere*. Oxford: Oxford University Press.

Voltmer, K. (2005). *Mass media and political communication in new democracies*. New York: Routledge.

Vukanovic, Z. (2011). Exploring and crossing communication and media industry frontiers: Creating a strategy to expand foreign direct investment (FDI) inflow in SEEC. *Eurolimes, (12)*, 61–88.

Waterman, D. (1988). World television trade: The economic effects of privatization and new technology. *Telecommunications Policy, 12*(2), 141–151.

Werner, S. (2002). Recent developments in international management research: A review of 20 top management journals. *Journal of Management, 28*(3), 277–305.

Wheeler, D., & Mody, A. (1992). International investment location decisions. *Journal of International Economics, 33*, 57–76.

Wildman, S. S. (1995). Trade liberalization and policy for media industries: A theoretical examination of media flows. *Canadian Journal of Communication, 20*(3), 367–388.

Wildman, S. S., & Siwek, S. E. (1987). The privatization of European television: Effects on international markets for programs. *Columbia Journal of World Business, 22*(3), 71–76.

Wildman, S. S., & Siwek, S. E. (1988). *International trade in films and television programs*. Cambridge, MA: Ballinger.

Wildman, S. S., & Siwek, S. E. (1993). The economics of trade in recorded media products in a multilingual world: Implications for national media policies. In E. M. Noam & J. C. Millonzi (Eds.), *The international market in film and television programs* (pp. 13–40). Norwood, NJ: Ablex.

Williams, G. (2003). *European media ownership: Threats on the landscape* (Working Paper). Brussels: The European Federation of Journalists.

Wolf, M. (2005). Will globalization survive? *World Economics, 6*(4), 1–10. Economic & Financial Publishing, 1 Ivory Square, Plantation Wharf, London, United Kingdom, SW11 3UE.

Yin, R. K. (1994). *Case study research design and methods* (2nd ed.). Thousand Oaks, CA: Sage.

Yin, R. K. (2003). *Case study research: Design and methods* (3rd ed.). Thousand Oaks, CA: Sage.

Yin, R. K. (2008). *Case study research: Design and methods*. Thousand Oaks, CA: Sage.

Zahra, S. A., & George, G. (2002). Absorptive capacity: A review, reconceptualization, and extension. *Academy of Management Review, 27*(2), 185–203.

Zlatev, O. (2011). Media accountability systems (MAS) and their applications in South East Europe and Turkey. In O. Zlatev et al. (Eds.), *Professional journalism and self-regulation. New media, old dilemmas in South East Europe and Turkey*. Paris: United Nations Educational, Scientific and Cultural Organization.

Printed by Printforce, the Netherlands